DARK GHETTO

DARK
GHETTO

Dilemmas of
Social Power

KENNETH B. CLARK

Second Edition With a New Introduction by
William Julius Wilson

Foreword by Gunnar Myrdal

Wesleyan University Press

WESLEYAN UNIVERSITY PRESS
Published by University Press of New England,
Hanover, NH 03755

Copyright © 1965 by Kenneth B. Clark
Introduction to the Wesleyan Edition copyright © 1989
by William Julius Wilson

Published by arrangement with Harper & Row, Publishers, Inc.

Printed in the United States of America 5 4 3 2

∞

LIBRARY OF CONGRESS CATALOGING-IN-PUBLICATION DATA
Clark, Kenneth Bancroft, 1914–
    Dark ghetto : dilemmas of social power / by Kenneth B.
Clark ; foreword by Gunnar Myrdal.—2nd ed. / with a new
introduction by William Julius Wilson.
        p.   cm.—(Wesleyan paperback)
    Originally published: New York : Harper & Row, c 1965.
    Includes bibliographical references and indexes.
    ISBN 0–8195–6226–2
    1. Afro-Americans—New York (N.Y.)—Social conditions.
2. Afro-Americans—New York (N.Y.)—Segregation.
3. Harlem (New York, N.Y.)—Social conditions.
4. New York (N.Y.)—Social conditions.   I. Title.
F128.9.N3C65   1989
305.8'9607307471—dc20   89–34554

To Mamie,
Who Has Endured
And Given Much

CONTENTS

INTRODUCTION TO THE
WESLEYAN EDITION[1]

By William Julius Wilson

The publication of *Dark Ghetto* in 1965 marked the beginning of a series of thoughtful studies of life in impoverished inner city neighborhoods in the latter half of the 1960s.[2] These studies were distinctive in their focus on the severe macrostructural constraints that have compelled many ghetto residents to live and to act in ways that do not conform to mainstream social norms and expectations.

Problems of poverty, joblessness, educational inequities, and family structure were highlighted in these studies, but so too were problems of crime, sexual exploitation, teenage pregnancy, alcoholism, drug addiction, and other forms of self-destructive behavior. As Kenneth B. Clark so ingenuously puts it in this volume,

The dark ghetto is institutionalized pathology; it is chronic, self-perpetuating pathology. . . . Not only is the pathology of the ghetto self-perpetu-

---

[1] Parts of this essay are based on the Godkin Lecture, "The American Underclass: Inner-City Ghettos and the Norms of Citizenship," delivered at the John F. Kennedy School of Government at Harvard University, April 1988. An extended version of this lecture will be published by Knopf in late 1990.

[2] In addition to *Dark Ghetto*, Lee Rainwater, "Crucible of Identity: The Negro Lower-Class Family," *Daedalus* 95 (Winter 1966): 176–216; Elliot Liebow, *Tally's Corner: A Study of Negro Streetcorner Men* (Boston: Little, Brown, 1967); Ulf Hannerz, *Soulside: Inquiries into Ghetto Culture and Com-

ating, but one kind of pathology breeds another. The child born in the ghetto is more likely to come into a world of broken homes and illegitimacy; and this family and social instability is conducive to delinquency, drug addiction, and criminal violence. Neither instability nor crime can be controlled by police vigilance or by reliance on the alleged deterring forces of legal punishment, for the individual crimes are to be understood more as symptoms of the contagious sickness of the community itself than as the result of inherent criminal or deliberate viciousness.[3]

Also, Lee Rainwater, in his now classic 1966 article "Crucible of Identity: The Negro Lower Class Family," noted that individuals in inner-city ghettos creatively adapt to this system of severely restricted opportunities "in ways that keep them alive and extract what gratification they can find, but in the process of adaptation they are constrained to behave in ways that inflict a great deal of suffering on those with whom they make their lives, and on themselves."[4]

Dark Ghetto and the other urban field research studies of the 1960s made it clear that ghetto behavior, which was said to be ultimately destructive to individuals and families, was at bottom a problem generated by the systematic blockage of opportunities. Although the problems of joblessness, teenage pregnancy, family dissolution, educational failure, violent crime, exploitative sexual relations, drug addiction, and alcoholism are not unique to black ghettos, they are more heavily concentrated there because of a unique combination of economic marginality and rigid racial segregation. Excluded from the stable employment sectors of the economy, inner-city residents have to rely on insecure and dead-end jobs that provide wages insufficient for the purchase of those goods and services that embody the prevailing standard of American life. Racially segregated from the larger society, they more frequently suffer discriminatory practices and encounter contemptuous attitudes from those in positions of social power, even though the latter know that the ghetto poor are forced by their very circumstances to endure superexploitative economic transactions from the private sector and inferior services from

munity (New York: Columbia University Press, 1970); and Lee Rainwater, *Behind Ghetto Walls: Black Families in a Federal Slum* (Chicago: Aldine, 1970).
[3] *Dark Ghetto,* 81.
[4] Rainwater, "Crucible of Identity," 164.

municipal authorities.[5] As Kenneth Clark so clearly shows in *Dark Ghetto,* stores and other business establishments are in a position to easily extract significantly higher prices for consumer goods. Public services are so inferior in quality to those enjoyed by the vast majority of other Americans that an outside visitor to the ghetto could hardly avoid a sense of shock at the insufficient sanitation, the inadequate police protection, the low quality of public schools, and the run-down parks and recreational facilities.

This absolute deprivation is rendered even more intolerable by relative deprivation. In an advanced industrial society it is impossible for ghetto residents to be unaware of the enormous discrepancy between their living standards and social experiences and those of the rest of society.[6] "The ghetto is not totally isolated," states Kenneth Clark.

The mass media—radio, television, moving pictures, magazines, and the press—penetrate, indeed, invade the ghetto in continuous and inevitable communication, largely one way, and project the values and aspirations, the manners and the style of life of the larger white-dominated society. Those who are required to live in congested rat-infested homes are aware that others are not so dehumanized. . . . Whatever accommodations they themselves must make to the negative realities which dominate their own lives, they know consciously or unconsciously that their fate is not the fate of mankind.[7]

The cumulative effects of racial oppression and economic marginality take their toll also on the structure of the ghetto neighborhoods, which lack the resources and organizational strength to provide basic support for and minimal stability to their residents. As the formal and informal means of social control weaken, levels of crime and street violence increase, leading to further neighborhood deterioration. Even those inner-city residents who are able to isolate themselves from constant awareness of such relative deprivation cannot elude the problems in their own neighborhoods, the problems, in the words of Lee Rainwater, in 1970, of confronting "a world full of

[5] For a good discussion of these problems see, especially, Rainwater, *Behind Ghetto Walls;* and Clark, *Dark Ghetto.* Also see, David Caplow, *The Poor Pay More* (New York: The Free Press, 1965).

[6] Rainwater, *Behind Ghetto Walls.*

[7] *Dark Ghetto,* 12.

dangers—not just the physical dangers of the ghetto world, but also the interpersonal dangers" of their exploitative milieu.[8]

In my view, the principal contribution of *Dark Ghetto* and the other urban field studies of the late 1960s is the systematic use of field research data to show how the experiences and the patterns of conduct of ghetto residents are shaped by powerful structural constraints in urban American society. These studies include a frank and concrete discussion of certain forms of behavior, "usually forgotten or ignored in polite discussion,"[9] so that the reader can clearly understand the consequences of living in a racially segregated and impoverished neighborhood. However, it is important to note, as Rainwater does, that ghetto residents "are not simply passive targets of the destructive forces which act upon them; they react adaptively, making use of the human resources available to work out strategies for survival."[10] For example, ghetto residents facing blocked opportunities through controlling institutional channels are far more likely to attempt to improve their own personal situations by exploiting or manipulating one of the few resources at their command: their own peers.

Such strategies of adaptation, described initially in *Dark Ghetto* and later elaborated systematically in Ulf Hannerz's *Soulside,* have resulted in the prevalence of female household dominance; male roles emphasizing toughness, flamboyant sexual activity, and liquor consumption; elaboration of adolescent sex codes that enhance and justify permissive attitudes toward extensive heterosexual relationships; conflict-ridden relations between males and females; flexible household composition; intensive participation in an informal social life outside the primary household; prevalent fear of crime; and hostility toward white America and its institutions.

The students of the ghetto described these traits as ghetto-specific because taken together they tend to be far more characteristic of ghetto neighborhoods than of mainstream American society. "Inimical to successful performance in the larger society,"[11] they enhance

---

[8] Rainwater, *Behind Ghetto Walls,* 372.
[9] Rainwater, "Crucible of Identity," 173.
[10] Rainwater, *Behind Ghetto Walls,* 372.
[11] Ibid., 7.

the probability of outcomes like crime, teenage pregnancy, and drug use and alcoholism—outcomes ultimately harmful both to the community and to the individual.

It is important to emphasize that several of the authors of the urban field studies were deeply concerned about the policy implications of their research. Kenneth Clark, for example, hoped that his graphic description and systematic explanation of the social ills that plague black ghettos would motivate those who care about social justice to move swiftly and forthrightly to correct those ills. Lee Rainwater believed that to ignore ghetto-specific strategies, however unflattering to the residents themselves, would only lead to public policies "that are unrealistic in the light of the actual day-to-day reality" of ghetto life.[12] Elliot Liebow, in *Tally's Corner,* intended his depiction of the plight of young males in a Washington D.C. ghetto to underline the urgent need for realistic social policies that would address the problems of economic dislocation among poor urban blacks.

It was clear, moreover, that the authors of these monographs wanted both policymakers and the general public to focus n the surface manifestation of the problems of inner-city poverty but more importantly on the *ultimate source* of ghetto social dislocations—*structural inequality in American society.* To these authors, ghetto-specific strategies represent limited, if creative, adaptations to deleterious structural and racial arrangements.

However, this message is difficult to communicate to policymakers and to the general public because it does not resonate with the basic belief system in the United States about the nature and causes of poverty and welfare, a belief system that accounts for economic and social outcomes strictly in individualistic terms. As the French social scientist Robert Castel has so appropriately argued, the paradox of poverty in affluent American society has rested on the notion that "the poor are individuals who themselves bear the chief responsibility for their condition. As a result the politics of welfare center around the management of individual deficiencies."[13]

[12] Rainwater, "Crucible of Identity," 161.
[13] Robert Castel, "The 'War on Poverty' and the Status of Poverty in an

Furthermore, the argument that ghetto-specific strategies represent adaptations to harmful structural and racial arrangements is difficult to convey because conservative intellectuals can easily overemphasize the negative aspects of certain forms of behavior in the inner city by playing on the key individualistic and moralistic themes of this dominant American belief system.

Finally, the association of ghetto-specific strategies with detrimental structural and racial arrangements is difficult to communicate because some liberal scholars, fully aware of the pervasiveness of this belief system, either shy away from describing or fail to even acknowledge ghetto-specific behavior. Indeed, some take it a step further by denouncing not only conservative studies but all studies that focus on such behavior.

It may, perhaps, be useful to discuss briefly two developments that began in the late 1960s and created an atmosphere leading to highly critical interpretations of studies such as *Dark Ghetto*. One was the controversy over the 1965 Moynihan Report on the black family[14] and the other was the attempt in the Afro-American community to identify a specific black perspective in the analysis of matters pertaining to race.

The controversy over the Moynihan report, like so many controversies, raged in large measure because his ideas were misrepresented and distorted by various interests and promulgated and elaborated by the popular media. Moynihan emphasized, first, that the socioeconomic system in the United States was ultimately responsible for producing unstable poor black families and, second, that this instability in turn "is a fundamental cause of other forms of pathology."[15] The critical commentary that followed ignored the first part of Moynihan's argument and left the erroneous impression that he had placed the blame for black social dislocations solely on black family

Affluent Society," *Actes de la recherche en sciences sociales* 19 (January 1979): 47–60. For a critical discussion of the American belief system on poverty and welfare see Wilson, "The American Underclass.

[14] *The Negro Family: The Case for National Action* (Washington, D.C.: Office of Policy Planning and Research, U.S. Department of Labor, March 1965).

[15] Ibid., 30.

instability. The report's reception was influenced, in addition, by a changing political climate in the black community. Some blacks were highly critical of the Moynihan report's emphasis on social patholo- gies within ghetto neighborhoods not simply because of its potential for embarrassment, but also because it conflicted with their claim that blacks were developing a community power base that could be- come a major force in American society and that would reflect the strength and vitality of the black community.[16]

This critical reaction reflected a new definition, description, and explanation of the black condition that accompanied the emergence of the Black Power movement. This new approach, proclaimed as the "black perspective," signaled an ideological shift from interra- cialism to black racial solidarity. It first gained currency among mili- tant black spokespersons in the late 1960s; by the early 1970s it had become a recurrent theme in the writings of a number of black aca- demics and intellectuals.[17] Although the "black perspective" rep- resented a variety of views and arguments on issues of race, the trumpeting of racial pride and self-affirmation was common to many of the writings and speeches on the subject.[18]

In this atmosphere of racial chauvinism, a series of scholarly stud- ies proclaiming a "black perspective" were published. The arguments set forth made clear a substantial and fundamental shift in both the

[16] Lee Rainwater and William L. Yancey, *The Moynihan Report and the Politics of Controversy* (Cambridge, Mass.: M.I.T. Press, 1967).

[17] See, for example, Robert B. Hill, *The Strength of Black Families* (New York: Emerson Hall, 1972); Nathan Hare, "The Challenge of a Black Scholar," *Black Scholar* 1 (December 1969): 58–63; Abd-el Hakim Ibn Alkalimat (Gerald McWorter), "The Ideology of Black Social Science," *Black Scholar* 1 (December 1969): 28–35; Robert Staples, "The Myth of the Black Ma- triarchy," *Black Scholar* 2 (February 1970): 9–16; Robert Staples, *The Black Family: Essays and Studies* (Belmont, Cal.: Wadsworth, 1971); and Joyce Ladner, ed., *The Death of White Sociology* (New York: Random House, 1973).

[18] As the sociologist Robert K. Merton has pointed out in this connection, "when a once powerless collectivity acquires a socially validated sense of grow- ing power, its members experience an intensified need for self-affirmation. Un- der such conditions, collective self-glorification, found in some measure among all groups, becomes a predictable and intensified counterresponse to long- standing belittlement from without." Robert K. Merton, "Insiders and Out- siders: A Chapter in the Sociology of Knowledge," *American Journal of So- ciology* 78 (July 1972): 18–19.

tone and focus of race relations scholarship. Consistent with the emphasis on black glorification and the quest for self-affirmation, analyses that described some aspects of ghetto life as pathological tended to be rejected by black activists in favor of those that emphasized black community strengths. (This rejection included even the thoughtful argument, so clearly articulated in *Dark Ghetto*, that the logical outcome of racial isolation and class subordination is that individuals are forced to adapt to the realities of the ghetto community and are therefore seriously impaired in their ability to function in any other community.) Arguments that focused on the deterioration of the poor black family were dismissed in favor of those that extolled the "virtues" and "strengths" of black families. Thus behavior described as self-destructive by scholars such as Clark and Rainwater was reinterpreted as creative by black-perspective proponents—creative in the sense that many blacks were displaying the ability to survive and even flourish in a ghetto milieu. Ghetto families were described as resilient and were seen as imaginatively adapting to an oppressive racist society.

The logic put forth by the proponents of the black-perspective explanation is interesting because it does not even acknowledge self-destructive behavior in the ghetto. This is a unique response to the dominant American belief system's emphasis on individual deficiencies, rather than on the structure of opportunity, as causes of poverty and welfare. Instead of challenging the validity of the underlying assumptions of this belief system, this approach sidesteps the issue altogether by denying that social dislocations in the inner city represent any special problem. Researchers who emphasize these dislocations, even those who reject the assumptions of individual deprivation of the dominant ideology on poverty and welfare and who focus instead on the structural roots of these problems, were denounced.

Accordingly, in the early 1970s, unlike in the middle 1960s when *Dark Ghetto* was published, there was little motivation to develop a research agenda that pursued the structural roots of ghetto social dislocations. The vitriolic attacks and acrimonious debate that characterized this controversy proved to be too intimidating to scholars, particularly to liberal scholars. Indeed, in the aftermath of this controversy and in an effort to protect their work from the charge of racism or of "blaming the victim," many liberal social scientists tended to avoid describing any behavior that could be construed as unflattering or stigmatizing to racial minorities. Accordingly, for a period of several years, and well after this controversy had subsided, the problems of social dislocation in the inner-city ghetto did not attract serious research attention. All of this was to change in the 1980s, after the nation's awareness of the problems in the ghetto was heightened by sensational media reports, and a new concept gained popularity—the urban "underclass." Let me briefly review this development.

After serious research on the ghetto ground to an abrupt halt in the early 1970s, several trends that had earlier worried Kenneth Clark became much more pronounced. First of all, poverty had become more urban, more concentrated, and more deeply rooted in large metropolises, particularly in older industrial cities with immense and highly segregated black and Hispanic populations.[19] For example, in the city of Chicago, poverty rates in the inner-city neighborhoods increased by an average of 12 percentage points from 1970 to 1980. In eight of the ten neighborhoods that represent the historic core of Chicago's "Black Belt," more than four families in ten were living in poverty by 1980. Accompanying this increase of poverty was a sharp growth in the number and percentage of single-parent households. In ghetto neighborhoods on Chicago's South Side the percent of all families headed by women climbed from an average of 40 percent in 1970 to about 70 percent in 1980. The growth and spread of receipt of public aid was even more spectacular. In 1980 seven of the ten "Black Belt" community areas experienced rates of receipt of AFDC and General Assistance in excess of the 50-percent mark of its total population, reaching such highs as 61 percent in the neighborhood of Grand Boulevard, 71 percent in Oakland, and 84 percent on the Near South Side.[20]

Nor are these changes unique to Chicago. In the ten largest Amer-

[19] Lois J. D. Wacquant and William Julius Wilson, "The Cost of Racial and Class Exclusion in the Inner City, *Annals of the American Academy of Social and Political Science* 501 (January 1989).
[20] Ibid.

ican cities, as of 1970,[21] the number of black residents residing in extreme poverty areas (that is, census tracts with a rate of poverty of at least 40 percent) doubled between 1970 and 1980; for Hispanics, the number tripled. In 1980, 16.5 percent of Hispanics and 21 percent of blacks lived in such areas, in contrast to only 1.7 percent of non-Hispanic whites.

Moreover, the poor residents of these ten large cities were more concentrated in extreme poverty areas in 1980 than they were in 1970. Indeed, the poorer the area, the greater the increase in poverty over that decade. As a result, the proportion of poor people who reside in nonpoor areas plunged from 45 percent in 1970 to 32 percent in 1980, while the proportion in extreme poverty areas soared from 13 to 27 percent.

In short, the 1970s witnessed a sharp growth in the population of blacks and Hispanics residing in extreme poverty areas; an increasing concentration of the poor in the most impoverished neighborhoods of these cities; and sharply divergent patterns of poverty concentration between racial minorities and whites. It is clear, then, that one of the legacies of historical racial and class subjugation in America is a unique concentration of minority and especially black residents in the inner-city ghettos of large central cities. The trend Kenneth Clark identified in 1965 had become even more pronounced by 1980.

Even though very little serious research on life in the ghetto was conducted during this period,[22] there was a general perception, as occasionally reported in the media, that things were getting worse. For example, following the New York city power shortage that occasioned widespread looting, *Time* magazine ran a cover story, in August 1977, that dramatized conditions in the ghettos of Chicago and New York. The article, entitled "The American Underclass: Minority within a Minority," was a trendsetter not only because it made the magazine the first major popular publication to feature

[21] These ten cities include New York City, Chicago, Los Angeles, Philadelphia, Detroit, Houston, Baltimore, Dallas, Cleveland, and Indianapolis.

[22] One notable exception was a study published in the late 1970s—Elijah Anderson, *A Place on the Corner* (Chicago: University of Chicago Press, 1978).

prominently the term "underclass," but also because it set the tone for future media reports on the world of the underclass. "Affluent people know little about this world," stated the *Time* report, "except when despair makes it erupt explosively onto Page One or the 7 o'clock news. Behind its crumbling walls lives a large group of people who are more intractable, more socially alien and more hostile than almost anyone had imagined. They are the unreachables: the American underclass." The *Time* article pointed out that the concept of "underclass," first used in "class-ridden Europe," was "applied to the U.S. by Swedish Economist Gunnar Myrdal and other intellectuals in the 1960s" and "has become a rather common description of people who are seen to be stuck more or less permanently at the bottom, removed from the American dream." The article goes on to state that

> though its members come from all races and live in many places, the underclass is made up mostly of impoverished urban blacks, who still suffer from the heritage of slavery and discrimination. . . . Their bleak environment nurtures values that are often at radical odds with those of the majority—even the majority of the poor. Thus the underclass minority produces a highly disproportionate number of the nations' juvenile delinquents, school dropouts, drug addicts and welfare mothers, and much of the adult crime, family disruption, urban decay, and demand for social expenditures.[23]

What is significant to note in this account is the strong emphasis on the allegedly unique "values" of the underclass and their connection with social pathologies. Arguments about the effects of the structural and racial arrangements of United States society are noticeably absent.

However, not until the first few years of the 1980s, following the publication of a series of well-publicized books written by conservative analysts, were arguments about the unique values and behavior of the underclass widely reflected in the media. In a political atmosphere created during the first term of the Reagan administration, one in which the dominant ideology of individual pathology in poverty and welfare was strongly reinforced, conservative analysts

---

[23] "The American Underclass," *Time,* August 29, 1977, 14–27.

rushed to explain the apparent paradox of a sharp rise in inner-city
social dislocations after the passage in the late 1960s of the most
sweeping antipoverty and antidiscrimination legislation in the nation's history.

These analysts, thrust to the fore of policy debate by the political
ascendancy of Reaganism, argued that the growth of liberal social
policies since the mid-1960s had exacerbated, not alleviated, ghetto-
specific cultural tendencies. Neoconservative books, such as George
Gilder's *Wealth and Poverty,* Charles Murray's *Losing Ground,* and
Lawrence Mead's *Beyond Entitlement,* presented a range of arguments dealing with the presumed adverse effects of liberal social
policies on urban underclass values and behavior.[24] Thus the Great
Society and other liberal programs were portrayed as self-defeating
because they ignored the behavioral problems of the underclass,
made them less self-reliant, increased their joblessness, and swelled
both their births outside of marriage and the number of female-
headed households. It did not seem to matter that these arguments
were not supported by any rigorous empirical research. Many liberal
intellectuals had retreated from a discussion of social dislocations in
inner-city ghettos and had no alternative explanations to advance.
This default allowed conservative analysts to dominate public discourse on the subject through the first half of the 1980s. Their
themes were echoed in a series of popular media reports on America's underclass that strongly reinforced individualistic explanations
of problems in the inner-city ghetto, explanations that resonated
with the dominant American belief system on poverty and welfare.[25]

Against this backdrop my most recent book, *The Truly Disadvantaged* was published.[26] When the first reviews appeared in late Oc-

[24] George Gilder, *Wealth and Poverty* (New York: Basic Books, 1981);
Charles Murray, *Losing Ground: American Social Policy, 1950–1980* (New
York: Basic Books, 1984); and Lawrence Mead, *Beyond Entitlement: The
Social Obligations of Citizenship* (New York: The Free Press, 1986).

[25] See, for example, Myron Magnet, "America's Underclass: What To Do?"
Fortune, May 11, 1987, 130–50; Chicago Tribune, *The American Millstone*
(Chicago: Contemporary Books, 1986); Mickey Kaus, "The Work Ethic State,"
New Republic, July 7, 1986, 22–23; and Nicholas Lemann, "The Origins of the
Underclass," *Atlantic,* June 1986, 31–55.

[26] William Julius Wilson, *The Truly Disadvantaged: The Inner City, The
Underclass, and Public Policy* (Chicago: University of Chicago Press, 1987).

tober 1987, I felt that the timing could not have been better. One of my purposes in *The Truly Disadvantaged* was to challenge the dominant themes on the underclass reflected in the popular media and in the writings of conservative intellectuals, not by shying away from using the concept "underclass," not by avoiding a description and explanation of unflattering behavior, but by attempting, as did Kenneth Clark in *Dark Ghetto,* to relate the practices and experiences of inner-city ghetto residents to the structure of opportunities and constraints in American society. And one of my principal arguments was that the vulnerability of poor urban minorities to changes in the economy since the early 1970s resulted in sharp increases in joblessness, in the concentration of poverty, in the number of single-parent families, and in welfare dependency despite the creation of Great Society programs and despite antidiscrimination and affirmative action programs.

Also, I argued that the effects of changes in the economy are most clearly felt in the concentrated poverty areas of the ghetto. The exodus of higher-income families, together with the sharp rise in joblessness, has transformed the social structure of these neighborhoods in ways that severely worsen the impact of the continuing industrial and geographic changes in the American economy since the 1970s, periodic recessions, wage stagnation, and the restriction of employment opportunities to the low-wage sector. Today the dwindling presence of middle- and working-class households in the ghetto makes it even more difficult than when Kenneth Clark wrote *Dark Ghetto* for the remaining residents of these communities to sustain basic formal and informal institutions in the face of high and prolonged joblessness and attendant economic hardships. And as the basic institutions decline, the social organization of inner-city ghetto neighborhoods disintegrates, further depleting the resources and limiting the life chances of those who remain mired in these blighted areas.[27]

[27] Ibid.; and William Julius Wilson et al., "The Ghetto Underclass and the Changing Structure of Urban Poverty," in *Quiet Riots: Race and Poverty in the United States,* eds. Fred R. Harris and Roger W. Wilkins (New York: Pantheon, 1988), 123–51.

The Truly Disadvantaged is just one of several recent studies from the scholarly community on the ghetto underclass.[28] Indeed, partly in response to heightened public awareness of and media attention to the problems of the underclass, research activity on the inner-city ghetto has been revived. Scholars are now researching and attempting to explain the growing concentration of urban poverty and the social transformation of the inner-city ghetto.

It is likely that many of these processes would have been better understood if studies such as *Dark Ghetto* had not been abruptly halted as the nation entered the 1970s. Kenneth Clark's brilliant depiction of the social and psychological dimensions of the ghetto still holds today. What is apparent is that many of the problems he carefully described have grown, even accelerated, in certain neighborhoods. Concepts that are now being discussed to explain ghetto experiences, such as "social isolation" and "concentration effects," certainly apply to the descriptions of inner-city life detailed in *Dark Ghetto*. What has changed is that Ghetto neighborhoods in large central cities like New York and Chicago are much more vulnerable to shifts in the broader economy because of the growing exodus of higher-income families after 1970. The combination of economic change and the departure of working- and middle-class families has created a process of "hyperghettoization."[29] But to repeat, this represents an acceleration, not a qualitative change, of a process discussed in considerable detail in *Dark Ghetto*. Students of urban life will find that Kenneth Clark's description and analysis of ghetto life continue to be relevant to impoverished inner-city neighborhoods in the nation's large metropolises.

Chicago
April 1989

[28] See, for example, the several articles in the special issue, "The Ghetto Underclass: Social Science Perspectives." *Annals of the American Academy of Political and Social Science,* Vol. 501, January 1989.

[29] Wacquant and Wilson, "The Cost of Racial and Class Exclusion."

FOREWORD
by Gunnar Myrdal

Following from a distance the rising Negro rebellion in America, I often think of a passage in W. E. B. Du Bois' *Dusk of Dawn:**

It is difficult to let others see the full psychological meaning of caste segregation. It is as though one, looking out from a dark cave in a side of an impending mountain, sees the world passing and speaks to it; speaks courteously and persuasively, showing them how these entombed souls are hindered in their natural movement, expression, and development; and how their loosening from prison would be a matter not simply of courtesy, sympathy, and help to them, but aid to all the world. One talks on evenly and logically in this way but notices that the passing throng does not even turn its head, or if it does, glances curiously and walks on. It gradually penetrates the minds of the prisoners that the people passing do not hear; that some thick sheet of invisible but horribly tangible plate glass is between them and the world. They get excited; they talk louder; they gesticulate. Some of the passing world stop in curiosity; these gesticulations seem so pointless; they laugh and pass on. They still either do not hear at all, or hear but dimly, and even what they hear, they do not understand. Then the people within may become hysterical. They may scream and hurl themselves against the barriers, hardly realizing in their bewilderment that they are screaming in a vacuum unheard and that their antics may actually seem funny to those outside looking in. They may even, here and there, break through in blood and disfigure-

* New York, Harcourt, Brace & Co., 1940.

ment, and find themselves faced by a horrified, implacable, and quite overwhelming mob of people frightened for their own very existence.

Du Bois could have added that some of the prisoners of American color caste seek escapes of one type or another which in different ways are all illusory; he commented upon this in other contexts.

This book by my friend, Kenneth B. Clark, is one of the many attempts now being made in greater numbers than ever by American intellectuals in that dark cave to speak so loudly, though calmly, that their voices pierce dramatically the invisible sheet of plate glass. He is desperately anxious that the ugly facts of life in the Negro ghetto become really known to the ruling white majority. Among these facts of life, one most difficult to convey is how it feels to be enclosed in segregation.

He speaks the language of reason and points to the immense wastage, not only in human happiness but in productivity. Obliterating in America the Negro ghetto and all other pockets of subhuman existence, involving even more non-Negroes than Negroes, is a necessary condition for President Johnson's Great Society. As long as they are permitted to exist, they constitute a drag on American prosperity generally. Even leaving aside the moral issue of justice and the more perfect realization of the American ideals of liberty and equality of opportunity, and speaking in cold financial terms, eradicating the rural and urban slums and giving the youth there an education for productive employment are probably the most profitable investments that can be made in America today.

But Clark is tired of the false objectivity, the "balanced view" of many of his liberal white friends on the other side of the horribly tangible plate glass, which is philosophically made possible by the inherited Anglo-Saxon naiveté and lack of clarity regarding the value problem. Therefore, he also speaks with passion but with honesty and, in the end, a belief in the possibility of integration as a two-way process. In the demand for true objectivity he must, indeed, demand human empathy and even compassion on the part of as many as possible of those who can read, think, and feel in free, prosperous, white America. He asks that they recognize that large reforms, far beyond the formal enactment of civil rights, have become necessary and urgent. He can press for these huge reforms with the better conscience as, without waiting for them, he threw himself first into constructive, healing work in the Haryou activity in Harlem upon which he reports in various parts of the book, and now continues his exploration of the relevance of social science for social change through his work as director of the Social Dynamics Research Institute of the City College of the City University of New York.

Institute for International Economic Studies
University of Stockholm

Stockholm
December 1964

INTRODUCTION TO AN EPILOGUE

It is difficult to know the source of a book. This book grows directly from the two years which the author spent as chief project consultant and chairman of the board of directors of the planning stage of Harlem Youth Opportunities Unlimited (Haryou). But, indirectly, its source is far more complex.

Haryou was financed by the President's Committee on Juvenile Delinquency and by the Mayor of the City of New York. In June 1962 its responsibilities were to set up the offices and hire a staff to study the conditions of youth in Harlem as background for a comprehensive program for these young people, and to submit within two years a report and a proposal for the funds necessary to implement these plans. With the publication of the report *Youth in the Ghetto: A Study of the Consequences of Powerlessness and a Blueprint for Change,* Haryou concluded its planning responsibility. In April 1964, the report was officially presented to the review panel of the President's Committee on Juvenile Delinquency. The review panel, headed by Dr. Leonard S. Cottrell, recommended an initial allocation of $1 million to put this program into action. The City of New York then allocated $3.5 million from its Anti-Poverty Program funds for general programming and the Department of Labor of the federal government granted $0.5 million to begin the job training and placement part of the Haryou program. I resigned from Haryou during this transition period between planning and implementation.

The action phase of the program is to be conducted by the combined forces of Haryou and Associated Community Teams (Act), an action program for the youth of Harlem, also financed by the President's Committee on Juvenile Delinquency during the same period when planning operations of Haryou were begun. Haryou-Act Inc. the new combined group, is charged with the responsibility of implementing the Haryou plans through operation of the multi-million dollar Harlem Youth Development program.

Initially, it was thought that the 620-page report *Youth in the Ghetto* should be published for more general distribution than it was possible to do privately. The board of directors of Haryou therefore established a committee with authority to make the necessary arrangements for such publication. The author of the book was chairman of the committee and was empowered to make the appropriate revisions. However, as work proceeded on the revisions and as one observed developments and problems related to the early stages of Haryou-Act, it became clear that a condensation and revision alone could not present a full and clear picture of the plight of Harlem's youth within the ghetto community. The Haryou report had been written for the specific purpose of presenting a plan for Harlem's youth to those review panels and groups in the federal, state and city governments and private foundations to whom requests would come for funds for the Haryou program. A book for the general public had to be broader and deeper in scope and purpose. While the Haryou report emphasized the plight of youth in Harlem, the present book concentrates on the problems of ghetto communities everywhere and with all of the inhabitants of the ghettos, not with youth alone. *Youth in the Ghetto,* therefore, became merely a point of departure for *Dark Ghetto.*

My two years of intense involvement with the Haryou planning project led to reflections that resulted in this study of the total phenomena of the ghetto. My direct involvement with the young people associated with Haryou, the countless committee meetings, board meetings, staff meetings, the inevitable contacts and communication with the newspapers of the community and the daily metropolitan press, and the meetings with federal, state and city officials brought me into the vortex of the ghetto community and in touch with the lives, the feelings, the thoughts, the strengths and weaknesses of the people who lived in the ghetto. *Dark Ghetto* attempts to communicate the momentum of this dynamic and, at times, personally threatening involvement. During this period the Harlem community became a laboratory in which I sought, not always successfully, to play the role of an "involved observer." It was hoped this concentrated project, with its clear and specific goals, would sharpen insight into problems which tend to become obscured for those who live in the ghetto and are required to struggle for their existence there.

But I could never be fully detached as a scholar or participant. More than forty years of my life had been lived in Harlem. I started school in the Harlem public schools. I first learned about people, about love, about cruelty, about sacrifice, about cowardice, about courage, about bombast in Harlem. For many years before I returned as an "involved observer," Harlem had been my home. My family moved from house to house, and from neighborhood to neighborhood within the walls of the ghetto in a desperate attempt to escape its creeping blight. In a very real sense, therefore, *Dark Ghetto* is a summation of my personal and lifelong experiences and observations as a prisoner within the ghetto long before I was aware that I was really a prisoner. To my knowledge, there is at present nothing in the vast literature of social science treatises and textbooks and nothing in the practical or field training of graduate students in social science to prepare them for the realities and complexities of this type of involvement in a real, dynamic, turbulent, and at times seemingly chaotic community. And what is more, nothing anywhere in the training of social scientists, teachers, or social workers now prepares them to understand, to cope with, or to change the normal chaos of ghetto communities. These are grave lacks which must be remedied soon if these disciplines are to become relevant to the stability and survival of our society.

The role and method of an "involved observer" is not an easy one to describe, but it is necessary to try. One owes an obligation to do so to one's colleagues who are also concerned with problems related to a systematic approach to the study of men in society. This role is particularly difficult to maintain when one is not only a participant in the community but when one brings to the attempt to use this method, with that degree of clarity and objectivity essential for social science accuracy, a personal history of association with and concern for many of the people in the very community one seeks to study. The method of study has much in common with the more traditional methods of a "participant observer" and the methods of the cultural anthropologist, who lives with primitive peoples in order to understand and describe their customs, their mores, and their total culture. All such methods require the observer to be a part of what is being observed, to join in the lives of the people while at the same time seeking to understand them and the forces which mold them and to which they respond. The role of the "involved observer," however, differs from the other two in that it demands participation not only in rituals and customs but in the social competition with the hierarchy in dealing with the problems of the people he is seeking to understand. While the observer of an alien group has the protection of the stranger to whom the group is required to show some degree of courtesy or hospitality, the "involved observer" runs the risk of joining in the competition for status and power and cannot escape the turbulence and conflict inherent in the struggle. He must be exposed at the same time that he seeks to protect himself and to protect his role of observer. He must run the risk of personal attacks, disappointments, personal hurts and frustrations, at the same time that he maintains a disciplined preoccupation with his primary goal of understanding. He must mobilize and use every personal resource, strength, and weakness in his struggle for clarity and perspective, though the personal and at times deeply subjective involvement would seem to work against achievement of clarity. Probably the most difficult assault to which he will be subjected is the questioning of his personal motives, the veiled and at times rather flagrant assertion that his concern with the problems of the community stem from a desire for personal power or material gain. In a ghetto community, where the material rewards are hard to come by, the motives of almost everyone are suspect. It is not easy for even the more intelligent or more sophisticated prisoners of the ghetto to believe that anyone could be motivated primarily, if not exclusively, by the desire to understand the depth of the human predicament. How much more difficult then for the scarred or hardened victims of the ghetto to believe that anyone could desire genuine social change or social justice. For the residents of the ghetto, who have learned from bitter experience, any form of altruism appears to be a ruse, a transparent disguise for the "hustle." The "hustle," the "cashing in," the smooth or crude exploiter, seem the realities.

Distortion of vision and confusion may harass the "involved observer," but the inevitable pressures of his role bring, also, gnawing self-doubt. It is the ultimate test of strength, which this observer did not always pass, as the pressures intensify and as the examples of equivocation and broken agreements accumulate, to discipline himself and attempt to control his defensiveness, his doubts concerning the adequacy of self, and above all, his desire to escape before the completion of his task. The only effective antidotes to this tropistic need to protect oneself in the face of engulfing pathology are a commitment to the quest for understanding and truth and a compulsion to persist in this quest in spite of personal hazards. In this regard the role of the "involved observer" is not unlike that of Bruno Bettelheim and Viktor E. Frankl, who used their skill and training to provide us with some understanding of the nature of the horror and the barbarity of the German concentration camps.* The circumstances of their initial observation were involuntary. The return of a former inhabitant to the Harlem ghetto appears to be a matter of personal choice, but who can say how free the choice really is. Can the prisoner ever fully escape the prison?

What are the possible antidotes to the deficiencies and pitfalls of

---

* Bruno Bettelheim, "Individual and Mass Behavior in Extreme Situations," *Journal of Abnormal and Social Psychology*, 1943, *38*, pp. 417–452; Viktor E. Frankl, *Man's Search for Meaning, An Introduction to Logotherapy.* (A newly revised and enlarged edition of *From Death-Camp to Existentialism.*) Boston, Beacon Press, 1962.

involved observations? One desirable countercheck would be made
by a parallel person who would test the observations, insights, and
conclusions of the primary observer. Such a person would have to be
more detached than he but at the same time fully cognizant of the
problems and processes of the situation. He must be of equal professional stature and capable of the same level of, if not more,
penetrating insight and intelligence. He must be protected and removed from direct competitive involvement with the community
and with the primary observer himself. He must be a person in whose
competence, but even more important, in whose critical judgment
and integrity, the observer has total confidence. In the Haryou
planning operation I had the good fortune of having available a
number of consultants, some of whom played this critical role most
effectively. Furthermore, for me, Dr. Hylan Lewis, professor of
sociology at Howard University and a consultant to Haryou from its
inception, assumed the burdens of this role with enthusiasm and at
times with awesome and prophetic insights. If I had not been able
to consult with him as the many crises arose I could not have continued my responsibilities through to their conclusion. Hylan Lewis's
counsel, advice, critical comments, and suggestions from the beginning of the Haryou process to the completion of the manuscript
of *Dark Ghetto* were, in the most literal sense, invaluable.

During the planning stage of Haryou some of the traditional social
science methods were used, including tape recordings of meetings
and of group and individual interviews. All of the statements of
Harlem residents presented in the first chapter, "Prologue: The Cry
of the Ghetto," were obtained by Willie Jones, Haryou staff interviewer, who has the capacity not only to talk naturally with the people
of Harlem but to elicit responses from them by blending into the
style and adopting the idiom of the particular group or individual
whose opinions he was seeking. It is of some methodological significance to note that the presence of a portable or stationary tape recorder and the inevitable microphone did not inhibit the responses
of these subjects even when they were discussing drug addiction or
police graft. On the contrary, it seemed that the starvation for serious

attention and respect which characterises so many of the forgotten people of the ghetto made the microphone a symbol of respect and status or a stimulus to vanity which encouraged free expression. This might not have been the case for more reserved middle-class people who might tend to view a microphone or tape recorder as invasion of their privacy and therefore to respond with appropriate protective defenses of repression, censoring, or distortion. Among the Haryou subjects, the posture of exaggeration, if not bombast, seemed more apparent than did inhibition. Intensity of feeling, anguish, and concern were freely and at times vehemently expressed. But even the most obvious hyperbole reflected a level of reality which can not be ignored if the complexities and potential explosiveness of the American ghettos are to be understood.

It became clear in the early stages of the Haryou study that while usual methods of data collection and analysis would contribute to an understanding of the demographic statistics of the community, the use of standardized questionnaires and interview procedures would result in stylized and superficial verbal responses or evasions. The outstanding finding at this time was that data obtained by these traditional methods did not plumb the depth or the complexities of the attitudes and anxieties, the many forms of irony and rage which form the truths of the lives of the people of Harlem. Methods which simplified these complex realities, subordinating the difficult and multifaceted realities to the constraints of the methods, could not be taken seriously without presenting and perpetuating a superficial and methodologically distorted social reality. The task confronting the Haryou research staff, then, was to discover and probe the dimensions of the ghetto with the most appropriate methods. It was hoped that the social phenomena would determine the methods instead of the methods distorting or determining the phenomena. It was necessary, therefore, to run risks, to establish as many contacts as possible with groups in the community; to organize groups of young people; to plan confrontations and conflicts among individuals within groups and between groups in order to draw forth deep feelings and ambivalences, and to see how these individuals responded to and interpreted and resolved those conflicts.

Probably the most distinctive fact about the Haryou process was the involving of hundreds of young people from various social, economic, and educational backgrounds in the research and planning. A group known as the Haryou Associates was formed by the young people themselves, who worked as volunteer research assistants and who pretested program ideas. Others, generally college students and the children of middle- or upper-class parents, found themselves able to establish only a peripheral or specifically limited relationship with the planning operation. They tended to see themselves more as "volunteers" or "missionaries" who would contribute as much time to Haryou as their other activities and demands would permit. Unlike the young people in Haryou Associates, they did not consider that they were directly involved in the goals of Haryou nor did they see any direct benefit to themselves. But all the youth associated with Haryou formed a valuable natural laboratory for direct observation and study of the human forces at work in the larger community. They were a microcosm of the Harlem community, though in a technical sense not totally representative of the people of Harlem. Through them it was possible to see more clearly the struggles and patterns of adjustment of the ghetto. Their problems, conflicts, defenses, and fantasies, their strengths and their weaknesses, their perspectives of themselves, their doubts and their aspirations, their defiance and their defeat or their affirmation and success were living experiences and more valuable than statistics.

Dark Ghetto attempts to go beyond the data gathered by Haryou. Though it relies in part upon material which formed a valuable factual basis for the report, it does so primarily as a point of departure. *Dark Ghetto* is, in a sense, no report at all, but rather the anguished cry of its author. But it is the cry of a social psychologist, controlled in part by the concepts and language of social science, and as such can never express the pure authenticity of folk spontaneity or the poetic symbolism of the artist. This book is and can be no wiser than its author. It is his interpretation of the meaning of the facts of the ghetto, the truths behind the delinquency, narcotics addiction, infant mortality, homicide and suicide statistics. In determining the value to be given to these impressions, the reader should know that the author is a Negro, a social psychologist, a college professor, and that he has long been revolted by those forces in American society which make for Harlems and by the fact of Harlem itself; and that he has not lived in Harlem in more than fifteen years. These and other facts do not make for absolute objectivity in judgment and they might lead a critical and exacting reader to suspect distortion and bias. Some form of subjective distortion seems inevitable whenever human beings dare to make judgments about any aspect of the human predicament.

Throughout my role as a student of the Harlem community, I was conscious of my biases and sought to correct them and test them against the biases and judgments of others with similar and different biases. A bias, used in this sense, is a starting hunch or hypothesis determined by a system of values with which one approaches and seeks to understand social reality. As Charles Beard said of himself and other social scientists in *The Discussion of Human Affairs,** I found that there was no one without some bias and that those who pretended to be most unbiased either were indifferent or reflected an insidious form of bias. An important part of my creed as a social scientist is that on the grounds of absolute objectivity or on a posture of scientific detachment and indifference, a truly relevant and serious social science cannot ask to be taken seriously by a society desperately in need of moral and empirical guidance in human affairs. Nor can it support its claims to scientific purity or relevance by a preoccupation with methodology as an end and by innumerable articles in scientific journals devoted to escapist, even though quantifiable, trivia. I believe that to be taken seriously, to be viable, and to be relevant social science must dare to study the real problems of men and society, must use the real community, the market place, the arena of politics and power as its laboratories, and must confront and seek to understand the dynamics of social action and social change. The appropriate technology of serious and relevant social science would have as its prime goal helping society move toward humanity and justice with minimum irrationality, in-

* New York, Macmillan, 1936.

stability, and cruelty. If social science and social technology cannot help achieve these goals then they will be ignored or relegated to the level of irrelevance, while more serious men seek these goals through trial and error or through the crass exercise of power.

This study of the Negro ghetto is an attempt to understand the combined problems of the confined Negro and the problems of the slum. Some of the problems of the lower status Negro are similar to and identical with the problems of poor people and slums in general. But in America, the white poor and slum dweller have the advantage of the social and psychological reality which is an essential aspect of American racism; that is, the belief that they can rise economically and escape from the slums. The Negro believes himself to be closely confined to the pervasive low status of the ghetto, and in fact usually is. This book's emphasis on the pathologies of American ghettos attempts to describe and interpret what happens to human beings who are confined to depressed areas and whose access to the normal channels of economic mobility and opportunity is blocked. This approach is not to be equated with assumptions of "inherent racial differences" or with the more subtly discriminatory "cultural deprivation" theories. It seeks answers to many questions, and among them are these: What are the personal and social consequences of the ghetto? What are the consequences of the victims' lack of power to change their status? What are the consequences of the inability or unwillingness of those with power to use it for constructive social change? The answers to these questions have implications beyond the important problems of American racial and economic ghettos, implications that may extend to an understanding of the chances of stability of relations between underdeveloped and developed nations of the world and that may hold the key to general international stability.

There have been a number of studies dealing with the American Negro and a number dealing with the American urban poor, but few concerned with the Negro ghetto itself. As a consequence, one finds meager data in other cities to compare with the Haryou studies of Harlem, hence the necessary reliance in *Dark Ghetto* on data relating to Harlem. For example, delinquency statistics may be available for a slum area of a given city or there may be national statistics for Negro unemployment, but little is available to describe the Negro ghetto itself, and certainly little has been done by social scientists to study the psychological—i.e., the human—significance of the ghetto.

A few years ago a highly respected friend, who is a psychiatrist, interrupted a humorous but somewhat serious discussion by observing that I would not permit "the facts to interfere with the truth." At the time we laughed in appreciation of the wit inherent in the seeming incongruity of the observation. Since then I have many times recalled that remark with increasing appreciation of its profound significance. Throughout my involvement in the study of the ghetto, in the collection of the data about Harlem, in my exposure to currents and cross currents of the community, it became increasingly clear to me that what are generally labeled as the *facts* of the ghetto are not necessarily synonymous with the *truth* of the ghetto. In fact, there are times when one feels that "facts" tend to obscure truth. *Dark Ghetto* seeks to move, as far as it can, beyond a narrow view of fact, beyond the facts that are quantifiable and are computable, and that distort the actual lives of individual human beings into rigid statistics. Probably such facts reflect or suggest some of the truth; delinquency and infant mortality rates do tell us that some people get in trouble with society and that others die early in life. But such facts do not relate the truths of the parents' emotions when confronted with the blight of defeat or death nor do they reveal the individual delinquent, his struggle for self esteem, his pretense at indifference or defiance of his fate, his vulnerability to hurt, his sense of rejection, his fears, his angers, or his sense of aloneness. These are rejected as facts by most social scientists because they are not now quantifiable.

To obtain the truth of Harlem one must *interpret* the facts. Certain social truths can be more painful and disturbing than facts, and this truth may account in some measure for social science's seemingly endless preoccupation with statistics. Statistics may be manipulated and played with, analyzed and treated in a way calculated to lead to minimum pain or personal involvement. They are "manageable." Figures on the extent of malnutrition in Southern states or rural areas are impersonal and are not especially disturbing. Direct encounter with a starving child, on the other hand, is a truth which is personal; it remains personally disturbing until the child is fed. To face social truths seems to require empathy, social sensitivity, and a peculiar type of courage.

Another basis for the confusion between social facts and social truths is that one fact may lead to different truths or assumptions of truth. There may be differences in the degree of empathy on the part of the interpreter or differences in the extent of personal encounter or in the resorting to devices like denial, repression, and rationalization. But also, differences in the nature of the interpretation may be the result of individual point of view or philosophy. A good illustration of this is found in the story that Otto Klineberg used to tell: Two alcoholics looked at the same bottle of whiskey in which half the content had been consumed. The optimistic alcoholic was glad that the bottle was half full; his pessimistic companion was depressed that it was half empty.

Similarly, one social scientist looking at the delinquency statistics in Harlem could rejoice in the *facts* that show that the vast majority of young people in the ghetto—nearly 90 percent—do not come in conflict with the law. Another social scientist might concentrate on the fact of the 10 percent who do become delinquent.

Truth is more complex, multifaceted and value-determined than is the usual fact. Fact is empirical while truth is interpretative. Fact is, in itself, unrelated to value; it merely *is*. Truth, as the understanding—in the fullest sense—of fact, is related to value and, for that reason, more fully human.

Dark Ghetto attempts to use some of the facts of Harlem to ascertain some of the truths of human ghettos. Since truth is not easy to grasp or recognize—it remains more of a quest than an attainment—one is obliged to seek it through a continuous process of observation, speculation, refinement of hypothesis, and testing of those hypotheses which are at present testable. It is my hope that the attempt presented in this book will stimulate further research and study in quest of truth and social justice.

To understand Harlem, one must seek the truth and one must dare to accept and understand the truths one does find. One must understand its inconsistencies, its contradictions, its paradoxes, its ironies, its comic and its tragic face, its cruel and its self-destructive forces, and its desperate surge for life. And above all one must understand its humanity. The truth of the dark ghetto is not merely a truth about Negroes; it reflects the deeper torment and anguish of the total human predicament.

ACKNOWLEDGMENTS

Many persons have contributed generally and specifically to this book. The basic support and help in the difficult period of gathering the data for the Haryou report came from an inspired Haryou staff. Most of the factual data concerning the Harlem community that is found in *Dark Ghetto* reflect the conscientious and indefatigable work of such members of the Haryou staff as James A. Jones, research director; Kenneth E. Marshall, program director; and Cyril D. Tyson, administrative director. These top staff members of Haryou were fortunate in having highly skilled associates and assistants who are too numerous to mention. Special note, however, must be made of the contribution of Olivia Frost and Lawrence Houston, who were largely responsible for gathering and interpreting the information on the economic and occupational status of Negroes in the Harlem ghetto, and Linda Tiger Bailey and Richard Hope who worked diligently with other staff members in gathering statistical and interview data on the schools in Harlem. Martha Blankenship, my administrative assistant at Haryou, was thoroughly involved in all aspects of the Haryou planning stage.

In addition to the staff, I was fortunate in having a panel of consultants of Haryou who included such outstanding social scientists as professors Isidore Chein, Allison Davis, Herbert Hyman, Hylan

Lewis, and Thomas Pettigrew. Dean John U. Monro of Harvard College; Whitney M. Young, executive director of the National Urban League; and Mark A. McCloskey, formerly chairman of the New York State Commission for Youth, gave valuable comments and criticisms of the initial report.

The magnitude and pressure of the Haryou operation required the cooperation and help of many groups of people, including its board of directors, the President's Committee on Juvenile Delinquency and its staff, and the deputy mayor-city administrator's staff, which had the responsibility for developing these community programs for the Mayor of the City of New York.

In preparing the manuscript for *Dark Ghetto,* I was fortunate in having the help of individuals who assumed the inescapable drudgery of checking and rechecking facts, typing and retyping various versions of the manuscript. It is difficult to express fully one's appreciation for this type of help, but I must try to express my thanks to Kate Clark, Gloria Edwards, Frances Farber, Dixie Moon, and Carolyn Atkinson, who took on these important responsibilities for me.

A special thanks must be given to my friend Gavin Thomson, who dared the limits of friendship by again typing the final draft of a book for me.

For an author to attempt to express his gratitude to his editor presents one with an awkwardness similar to that of trying to express the depth of one's feelings for a member of the family. My editor, Jeannette Hopkins, made this book possible because she believed in it even before I could permit myself to accept it as a possibility. She understood the book in terms of itself, and forced me into that most difficult of all confrontations, the confrontation of myself with my beliefs. She raised many of the most disturbing questions. She saw some of the gaps and she assumed the risk of pushing me to the limits of my insights. She brought to her work with me and *Dark Ghetto* not only her exceptional professional skills, her clarity, her precision, her versatility and breadth of knowledge, but also her personal depth of social commitment. Her friendship, understanding, and compassion controlled somewhat my procrastination and prevented me from escaping the responsibility of producing this book.

In spite of the help of the many people who made this book possible, its flaws reflect my own limitations. Whatever are its virtues must be shared.

K. B. C.

New York City
January 1965

DARK GHETTO

Perchance hee for whom this Bell tolls, may be so ill, as that he knowes not it tolls for him; And perchance I may thinke my selfe so much better than I am, as that they who are about mee, and see my state, may have caused it to toll for mee, and I know not that.

—JOHN DONNE, *Meditations from "Devotions upon Emergent Occasions," XVII*

1

PROLOGUE: THE CRY OF THE GHETTO

A lot of times, when I'm working, I become as despondent as hell and I feel like crying. I'm not a man, none of us are men! I don't own anything. I'm not a man enough to own a store; none of us are.

—Man, age about 30

You know the average young person out here don't have a job, man, they don't have anything to do. They don't have any alternative, you know, but to go out there and try to make a living for themselves. Like when you come down to the Tombs down there, they're down there for robbing and breaking in. They want to know why you did it and where you live, but you have to live. You go down to the employment agency and you can't get a job. They have you waiting all day, but you can't get a job. They don't have a job for you. Yet you have to live. I'm ready to do anything anyone else is ready to do—because I want to live—I want to live. No one wants to die. I want to live.

—Drug addict, male, age 30

If a man qualifies, it should be first come, first serve. You understand what I mean? Regardless of whether we're black or white, we

all have families! It should be first come, first serve. But that's not
how they do you! If you're black, you're automatically turned down
on a lot of jobs. They'll take your application, but no sooner than you
walk out of the office, or wherever it is, they take the application
and put it in the wastebasket, and tell you they'll let you know in a
couple of weeks.

—Man, age about 24

No one with a mop can expect respect from a banker, or an attorney, or men who create jobs, and all you have is a mop. Are you
crazy? Whoever heard of integration between a mop and a banker?

—Man, age about 38

The way the Man has us, he has us wanting to kill one another.
Dog eat dog, amongst us! He has us, like we're so hungry up here,
he has us up so tight! Like his rent is due, my rent is due. It's Friday.
The Man wants sixty-five dollars. If you are three days over, or don't
have the money; like that, he wants to give you a dispossess! Take
you to court! The courts won't go along with you, they say get the
money or get out! Yet they don't tell you how to get the money, you
understand? They say get the money and pay the Man, but they
don't say how to get it. Now, if you use illegal means to obey his
ruling to try to get it—which he's not going to let you do—if you
use illegal means to pay your bills according to his ruling—he will
put you in jail.

—Man, age 31

They are raising the rents so high, like that, with a job, the menial
jobs that we have or get, the money we will receive—we won't be
able to pay the rent! So where we going to go? They are pushing
us further, and further, and further—out of Harlem.

—Man, age 31

If you could get onto the ninth floor of the Tombs, you would see
for yourself. They are lying there like dogs, vomiting and what not,

over one another. It is awful. It smells like a pigpen up there. If you look, you'll see nothing but Spanish. And the black man. You'll seldom see a white man. When you do, he is from a very poor group. They are 20 years old, looking like they were 40.

—Drug addict, male, age about 37

I want to go to the veins.
You want to do what?
I want to go to the veins.
You want to go to the veins; you mean you want to get high?
Yeah.
Why do you want to get high, man?
To make me think.
You can't think without getting high?
No.

Discrimination is even in the school I attend right now. I know my teacher is very prejudiced because I have certain questions that have to be answered for my knowledge, but he will never answer. He would always call on a little white boy to give the answer. I told him one night, to his face, that if he didn't want to answer my questions just tell me and I would leave. There are always other teachers. He didn't say anything. He just looked at me and figured I was going to—so he said, "Well, maybe next time." There is no next time—this is the time and I'm not taking second best from any white man.

—Boy, age 17

Well, the gang, they look for trouble, and then if they can't find no trouble, find something they can do, find something they can play around. Go in the park, find a bum, hit him in the face, pee in his face, kick him down, then chase him, grab him and throw him over the fence.

—Boy, age 15

The conditions here are the way they are because of white domination of this community, and when that changes, as is being attempted here, by these [Black] Nationalists, or by any other nationalist groups, or by the Muslims; when they can unite and change these conditions, change the white domination for Black domination, the conditions will change.

—Man, age 28

Why in the hell—now this is more or less a colored neighborhood—why do we have so many white cops? As if we got to have somebody white standing over us. Not that I am prejudiced or anything, but I can't understand why we have to have so many white cops! Now if I go to a white neighborhood, I'm not going to see a lot of colored cops in no white neighborhood, standing guard over the white people. I'm not going to see that; and I know it, and I get sick and tired of seeing so many white cops, standing around.

—Woman, age 38

My wife was even robbed coming back from the store. They tried to snatch her pocketbook, and she came upstairs crying to me. What could I do? Where was the police? Where is the protection?

—Man, age about 50

The white cops, they have a damn sadistic nature. They are really a sadistic type of people and we, I mean me, myself, we don't need them here in Harlem. We don't need them! They don't do the neighborhood any good. They deteriorate the neighborhood. They start more violence than any other people start. They start violence, that's right. A bunch of us could be playing some music, or dancing, which we have as an outlet for ourselves. We can't dance in the house, we don't have clubs or things like that. So we're out on the sidewalk, right on the sidewalk; we might feel like dancing, or one might want to play something on his horn. Right away here comes a cop. "You're disturbing the peace!" No one has said anything, you understand; no one has made a complaint. Everyone is enjoying themselves. But here comes one cop, and he'll want to chase everyone. And gets mad. I mean, he gets mad! We aren't mad. He comes into the neighborhood, aggravated and mad.

—Man, age about 33

Last night, for instance, the officer stopped some fellows on 125th Street, Car No. _____, that was the number of the car, and because this fellow spoke so nicely for his protection and his rights, the officer said, "All right, everybody get off the street or inside!" Now, it's very hot. We don't have air-conditioned apartments in most of these houses up here, so where are we going if we get off the streets? We can't go back in the house because we almost suffocate. So we sit down on the curb, or stand on the sidewalk, or on the steps, things like that, till the wee hours of the morning, especially in the summer when it's too hot to go up. Now where were we going? But he came out with his nightstick and wants to beat people on the head, and wanted to—he arrested one fellow. The other fellow said, "Well, I'll move, but you don't have to talk to me like a dog." I think we should all get together—everybody—all get together and every time one draws back his stick to do something to us, or hits one of us on the head, take the stick and hit *him* on *his* head, so he'll know how it feels to be hit on the head, or kill him, if necessary. Yes, kill him, if necessary. That's how I feel. There is no other way to deal with this man. The only way you can deal with him is the way he has been dealing with us.

—Man, about 35

Everything is a big laugh in this dump unless you kill a cop. Then they don't laugh. I had a cop walk up to me a couple of days ago. You know what he said? "Move over." They have the street blocked up and he's going to tell me you can go around them. I said, "Hell if I do." He said, "What did you say?" I said, "Hell if I do." He said, "I'll slap your black ass." I told him, "That's one day you'll know if you're living or dying." He just looked at me. I said, "Why don't you say it? You want to say nigger so bad."

—Man, age 21

The flag here in America is for the white man. The blue is for justice; the fifty white stars you see in the blue are for the fifty white states; and the white you see in it is the White House. It represents white folks. The red in it is the white man's blood—he doesn't even respect your blood, that's why he will lynch you, hang you, barbecue you, and fry you.

—Man, age about 35

A stereotyped Negro you see him in the movies or on TV, walking down the levee with a watermelon in his hand, his shiny teeth, and his straw hat on his head. That's the one you see on television, yassuh, yassuh, and the showboys come in Stepin Fetchit, because that's what every Negro is associated with. To me, the middle-class Negro and the upper-class Negro is one that's trying to get away from that stereotype. They're the ones trying to get away.

—Man, age 18

I don't see why we've got to always look up to the white man's life. That's what we've been exposed to, you know. Be like the white man. I think we have to have criteria of our own. They had "Amos and Andy" on radio, they were done by white men. You hear the fellows saying, "Oh, I'm going to get me a white broad." We should form our own criteria. We should try and have some more people like Martin Luther King, like James Baldwin. We can send some draftsmen to school, some engineers; people can come back and build a city for Negroes to live in, or you know, not just for Negroes but for Negroes and anyone else who wants to live there. Why do we always have to get up—come up to the white man's level? We struggle like the devil to get up there, and we hardly ever do it. Why can't we form our own level?

—Girl, age 15

I have been uncomfortable being a Negro. I came from the South— Kentucky, on the Ohio River line—and I have had white people spit on me in my Sunday suit.

—Woman

The main thing is to know just where he comes from, knowing about his race. The main thing. He will then disregard every time he turns on the television that he sees a white face. That won't mean anything to him; it will be just another program because he will know that the conditions of the way of this world are based on only the white man's psychology, that makes these things. It won't be because this man is better fitted than he is on the television; it is because he dominates, he capitalizes, he corrupts.

—Man, age 35

First stop wearing the white man's clothes. Dress in your ancestral clothes. Learn your history and your heritage. This is part of my culture and I'm proud. Wear your clothes! Put on your *abdaba,* your *dashiki* and your *fella.* You can do it.

—Woman, age about 45

The Honorable Elijah Mohammed teaches, but the only thing is, some of our people still don't take that old blue-eyed, hook-nosed picture of Christ off their wall—take it down and step on it. These people have been exploiting us for years.

—Man, age about 35

Hear me now, hear me. Thy kingdom come, thy will be done, on earth as it is in Heaven. The kingdom is ours, black man's kingdom. We want our own God, our own paradise, our own joys on this earth, and if we are not getting that, then something must be wrong somewhere, so with all of your Gospel and all your preaching, if you cannot benefit the children, it has no value.

—Man, age about 50

Churches don't mean us no good. We've been having churches all our lives under the same conditions, and look at the condition we're still in. The church must not have meant anything. See, when you go to church you don't learn how to read and write, and count, at church. You learn that in school. See what I mean? So what good the churches doing us? They are not doing us any good! You could build some factories or something in Harlem and give our people some work near home. That would do us more good than a church.

—Man, age about 45

The preacher is a hustler. He creates a system for people to believe in that makes faggots, homosexuals, and lesbians out of the population of the black people, and this is exactly what Whitey wants him to do. If you keep the damn preachers out of it, we'd solve our whole problem, just like the NAACP and the CORE over here in Brooklyn now; they don't want no part of the medicine, so that's it. But I'm a U-Pad member of the National Black Nationalists, and that's all I have to say. I don't go with this. His members that are here can believe him, they can fall behind or whatsoever. The only thing he wants—you never see a rabbi ride in a Cadillac, you never see a Jew rabbi, a charity rabbi, ride in nothing. They walk—They're doing a big enough job in the church, we don't need any leaders out here. In fact, we need to get rid of preachers like this because they are the very first ones who are going to sell us down the creek like he has done, like ministers have been doing over and over again. And incidentally, there was a big crook over in Brooklyn who sold everybody out on the picket line.

—Man, age 35

We don't want any bloodshed if we can help it, but if there has to be a little bloodletting, well and good. But this is only the beginning —what happened here today. Our next big step is the Harlem Police Department—we want black captains and we're going to have them. I've been fighting for dozens of years here in Harlem, where the so-called leaders play—Uncle Tom—play politics and let the people starve. You have district leaders here that draw a big fat salary. You can't hardly walk the street for trash. You have captains here—district captains and what not—all kinds of leaders here in Harlem. You never see them until election.

—Woman, age about 30

I think there's a great lack of offensive direction and most of the adults have, more or less, succumbed to the situation and have decided, what the hell can I do? This is the attitude; that we can do nothing, so leave it alone. People think you're always going to be under pressure from the white man and he owns and runs everything, and we are so dependent on him that there's nothing I can do. This is the general impression I've gotten from most of the adults in Harlem.

—Girl, age 15

It's got to get better. It can't get worse—it's got to get better, and they'll open up. They have to open up because they will find themselves going down all over the world, not only here. It's not just us picketing that forced them to do this; all over the world people are talking about American imperialism, and it's forcing them to do all these things. Because whether I walk the line or not, whoever walks the line that has a black face is walking the line for me. Whether they are walking in Alabama, Arizona, Mississippi, or wherever they're walking. And there isn't anything for the Man to do but begin giving us an equal chance if he wants to save himself, because he's going down and we're the only ones that are holding him up.

—Man, age about 45

All right, so you get into the school and you get your rights, but in the whole scope of the black man in America, how can you accomplish anything by doing this? Yes, all right, you are accepted into Woolworths; you fought and got your heads beat in. But what do your children think of you? Do you have any economic or political power? The people like you who're going into Greenwood, Mississippi, say, where the people are living—you are all dependent. It's unthinkable. The people have nothing. At this point they are living on things that are being sent to them from New York, Chicago, and other places in the United States. Do you know how much money we spend on foreign aid while here in the United States we people are starving?

—Man, age 18, and girl, age 15

When the time comes, it is going to be too late. Everything will explode because the people they live under tension now; they going to a point where they can't stand it no more. When they get to that point. . . . They want us to go to Africa, they say.

That would be the best thing they would want in the world because then they could get all of us together. All they would have to do is drop one bomb and we're dead.

—Men, ages 30 to 35

I would like to see the day when my people have dignity and pride in themselves as black people. And when this comes about, when they realize that we are capable of all things, and can do anything under the sun that a man can do, then all these things will come about—equality, great people, presidents—everything.

—Man, age 19

I would like to be the first Negro president.

—Boy, age about 17

2

THE INVISIBLE WALL

"Ghetto" was the name for the Jewish quarter in sixteenth-century Venice. Later, it came to mean any section of a city to which Jews were confined. America has contributed to the concept of the ghetto the restriction of persons to a special area and the limiting of their freedom of choice on the basis of skin color. The dark ghetto's invisible walls have been erected by the white society, by those who have power, both to confine those who have *no* power and to perpetuate their powerlessness. The dark ghettos are social, political, educational, and—above all—economic colonies. Their inhabitants are subject peoples, victims of the greed, cruelty, insensitivity, guilt, and fear of their masters.

The objective dimensions of the American urban ghettos are overcrowded and deteriorated housing, high infant mortality, crime, and disease. The subjective dimensions are resentment, hostility, despair, apathy, self-depreciation, and its ironic companion, compensatory grandiose behavior.

The ghetto is ferment, paradox, conflict, and dilemma. Yet within its pervasive pathology exists a surprising human resilience. The ghetto is hope, it is despair, it is churches and bars. It is aspiration for change, and it is apathy. It is vibrancy, it is stagnation. It is courage, and it is defeatism. It is cooperation and concern, and it is suspicion, competitiveness, and rejection. It is the surge toward

11

assimilation, and it is alienation and withdrawal within the protective walls of the ghetto.

The pathologies of the ghetto community perpetuate themselves through cumulative ugliness, deterioration, and isolation and strengthen the Negro's sense of worthlessness, giving testimony to his impotence. Yet the ghetto is not totally isolated. The mass media— radio, television, moving pictures, magazines, and the press—penetrate, indeed, invade the ghetto in continuous and inevitable communication, largely one-way, and project the values and aspirations, the manners and the style of the larger white-dominated society. Those who are required to live in congested and rat-infested homes are aware that others are not so dehumanized. Young people in the ghetto are aware that other young people have been taught to read, that they have been prepared for college, and can compete successfully for white-collar, managerial, and executive jobs. Whatever accommodations they themselves must make to the negative realities which dominate their own lives, they know consciously or unconsciously that their fate is not the common fate of mankind. They tend to regard their predicament as a consequence of personal disability or as an inherent and imposed powerlessness which all Negroes share.

The privileged white community is at great pains to blind itself to conditions of the ghetto, but the residents of the ghetto are not themselves blind to life as it is outside of the ghetto. They observe that others enjoy a better life, and this knowledge brings a conglomerate of hostility, despair, and hope. If the ghetto could be contained totally, the chances of social revolt would be decreased, if not eliminated, but it cannot be contained and the outside world intrudes. The Negro lives in part in the world of television and motion pictures, bombarded by the myths of the American middle class, often believing as literal truth their pictures of luxury and happiness, and yet at the same time confronted by a harsh world of reality where the dreams do not come true or change into nightmares. The discrepancy between the reality and the dream burns into their consciousness. The oppressed can never be sure whether their failures reflect personal inferiority or the fact of color. This persistent and agonizing conflict dominates their lives.

The young people in Harlem, in the Negro ghettos of Chicago, Washington, Cleveland, Detroit, Los Angeles, and other cities, who persist, in spite of obstacles, in seeking an education, who insist upon going to night school and then the day session of a municipal college, whose parents, friends, or teachers encourage and support them demonstrate that a positive resolution of the ghetto's nuclear conflict is possible. But many resolve the conflict negatively—in either a passive or defiant way. Those within the ghetto who are defeated—those who accept the "evidence" of their personal inferiority and impotence, those who express a pervasive sense of personal failure through stagnation and despair, who drop out of school, who depend on marijuana and narcotics—demonstrate a passively negative and self-destructive solution.

The overt delinquent, the acting-out rebel, on the other hand, seeks his salvation in defiant, aggressive, and in the end self-destructive forms. Because the larger society has clearly rejected him, he rejects—or appears to reject—the values, the aspirations, and techniques of that society. His conscious or unconscious argument is that he cannot hope to win meaningful self-esteem through the avenues ordinarily available to more privileged individuals. These avenues have been blocked for him through inadequate education, through job discrimination, and through a system of social and political power which is not responsive to his needs. When a warlord of one of the last of Harlem's active fighting gangs was asked why he did not "go downtown and get a job," he laughed and replied:

Oh come on. Get off that crap. I make $40 or $50 a day selling marijuana. You want me to go down to the garment district and push one of those trucks through the street and at the end of the week take home $40 or $50 if I'm lucky? They don't have animals doing what you want me to do. There would be some society to protect animals if anybody had them pushing them damn trucks around. I'm better than an animal, but nobody protects me. Go away, mister. I got to look out for myself.

Such rebels are scornful of what they consider the hypocrisy and the dishonesty of the larger society. They point to corruption and criminal behavior among respected middle-class whites. Almost every delinquent or marginal adolescent in a Negro urban ghetto claims to know where and how the corrupt policeman accepts graft from the numbers runners and the pimps and the prostitutes. The close association, collaboration, and at times identity, of criminals and the police is the pattern of day-to-day life in the ghetto as these young people come to know and accept it. Not only do they not respect the police, but they see the police as part of their own total predicament.

Large numbers of other ghetto youth, however, are caught in the paradox of the ghetto unable to resolve their personal conflicts either in positive and socially acceptable forms of adjustment or in direct and assertive antisocial behavior. They are aware of the values and standards of the larger society, but they know that they are not personally equipped to meet its demands. They have neither succumbed totally to pathology nor have they been able to emerge from it. As adults they live out lives they feel helpless to change, in a kind of unstable equilibrium, aware of their plight and yet accepting it. They are the ones who listen to Malcolm X but do not join; who vote Democratic if they bother to register but recognize at the same time that City Hall will do little for them. They are momentarily stimulated by the verbal militance of certain Negro newspaper editors and soapbox orators; they gain vicarious satisfaction through temporary identification with the flamboyance and antiwhite verbal extremisms of charismatic Negro politicians. They send their children to bad public schools reluctantly because they do not have the money for private schools. They are the great potential who could engage in constructive social action or who could become the pawns of the demagogues. They have no inner-determined direction. Whoever develops any movement toward power in the ghetto finally does so through winning the allegiance of this group—the largest in the ghetto—not of the semicriminal and certainly not of the elite and comfortable.

The ferment within Negro communities throughout the nation—hitherto more obvious in certain Southern communities, but beginning to express itself with increasing intensity and even spasmodic ferocity in such Northern urban communities as Chicago, Boston, Philadelphia, Rochester, and New York—suggests that the past cycle, in which personal and community powerlessness reinforces each other, is being supplanted by a more forceful pattern of personal and community action. This is proof that the reservoir of energy was there, ready to be stirred by hope, for effective or even sporadic protest could never have emerged out of total stagnation.

Although the civil rights movement gives Negroes more leverage, enabling many to channel their energies into constructive protest, there is a possibility that these energies could also be diluted into meaningless catharsis. Demonstrations that do not lead to results may become only one more safety valve—as the church has long been for Negroes—releasing Negro energies without the transformation of society, without any actual change in their relative status.

If mobilized community power and protest do succeed in winning concrete positive changes, Negro self-confidence and pride will grow, and a new cycle of greater personal and community effectiveness should emerge. But it would not be realistic for the white community to expect protest to subside in the face of gains, for the closer the Negro community gets to the attainment of its goals—the removal of the causes and effects of racial exploitation and powerlessness—the more impatient will Negroes become for total equality. In the complex turbulence of the Negro ghetto, and consistent with the affirmative dynamics of the civil rights thrust, success feeds hope and provides the strength and the motivation for further activity. This, in turn, makes existing barriers even more intolerable. Accelerated impatience and the lowering of the threshold of frustration toward remaining inequities, paradoxically increase the chances of racial tensions and ferment and conflict. Failure would reinforce the sense of stagnation and despair and establish as fact the sense of personal and group powerlessness. A truly hopeless group makes no demands and certainly does not insist upon stark social confrontations.

The summer of 1964 brought violent protests to the ghettos of America's cities, not in mobilization of effective power, but as an outpouring of unplanned revolt. The revolts in Harlem were not led by a mob, for a mob is an uncontrolled social force bent on irrational destruction. The revolts in Harlem were, rather, a weird social defiance. Those involved in them were, in general, not the lowest class of Harlem residents—not primarily looters and semicriminals—but marginal Negroes who were upwardly mobile, demanding a higher status than their families had. This was not a race riot in the sense that mobs of whites were assaulting mobs of Negroes or vice versa, yet the fact of race was pervasive. The 1964 Harlem riot was indeed in many respects more frightening than a race riot and the participants' deliberate mockery more threatening than a mob. Small groups of young people seemed to take delight in taunting the police, whose white faces were accentuated by their white helmets: "Here's a nigger, kill me." Even those Negroes who threw bottles and bricks from the roofs were not in the grip of a wild abandon, but seemed deliberately to be prodding the police to behave openly as the barbarians that the Negroes felt they actually were. You cannot hear conversations of a mob, but during the disturbance in Harlem, groups of young people discussed their plans: "I'll go home and come back tomorrow. Whitey will still be here." "I don't want to be killed tonight; tomorrow will be all right." There was an eerie, surrealistic quality, a silence within the din, punctuated by gunfire and sporadic shattering of glass, a calm within the chaos, a deliberateness within the hysteria. The Negro seemed to feel nothing could happen to him that had not happened already; he behaved as if he had nothing to lose. His was an oddly controlled rage that seemed to say, during those days of social despair, "We have had enough. The only weapon you have is bullets. The only thing you can do is to kill us." Paradoxically, his apparent lawlessness was a protest against lawlessness directed against *him*. His acts were a desperate assertion of his desire to be treated as a man. He was affirmative up to the point of inviting death; he insisted upon being visible and understood. If this was the only way to relate to society at large, he would die rather than be ignored.

At times of overt social unrest, many white persons who claim to be in favor of civil rights and assert that they are "friends" of the Negro will admonish the Negro not to engage in disruptive and lawless demonstrations lest he incite racism and reverse the progress made in his behalf. These often well-meaning requests may reflect the unconscious condescension of benign prejudices. They demonstrate mistaken assumptions concerning the nature and dynamics of Negro protest. It is argued, for example, that Negroes should "choose" only those techniques, tactics, and demonstrations which do not inconvenience the dominant white society; the oppressed are urged to be concerned about the comfort and sensitivities of those they regard as their oppressors. The implication is that if they do not, middle-class whites will use their own power to retaliate against all Negroes. Negroes are increasingly reminded of the sting of the "white backlash." Many middle-class Negroes as well as whites accept these arguments and behave accordingly. Yet the threat is not new. The struggle of those with power to deny power to those who have none is age-old, and accommodation and appeasement have not resolved it. The "white backlash" is a new name for an old phenomenon, white resistance to the acceptance of the Negro as a human being. As the Negro demands such status—as he develops more and more effective techniques to obtain it, and as these techniques come closer to success—the resistance to his demands rises in intensity and alarm. The forms it takes vary from the overt and barbaric murders and bombings to the more subtle innuendo of irritation and disparagement.

Many whites also assume that a governing group of Negro leaders chooses tactics for the Negro masses. Yet leaders of the stature and responsibility of Roy Wilkins and Whitney M. Young, Jr., James Farmer or Martin Luther King cannot impose tactics upon the masses of marginal Negroes, who are not disciplined members of any group. And the masses of Negroes do not "choose" tactics at all. They respond to the pressures of their lives and react spontaneously to incidents which trigger explosions or demonstrations. When a bewildered white liberal asks why, in the face of the passage of the Civil Rights Bill of 1964, "they" still revolt—and not in the dignified, respectable nonviolent way of the earlier student sitins—he betrays his own alienation from the Negroes whose cause he espouses. The Civil Rights Act was so long coming it served merely to remind many Negroes of their continued rejected and second-class status. Even well-meaning whites continue to see and talk of Negroes as "they," clearly differentiated from "we," the "outgroup" from the "ingroup." As long as this alienation remains, the masses of whites will be irritated and inconvenienced by any meaningful activity by Negroes to change their status. No real revolt can be convenient for the privileged; no real revolt can be contained within comfortable bounds or be made respectable.

In the face of the growing unrest, careful, thoughtful, and realistic planning becomes starkly imperative. Some whites would react to renewed protest by warning Negroes not to go too far too fast, not to alienate the white liberals who have, even if often timidly, supported them. To others, less well-intentioned, Negro unrest is but confirmation of their own prejudice: Negroes are, after all, behaving as the uncivilized do. But unrest *is* a characteristic of civilization, and to fight against oppression—even unwisely—is a sign that men have begun to hope. As studies on social disasters have demonstrated, people who feel there is no escape submit to their fate; it is those who see an exit sign and an open door who struggle to reach it.

Furthermore, energies devoted to a struggle for constructive social change are clearly not simultaneously available for antisocial and self-destructive patterns of behavior. In those communities such as Montgomery, Alabama, where Negroes mobilized themselves for sustained protest against prevailing racial injustice, *the incidence of antisocial behavior and delinquency decreased almost to a vanishing point during the period of protest.*

The Negro cannot any longer feel, if he ever did, that he should have to prove himself "worthy" in order to gain his full freedom—the rights guaranteed to all other American citizens, including those most recently naturalized. The Negro cannot be asked to prove that he "deserves" the rights and responsibilities of democracy, nor can he be told that others must first be persuaded "in heart and mind" to accept him. Such tests and trials by fire are not applied to others. To impose them on the Negro is racist condescension. It is to assume that the Negro is a special type of human being who must pass a special test before admission to a tenuous status worthy of governmental protection. It is to place upon the Negro a peculiar burden reflecting and exploiting his powerlessness, and it is, paradoxically, to deny him the essential human rights of frailty and imperfection. The experience of inferior racial status has not transformed the Negro into a super human being. To demand that he demonstrate virtues not ordinarily found in more privileged people, before he may enjoy the benefits of democracy, is not only irrational and inconsistent but gratuitously cruel. And above all it is evidence that the invisible wall is opaque from outside in.

No one ought to expect the transition from a system of injustice to a system of social justice to occur without personal and social trauma for the Negro as well as the white. The intensification of conflict and resistance inherent in the immediacy of the Negro's demands, and the dramatic methods which he is now using to attain his goals, understandably obscure some of the more profound human problems involved in progressing from a racially segregated to a nonsegregated society. But, when the cries of anguish of the segregationists have subsided, as they will eventually, the Negro will be confronted with his own inner anxieties, conflicts, and challenges as he dares to move into a society of open competition. It will then be clear that though the problems of adjusting to change are difficult for whites, in even more insidious ways they are quite painful for Negroes. The invisible walls of a segregated society are not only damaging but protective in a debilitating way. There is considerable psychological safety in the ghetto; there one lives among one's own and does not risk rejection among strangers. One first becomes aware of the psychological damage of such "safety" when the walls of the ghetto are breached and the Negro ventures out into the repressive, frightening white world. Some Negroes prefer to stay in the ghetto, particularly those who have developed seemingly effective defenses to protect themselves against hurt, those who fear for their children, and those who have profited from the less competitive segregated society. Other Negroes, particularly the young, are militant in their efforts to crash the remaining barriers of race. But even among this group it is not always easy to tell who is totally committed and willing to assume the risks and who is only talking militance. Most Negroes take the first steps into an integrated society tentatively and torn with conflict. To be the first Negro who is offered a job in a company brings a sense of triumph but also the dread of failure. To be the "show" Negro, the symbol of a new-found policy of racial democracy in an educational institution, private industry, or governmental agency, imposes demands for personal restraint, balance, and stability of character

rare among any group of mere human beings. For a Negro to be offered friendship and to find himself unable to accept it fully, to find
that he is himself in the grip of hitherto unrealized racial prejudice
—or, more precisely racial anger—is to look into the hidden recesses
of his own mind. A person—or a race—who has been forced to be
ashamed of his identity cannot easily accept himself simply as a human being and surrender either the supportive group identification or
hostility toward those who have rejected him.

The newly emerging Negro—the assertive, militant, defiant, self-
affirming Negro seeking his identity—will probably at first seem a
caricature, a person who wears the mask of race with its fixed artificial
expression. No more than the white bigot who succumbs to his passion of hatred and fear, or the white "liberal" who struggles to reconcile his affirmation of racial justice with his visceral racism, has the
Negro escaped domination of his own individuality by the role of race.
Only when the need to play such a role is no longer urgent will the
individual Negro and white feel free to be merely themselves, without defenses.

3

THE SOCIAL DYNAMICS
OF THE GHETTO

White America is basically a middle-class society; the middle class sets the mores and the manners to which the upper class must, when it wishes influence, seek to conform, at least in appearances, and which the lower class struggles to attain or defensively rejects. But dark America, of the rural and of the urban Negro, has been automatically assigned to be a lower-class society; the lower class sets the mores and manners to which, if the Negro upper class wishes influence, it must appeal; and from which the Negro middle class struggles to escape. As long as this chasm between white and dark America is allowed to exist, racial tensions and conflict, hatred and fear will spread. The poor are always alienated from normal society, and when the poor are Negro, as they increasingly are in American cities, a double trauma exists—rejection on the basis of class and race is a danger to the stability of society as a whole. Even though Negroes are a minority in America—approximately one-tenth of the population—a minority that is sick with despair can poison the wellsprings from which the majority, too, must drink. The social dynamics of the dark ghettos can be seen as the restless thrust of a lower-class group to rise into the middle class.

The problem of the American Negro, once predominantly Southern, has gradually over the past few decades become predominantly a Northern problem. Millions of Negroes have come North seeking escape from the miasma of the South, where poverty and oppression kept the Negro in an inferior caste. Three out of every four Negroes live in cities; approximately one of two lives in Northern cities. A million and a half left the South in the years 1950–1960, the largest number heading for California, New York, Illinois, and Michigan. Of the Negroes who live in the North, 95 percent now live in cities (in 1890 it was 65 percent).

There are Negro residential areas in such Southern cities as Atlanta, Birmingham, and New Orleans, but the Negro ghetto in America is essentially a Northern urban invention. There are racially mixed residential areas in a number of Southern cities, few in Northern cities. Although the South often criticizes the North for its urban segregation and explains its own comparatively mixed residential patterns as illustrative of a more intimate and more tolerant relationship to the Negro, the fact is that in the South mixed neighborhoods are permitted only so long as Negroes are not seen as a threat In Charleston, South Carolina, for example, racial residential patterns reflect slavery days, and whites and Negroes tend to live in the same area as they did before Emancipation. Negro servants can come into any area and live in white homes without a lifted eyebrow. Racial problems have not been problems of racial contact—despite the implications of those who refuse to join Negroes at a college dormitory table or to use the common washroom in a factory. It is not the sitting next to a Negro at a table or washing at the next basin that is repulsive to a white, *but the fact that this implies equal status*. Historically, the most intimate relationships have been approved between Negro and white so long as status of white superiority versus Negro inferiority has been clear. Trouble comes only when Negroes decide not to be servants or mistresses and seek a status equal to that of whites. When Negroes start to assume symbols of upward mobility, then a pattern of residential segregation develops in the South, too. In Little Rock and Pine Bluff, Arkansas, and Atlanta, Georgia, to illustrate, as the status of Negroes improved, housing segregation increased. The South is today becoming more "Northern" in its discriminatory pattern. As its economic level rises, it will steadily become more and more like the North. Then urban ghettos will be created, and the Negro will be forced to deal with a different kind of rejection. Part of the social dynamics of the ghetto is the tension between those Negroes who wish to resist and eventually to destroy the ghetto and those whites who seek to maintain and strengthen it.

Eleven metropolitan areas have Negro communities of between 200,000 and one million: New York, Chicago, Los Angeles, Detroit, Philadelphia, Washington, D.C., St. Louis, Baltimore, Cleveland, Houston and New Orleans. (See Tables 1, 2, 2A, 3.) In Washington,

TABLE 1

RESIDENTIAL CONCENTRATION OF NEGROES

Tracts with 90 percent + Negro population	City	In city	In tracts 90 percent + Negro	Percentage in tracts 90 percent + Negro
122	Chicago, Ill.	812,637	533,214	65.6
31	Baltimore, Md.	325,589	184,992	56.8
27	Cleveland, Ohio	250,818	134,142	53.5
29	Washington, D.C.	411,737	200,380	48.7
10	St. Louis, Mo.	214,377	94,041	43.9
8	Houston, Texas	215,037	87,222	40.6
27	Philadelphia, Penn.	529,240	207,627	39.2
17	New Orleans, La.	233,514	85,968	36.8
71	New York, N.Y.	1,087,931	362,370	33.3
45	Detroit, Mich.	482,223	140,546	29.1
19	Los Angeles, Calif.	334,916	68,715	20.5

SOURCE: U.S. Census of Population: 1960. The data presented in Tables 1 through 3 were prepared by James A. Jones, research director of Haryou, for this book.

D.C., Negroes are in the majority; in Philadelphia, one in four persons is Negro. In the half century between 1910 and 1960 when the nation's Negro population doubled, New York City's Negro population multiplied ten times over.* Now the largest concentration of Negroes

* E. Franklin Frazier noted in *Condition of Negroes in American Cities*, when the first federal census was taken, Negroes constituted 13.1 percent of the New York City population and 5.7 percent of Philadelphia's.

TABLE 2
CITIES WITH 200,000 OR MORE NEGROES

| City | Total Population | Negroes | | | Percent Negro |
		Total	Males	Females	
New York, N.Y.	7,781,984	1,087,931	498,167	589,764	% 14.0
Chicago, Ill.	3,550,404	812,637	387,718	424,919	22.9
Philadelphia, Penn.	2,002,512	529,240	250,256	278,984	26.4
Detroit, Mich.	1,670,144	482,223	232,829	249,394	28.9
Washington, D.C.	763,956	411,737	196,257	215,480	53.9
Los Angeles, Calif.	2,479,015	334,916	160,118	174,798	13.5
Baltimore, Md.	939,024	325,589	157,130	168,459	34.7
Cleveland, Ohio	876,050	250,818	120,873	129,945	28.6
New Orleans, La.	627,525	233,514	110,096	123,418	37.2
Houston, Texas	938,219	215,037	103,471	111,566	22.9
St. Louis, Mo.	750,026	214,377	100,159	114,218	28.6

A Sampling of Other Cities

City	Total Population	Total	Males	Females	Percent Negro
Pittsburgh, Penn.	604,332	100,692	48,670	52,022	% 16.7
Kansas City, Mo.	475,539	83,146	39,723	43,423	17.5
Boston, Mass.	697,197	63,165	30,081	33,084	9.1
Rochester, N.Y.	318,611	23,586	11,491	12,095	7.4
Minneapolis, Minn.	482,872	11,785	5,792	5,993	2.4

TABLE 2A
CITIES WITH 200,000 OR MORE NEGROES IN TERMS OF PERCENTAGES OF NEGROES

City	Percent Negro
Washington, D.C.	% 53.9
New Orleans, La.	37.2
Baltimore, Md.	34.7
Detroit, Mich.	28.9
Cleveland, Ohio	28.6
St. Louis, Mo.	28.6
Philadelphia, Penn.	26.4
Chicago, Ill.	22.9
Houston, Texas	22.9
New York, N.Y.	14.0
Los Angeles, Calif.	13.5

Sample Cities in Terms of Percentage of Negroes

City	Percent Negro
Kansas City, Mo.	% 17.5
Pittsburgh, Penn.	16.7
Boston, Mass.	9.1
Rochester, N.Y.	7.4
Minneapolis, Minn.	2.4

SOURCE: U.S. Census of Population: 1960.

TABLE 3
NEGRO RESIDENTIAL CONCENTRATION BY AREAS OF CITIES

City and Area	Population	Negroes	Percent
New York, N.Y.			
Brooklyn ghetto	91,391	87,654	% 95.9
Queens ghetto	20,324	19,091	93.9
Manhattan ghetto	241,125	236,051	97.9
Los Angeles, Calif.			
Area I	48,806	46,865	96.0
Area II	15,489	14,990	96.8
Baltimore, Md.			
Area I	149,197	143,849	96.4
Washington, D.C.			
Area I	120,060	115,552	96.2
Area II	66,043	64,196	97.2
Cleveland, Ohio			
Area I	70,060	68,700	98.1
Area II	49,815	46,863	94.1
St. Louis, Missouri			
Area I	97,144	93,807	96.6
New Orleans, Louisiana			
Area I	45,111	44,044	97.6
Chicago, Illinois			
Area I	347,806	340,599	97.9
Area II	105,307	102,096	97.0
Area III	21,133	20,401	96.5
Area IV	22,168	21,347	96.3

SOURCE: U.S. Census of Population: 1960.

in an urban ghetto area is in Chicago; the largest number of Negroes lives in New York; and the largest percentage of Negroes (of total population) is in Washington, D.C.

In every one of these cities, Negroes are compelled to live in concentrated ghettos where there must be a continuous struggle to prevent decadence from winning over the remaining islands of middle-class society. A possible exception to this picture of creeping blight seems to be the Bay Area of San Francisco, Berkeley, and Oakland, where the Negro residential areas do not stand out from the other middle-class areas; the usual signs of congestion, deterioration, dirt, ugliness are not yet present there. In all of these ghettos whites had lived before and, as Negroes came, gradually moved away. The origin of Harlem—symbol of Negro ghettos everywhere—is, in many ways, typical of the blight that has already affected almost all.

In the early years of the century an upper-class community of luxury, Harlem by World War I became a moderately populated area of middle-class Jews, Italians, Irish, Germans, and Finns and then, during the twenties and thirties, was transformed into one of the largest and most densely populated Negro communities in the country.

The Negro came to Harlem, as all migrants do, seeking better living conditions and expanded economic opportunities. Harlem became the center of Negro culture and talent. It is here that most Negro artists and intellectuals lived, drawing their ideas and inspiration from the life of the community. But the Negro in Harlem found himself increasingly isolated culturally, socially, and economically by a wall of racial prejudice and discrimination. He was blocked from the training necessary to prepare himself for the highly skilled jobs in private industry or government, and he was pushed into the most menial occupations. His housing and schools deteriorated, and he was forced to pay more for less. He discovered that his new neighbors resented his presence, his aspirations, and his talents. They left in droves, and Harlem became a prison of its new residents. During the thirties Harlem seethed with discontent and racial strife, gaining an exaggerated reputation as a center of vice and crime. White persons ventured into the community only in search of exotic primitive glamour. Today, Harlem, no longer the mecca for white bohemia, is a center both of trouble and potential talent, the fountainhead of Negro protest movements. Despite the apathy and despair of many of its residents, it is a vibrant, exciting and, all too frequently, a turbulent community.*

In most important ways—social and economic structure, community culture, quality of education, and the like—all urban ghettos in America are similar. As one Negro told a Haryou interviewer: "I don't limit the black man to Harlem alone. Harlem is only one of the accidents in time that have beset the children along the way. Problem of the black man is universal, the world over."

---

* The name "Harlem," as used in this book, refers to that section of Manhattan sometimes referred to as Central Harlem, and excluding Spanish Harlem. Its boundaries are: 110th Street on the south; Third Avenue on the east; Harlem River, northeast; the parks bordering St. Nicholas, Morningside, and Manhattan avenues on the west.

Economic and Social Decay

The symptoms of lower-class society afflict the dark ghettos of America—low aspiration, poor education, family instability, illegitimacy, unemployment, crime, drug addiction and alcoholism, frequent illness and early death. But because Negroes begin with the primary affliction of inferior racial status, the burdens of despair and hatred are more pervasive. Even initiative usually goes unrewarded as relatively few Negroes succeed in moving beyond menial jobs, and those who do find racial discrimination everywhere they go.

The most concrete fact of the ghetto is its physical ugliness— the dirt, the filth, the neglect. In many stores walls are unpainted, windows are unwashed, service is poor, supplies are meager. The parks are seedy with lack of care. The streets are crowded with the people and refuse. In all of Harlem there is no museum, no art gallery, no art school, no sustained "little theater" group; despite the stereotype of the Negro as artist, there are only five libraries—but hundreds of bars, hundreds of churches, and scores of fortune tellers. Everywhere there are signs of fantasy, decay, abandonment, and defeat. The only constant characteristic is a sense of inadequacy. People seem to have given up in the little things that are so often the symbol of the larger things.

The dark ghetto is not a viable community. It cannot support its people; most have to leave it for their daily jobs. Its businesses are geared toward the satisfaction of personal needs and are marginal to the economy of the city as a whole. The ghetto feeds upon itself; it does not produce goods or contribute to the prosperity of the city. It has few large businesses. Most of the businesses are small, with what that implies in terms of degree of stability. Even the more substantial-appearing businesses (e.g., real estate and insurance companies) are, by and large, marginal. Of 1,617 Harlem businesses listed in the yellow pages of Manhattan's telephone directory, 27 percent are barber shops, beauty shops, or cleaning establishments—all devoted to tidying up, a constantly renewable service. Thirty-five percent are involved in the consumption of food and drink (bakeries, caterers, grocery stores, liquor stores, luncheonettes, restaurants, bars, and taverns). In general, a ghetto does not produce goods of lasting worth. Its products are used up and replaced like the unproductive lives of so many of its people. There are 93 funeral homes in Harlem.

Even though the white community has tried to keep the Negro confined in ghetto pockets, the white businessman has not stayed out of the ghetto. A ghetto, too, offers opportunities for profit, and in a competitive society profit is to be made where it can.

In Harlem there is only one large department store and that is owned by whites. Negroes own a savings and loan association; and one Negro-owned bank has recently been organized. The other banks are branches of white-owned downtown banks. Property—apartment houses, stores, businesses, bars, concessions, and theaters—are for the most part owned by persons who live outside the community and take their profits home. Even the numbers racket, a vital and indestructible part of Harlem's economy, is controlled by whites. Here is unproductive profit-making at its most virulent, using the Negro's flight from despair into the persistent dream of quick and easy money as the means to take from him what little money he has.

When tumult arose in ghetto streets in the summer of 1964, most of the stores broken into and looted belonged to white men. Many of these owners responded to the destruction with bewilderment and anger, for they felt that they had been serving a community that needed them. They did not realize that the residents were not grateful for this service but bitter, as natives often feel toward the functionaries of a colonial power who, in the very act of service, keep the hated structure of oppression intact. Typical of this feeling are the following views expressed to Haryou investigators in 1962 and 1963. None who heard their contempt, their anti-Semitic overtones, would have been surprised at the looting of 1964—rarely does a social revolt occur without decades of advance warning.

That Jew, he's got a wagon out here, and he will send his son through college, you understand? Nothing but a wagon, selling to these people in this junky neighborhood right here, and he's got a house in the Bronx, and he's paying for it, and the child is going to college, and he's selling you stringbeans at fifteen cents a pound.

—Man, age 27

Another thing I am sick and tired of, I am sick and tired of all these Jew business places in Harlem. Why don't more colored business places open? This is our part of town. They don't live here but they got all the businesses and everything.

—Woman, age 38

Negroes have left business in the ghettos to whites not from a dislike of business but for a complex of other reasons. In those Southern cities like Birmingham, Atlanta, and Memphis, where the pattern of segregation is so complete that the dark ghettos must be almost self-sufficient, there are a number of Negro-owned stores, restaurants, and banks. But, in the North, the Negro is allowed to involve himself partially in the total city, and whites are willing to open businesses within the ghetto, sensing a profit among the tenements. The white power structure has collaborated in the economic serfdom of Negroes by its reluctance to give loans and insurance to Negro business. Eugene P. Foley, administrator of the Small Business Administration, told a meeting called in August 1964 to encourage economic investment among minorities that, before its field office opened in Philadelphia in that year, "I am ashamed to admit that my agency had made seven loans to Negroes in ten years." The situation has somewhat improved since then; in the six months after the field office opened fifty-five loans were granted and sixteen new businesses opened; new field offices were organized, also, in Harlem and in Washington, D.C.

There are insufficient economic resources within the ghetto to support its future development. Therefore any economic growth—as in fact is true of suburbs—must be supported and developed from without. But unlike the suburbs, where residents have high income and good credit, the ghetto has inadequate resources to command the attraction of economic power outside and cannot lure capital into its limits. Most ghetto residents are permitted only menial jobs and marginal income. The suburbs drain the economy of the city—through subsidized transportation, housing development, and the like. The economy of the ghetto is itself drained and is not replenished.

Housing Decay

Another important aspect of the social dynamics of the Northern urban ghettos is the fact that all are crowded and poor; Harlem houses 232,792 people within its three and one half square miles, a valley between Morningside and Washington Heights and the Harlem River. There are more than 100 people per acre. Ninety percent of the 87,369 residential buildings are more than thirty-three years old, and nearly half were built before 1900. Private developers have not thought Harlem a good investment: Few of the newer buildings were sponsored by private money, and almost all of those buildings erected since 1929 are post-World War II public housing developments, where a fifth of the population lives.

The condition of all but the newest buildings is poor. Eleven percent are classified as dilapidated by the 1960 census; that is, they do "not provide safe and adequate shelter," and thirty-three percent are deteriorating (i.e., "need more repair than would be provided in the course of regular maintenance"). There are more people in fewer rooms than elsewhere in the city. Yet the rents and profits from Harlem are often high, as many landlords deliberately crowd more people into buildings in slum areas, knowing that the poor have few alternatives. The rent per room is often higher in Harlem than for better-equipped buildings downtown. Slum landlords, ready enough when the rent is due, are hard to find when repairs are demanded. Even the city cannot seem to find some of them, and when they go to trial for neglect, they are usually given modest and lenient sentences —compared to the sentences of Harlem teen-agers who defy the law. Cruel in the extreme is the landlord who, like the store owner who charges Negroes more for shoddy merchandise, exploits the powerlessness of the poor. For the poor are not only poor but unprotected and do not know how to seek redress. One is reminded of the Biblical admonition: "For whosoever hath, to him shall be given, and he shall have more abundance: but whosoever hath not, from him shall be taken away even that he hath."

The effects of unsafe, deteriorating, and overcrowded housing upon physical health are well documented and understood.* The multiple use of toilet and water facilities, inadequate heating and ventilation, and crowded sleeping quarters increase the rate of acute respiratory infections and infectious childhood diseases. Poor facilities for the storage of food and inadequate washing facilities cause enteritis and skin and digestive disease. Crowded, poorly equipped kitchens, poor electrical connections, and badly lighted and unstable stairs increase the rate of home accidents and fires. Nor is the street any safer. Harlem's fourteen parks, playgrounds, and recreational areas are inadequate and ugly, and many of the children play in the streets where heavy truck traffic flows through the community all day. Far more children and young adults are killed by cars in Harlem than in the rest of the city (6.9 per 100,000 population compared to 4.2 per 100,000 for New York City as a whole).

The physical health of the residents of the ghetto is as impaired as one would expect based on knowledge of its housing conditions. The best single index of a community's general health is reputed to be its infant mortality rate. For Harlem this rate in 1961 was 45.2 per 1,000 live births compared to 25.7 for New York City. For Cleveland's Hough area the infant deaths are also about double that of the rest of the city. Poor housing conditions, malnutrition, and inadequate health care are undoubtedly responsible; where flies and maggots breed, where the plumbing is stopped up and not repaired, where rats bite helpless infants, the conditions of life are brutal and inhuman. All are symptoms of the underlying fact of poverty. Perhaps even more extraordinary than the high rate of disease and death is the fact that so many human beings do survive.

The effect of housing upon the social and psychological well being

* Among others, see D. M. Wilner, R. P. Price, and M. Tayback, "How Does the Quality of Housing Affect Health and Family Adjustment?" *American Journal of Public Health*, June 1956, pp. 736–744; "Report of the Subcommittee on Housing of the Committee on Public Health Relations," *Bulletin of the New York Academy of Medicine*, June 1954; M. Allen Pond, "The Influence of Housing on Health," *Marriage and Family Living*, May 1957, pp. 154–159; Alvin L. Schorr, *Slums and Social Insecurity*, Social Security Administration, Division of Research and Statistics, no date; D. M. Wilner, R. P. Walkley, T. Pinkerton, and M. Tayback, *The Housing Environment and Family Life: A Longitudinal Study of the Effects of Housing on Morbidity and Mental Health*, Baltimore, Johns Hopkins Press, 1962.

of its occupants is much discussed but less well documented. The most careful of the few relevant studies (those by Wilner, Walkley, Pinkerton and Tayback) on the psychological effects of poor housing have produced findings less dramatic than one would expect. The link between housing and mental health is not clearly established, but residents of public housing do have higher morale and greater pride in their neighborhoods than those who live in slums, and they are more likely to say that they have improved their lot in life and are "rising in the world." Nevertheless, their pride is generally not followed by genuine aspiration. They often express hope, but it usually is, alas, a pseudohope unaccompanied by an actual struggle to win better jobs, to get their children into college, to buy homes. Real hope is based on expectations of success; theirs seems rather a forlorn dream. Wilner and Walkley point out that "for all the housing improvement, many other circumstances that would be expected to affect the way of life [of these families] remained substantially the same. These were still families at the lowest end of the economic scale; practical family situations remained materially unimproved; in one-third of the families there was no husband present; and one-third were on public welfare."* Housing alone does not lead to sound psychological adjustment, for to build new housing or to spruce up the old is not to abolish the multiple pathology of the slums. Still, at the very least, good housing improves health, lifts morale, and thereby helps to generate a restless eagerness for change, if not in the adult generation then in their children; a fact, incidentally, that might give pause to some of those in society who support aid to public housing believing it will decrease the demands of Negroes. It will, in fact, stimulate them to further demands, spurred by hope for a further identification with middle-class society. Housing is no abstract social and political problem, but an extension of a man's personality. If the Negro has to identify with a rat-infested tenement, his sense of personal inadequacy and inferiority, already aggravated by job discrimination and other forms of humiliation, is reinforced

* Daniel M. Wilner and Rosabelle Price Walkley, "Effects of Housing on Health and Performance," in *The Urban Condition*, L. J. Duhl, editor, New York, Basic Books, 1963, p. 224.

by the physical reality around him. If his home is clean and decent and even in some way beautiful, his sense of self is stronger. A house is a concrete symbol of what the person is worth.

In Harlem, a Haryou interviewer had a conversation with a little girl about her home that revealed both the apathy and the hope of the ghetto:

INTERVIEWER: Tell me something about you—where you were born, you know, where you grew up, how everything went for you?

GWEN D: When I was born I lived on 118th Street. There was a man killed in the hallway, and a man died right in front of the door where I lived at. My mother moved after that man got killed.

   I liked it in 97th Street because it was integration in that block. All kinds of people lived there.

INTERVIEWER: Spanish people? White people?

GWEN D: Spanish people, Italian people, all kinds of people. I liked it because it wasn't one group of whites and one group of Negroes or Spanish or something like that; everybody who lived in that block were friends.

INTERVIEWER: How come you moved?

GWEN D: Well, my mother she didn't like the building too well.

INTERVIEWER: What didn't she like about it?

GWEN D: Well, it was falling down!

INTERVIEWER: In your whole life, has anything happened to you that you really got excited about?

GWEN D: I can't remember.

INTERVIEWER: Tell me about some real good times you've had in your life.

GWEN D: In Harlem?

INTERVIEWER: In your life, that you've really enjoyed.

GWEN D: One year we was in summer school, and we went to this other school way downtown, out of Harlem, to give a show, and everybody was so happy. And we were on television, and I saw myself, and I was the only one there with a clean shirt and blouse.

INTERVIEWER: And you really got excited about that. Anything else
                ever happen to you that you had a really good time?

GWEN D: No.

INTERVIEWER: What kind of changes would you want to make?
                Changes so that you can have a better chance, your sis-
                ters can have a better chance and your brother?

GWEN D: Well, I just want a chance to do what I can.

The Dynamics of Under-Employment

The roots of the pathology of ghetto communities lie in the menial,
low-income jobs held by most ghetto residents. If the occupational
level of the community could be raised, one would expect a corres-
ponding decrease in social pathology, in dependency, disease, and
crime.

With the growth of the civil rights movement, Negroes have won
many footholds earlier forbidden to them, and it would seem logical to conclude, as many do, that Negroes are better off than ever
before in this gradually desegregating and generally affluent society.
But the fact is that in many ways the Negro's situation is deteriorating.
The Negro has been left out of the swelling prosperity and social progress of the nation as a whole. He is in danger of becoming a permanent economic proletariat.

About one out of every seven or eight adults in Harlem is unemployed. In the city as a whole the rate of unemployment is half that.
Harlem is a young community, compared to the rest of New York,
and in 1960 twice as many young Negro men in the labor force, as
compared to their white counterparts, were without jobs. For the
girls, the gap was even greater—nearly two and one-half times the
unemployment rate for white girls in the labor force. Across the
country the picture is very much the same. Unemployment of Negroes
is rising much faster than unemployment of whites. Among young
men eighteen to twenty-four, the national rate is five times as high
for Negroes as for whites.

An optimist could point to the fact that the average family income
of Negroes has increased significantly within the two decades 1940–

1960, but a more realistic observer would have to qualify this with the fact that the *discrepancy* between the average family income of whites and that of Negroes has increased even more significantly. The real income, the relative status income, of Negroes has gone down during a period when the race was supposed to have been making what candidates for elective office call, "the most dramatic progress of any oppressed group at any period of human history."

The menial and unrewarding jobs available to most Negroes can only mean a marginal subsistence for most ghetto families. The median income in Harlem is $3,480 compared to $5,103 for residents of New York City—a similar gap exists in the country as a whole. Half the families in Harlem have incomes under $4,000, while 75 percent of all New York City residents earn more than $4,000. Only one in twenty-five Negro families has an income above $10,000, while more than four in twenty-five of the white families do.

Nor do Negroes with an education receive the financial benefits available to whites. Herman P. Miller in his book, *Rich Man, Poor Man,** states that Negroes who have completed four years of college *"can expect to earn only as much in a lifetime as whites who have not gone beyond the eighth grade."* This is true both in the North and in the South. The white high school graduate will earn just about as much as a Negro who has gone through college and beyond for graduate training. One young man in Harlem asked: "What is integration into poverty?" The question is not easy to answer.

Both the men and the women in the ghetto are relegated to the lowest status jobs. Sixty-four percent of the men in Harlem compared to only 38 percent of New York City's male population, and 74 percent of the women, compared to 37 percent for New York City, hold unskilled and service jobs. Only 7 percent of Harlem males are professionals, technicians, managers, proprietors, or officials. Twenty-four percent of the males in the city hold such prestige posts.

An eighteen-year-old Negro boy protested: "They keep telling us about job opportunities, this job opportunity, and that, but who wants a job working all week and bringing home a sweat man's pay?"

* New York, Thomas Y. Crowell Co., 1964.

Most of the men in the dark ghetto do work for a "sweat man's pay," and even *that* is now threatened by the rise of automation.

Many of the jobs now held by Negroes in the unskilled occupations are deadend jobs, due to disappear during the next decade. Decreases, or no expansions, are expected in industries in which more than 43 percent of the labor force in Harlem is now employed (i.e., transportation, manufacturing, communication and utilities, and wholesale and retail trades). Employment in those industries and occupations requiring considerable education and training is expected to increase. As the pressure of unemployed white workers in the few expanding areas of unskilled jobs grows, the ability of ghetto residents to hold on to such jobs becomes doubtful. And by 1970 there will be 40 percent more Negro teen-agers (16–21) in Harlem than there were in 1960. The restless brooding young men without jobs who cluster in the bars in the winter and on stoops and corners in the summer are the stuff out of which riots are made. The solution to riots is not better police protection (or even the claims of police brutality) or pleas from civil rights leaders for law and order. The solution lies in finding jobs for the unemployed and in raising the social and economic status of the entire community. Otherwise the "long hot summers" will come every year.

By far the greatest growth in employment in New York City is expected in professional, technical, and similar occupations—some 75,000 to 80,000 jobs by the end of the present decade.* Of the 3 percent of Harlem residents in this group, the major portion are in the lower-paying professions: clergymen, teachers, musicians, and social welfare and recreation workers. A substantial increase of 40 percent in the number of managers, officials, and proprietors is expected in business and government, but the Negro has made few advances here. This will be offset by declines expected in retail business, where the trend toward bigness will result in fewer small store proprietors, another prophecy with grim implications for Negroes since the only business where Negro ownership exists in number is small stores. The number of clerical positions is due to grow in New

---

* *Manpower Outlook 1960–1970,* New York City Department of Labor, 1962, pp. 1 and 12, provides the projections that pertain to job expectations.

York by 35,000 to 40,000 jobs. Approximately 14 percent of the residents of Harlem have such jobs, but most of them are in the lower-paying positions. Electronic data-processing systems will soon replace many clerks in routine and repetitive jobs, such as sorting, filing, and the operation of small machines—the kind of jobs Negroes have—while workers in jobs requiring contact with the public, such as claim clerks, complaints clerks, and bill collectors—usually white—will be least affected by office automation. The number of sales workers will decline as self-service increases, and here too, Negroes who have been successfully employed will lose out.

Jobs for skilled workers are due to grow in New York State by 28,000 yearly. Building trades craftsmen will be particularly in demand. But the restrictions to apprenticeship training programs in the building trades industry have kept Negroes from these jobs. Semiskilled and unskilled jobs (excluding service workers) will decrease by 70,000 to 80,000 jobs between 1960 and 1970. Thirty-eight percent of the Negro male workers living in Harlem have such jobs now. If present employment patterns persist, Negro and white workers who might ordinarily qualify for semiskilled jobs will undoubtedly be pushed into the unskilled labor force or become unemployed in the face of increasing competition with those who are better trained. Negro unemployment will rise as the unskilled labor supply exceeds the demand. The only jobs that will increase, and in which Negroes now dominate, are jobs as servants, waitresses, cooks—the traditional service jobs which have added to the Negro's sense of inferiority. But as the requirements for skilled jobs grow stiffer and as semiskilled jobs decline, Negroes will face strong competition from whites to hold even these marginal jobs.

It is illegal in New York to deny a job to anyone on the basis of skin color, but it is common practice anyway. First, Negro applicants are often said to lack the qualifications necessary for a particular job. Who can prove this to be disguised racial discrimination? Like any charge with some truth, the extent of the truth is hard to determine. Second, often working against the Negro applicant, though sometimes in his favor, are ethnic quotas applied to certain types of jobs, employed with the conscious intent of maintaining an "ethnic balance" in the work force. When the quota is filled, the Negro applicant, no matter how well qualified, is told that there are no openings. Third, and much more subtle, although no less discriminatory, is the practice employed by some unions of requiring that a member of the union vouch for an applicant. When the union has no Negro members, the possibility of finding someone to vouch for a Negro applicant is extremely remote.

Through historical processes certain ethnic or religious minority groups come to predominate in certain kinds of jobs: in New York, the waterfront for the Italians, the police force for the Irish, the school system for Jews, and the personal services for Negroes.*

A study by the Bureau of Social Science Research, Inc., showed a fourth technique of exclusion; that employers tend to label some jobs, usually the lowest, as "Negro jobs"—Negroes are hired by many firms, but at "Negro jobs," with menial status, minimum wages, and little if any security.

Furthermore, many Negroes are discouraged before they begin. Guidance counselors often in the past advised Negro students not to prepare for jobs where employment opportunities for Negroes were limited. Doubtless they believed they did so in the best interests of the youth—better not to encourage him to pursue a career which is likely to end in bitter frustration and unemployment. There is some evidence that this form of root discrimination is now being reduced under persistent pressure from groups like the Urban League and the National Scholarship Service and Fund for Negro Students. The plethora of ineffective antidiscrimination and equal opportunities legislation—contrasted with the clear evidence of actual exclusion—leads one to suspect that this type of discrimination works in such a way as to be relatively immune to laws. It would appear that effective techniques for reducing discrimination in employment must, therefore, be as specific, subtle, and as pervasive as the evil they seek to overcome.

It has been charged over and over again that Negro youth lack

* A similar conception has been formulated by Eli Ginsberg in *A Policy for Skilled Manpower,* New York, Columbia University Press for the National Manpower Council, 1954, especially p. 249.

motivation to succeed. To the extent that this is true, it is largely a consequence of ghetto psychology. Teen-age boys often help to support their families, and they have neither the time nor money nor encouragement to train for a white-collar job or skilled craft. Negroes often dread to try for jobs where Negroes have never worked before. Fear of the unknown is not peculiar to one racial group, and Negroes have had traumatic experiences in seeking employment. The Negro youth is caught in a vicious cycle: Poor preparation means poor jobs and low socio-economic status. Low status and poor jobs result in poor preparation for the next generation to come.

A comprehensive employment program for the youth of dark ghettos everywhere must be geared toward revamping the various systems which feed upon one another. It must upgrade the educational system which spawns functional illiterates and which helps perpetuate personnel practices which exclude Negro youth. Even if a personnel officer is free of racial prejudice, the majority of Negro applicants can be rejected for jobs which require basic educational skills. Inferior schools, which discriminate against the masses of Negroes, have made Fair Employment Practices regulations virtually irrelevant. A crash program of rehabilitation with specific skill training is imperative. So, too, is a systematic procedure to inform ghetto youth about the occupations for which they might qualify. A realistic and comprehensive occupational training and employment program would include a counseling service not only to develop motivation and self-respect but also to help young people with concrete problems related to getting and keeping a job—many do not know how to apply for a job, how to speak to an employer, how to fill in an application blank. Many must learn the importance of promptness, appropriate dress and speech, and to modify habits that had been appropriate in the menial jobs to which Negroes had been relegated in the past. They must learn to appear and to behave like other middle-class applicants with whom they will be required to compete.

The Haryou proposal* to the City of New York included such a many-pronged attack. Over a three-year period, 7,000 Harlem youths,

* See author's introduction and *Youth in the Ghetto, A Study of the Consequences of Powerlessness and a Blueprint for Change,* Harlem Youth Opportunities Unlimited, Inc., New York, 1964.

ages 16 through 21, were to receive job training. In on-the-job training the youth was to be paid the standard wage of the job for which he was being trained, with the employer and the project sharing the cost. As he improved, the employer would assume more of the salary costs. Also part of the Haryou plan was to establish a special counseling and guidance program for high school dropouts, for those who could be encouraged to re-enter high school. Those who chose not to return to school were to be referred to training programs appropriate to their specific needs and interests. High school graduates with marketable work skills were to be referred for employment through the program placement services. Graduates in need of further training would get it.

The young people associated with Haryou during its planning stage (the Haryou Associates) pointed out that Negro youth in Harlem did not have the opportunity to learn how to manage even a small business or store since, unlike other lower-middle-class groups in the city, their parents did not own stores. They believed that this was a major handicap and suggested the organization of a Harlem Youth Enterprises, Unlimited, which would sponsor a cluster of local business enterprises owned by youth so as to provide them with on-the-job training opportunities.

For those who have been so severely damaged that they are not at present able to profit from organized job training and not able to benefit from the small-business management program, Haryou proposed to recruit in the poolrooms and other hangouts for a Community Service Corps, designed to perform various needed community services at whatever level of competence these young people had. The corps would try to raise their level of competence so that they would eventually be able to move into a more demanding job training program. Since each corps trainee would get enough money to meet his normal living needs, it might turn out that in a time of severe job scarcity, young people would "make a career" of job training. The alternative—larger welfare rolls, more jails, bigger police force to constrain hordes of desperate, jobless young people—is clearly more expensive. But the emphasis in all these programs would not be on "make-work" jobs designed to provide pocket money or to keep youths out of trouble during the stormy adolescent years. Rather, they would concentrate on providing young people with salable skills and insure a boost to the socio-economic status of ghetto residents of all America's urban ghettos, crucial if the pathology rooted in social and economic inferiority is to be remedied. One man expressed to a Haryou interviewer the view of many in the dark ghettos of America:

Most of all, I am trying to impress on them that the people are not chaining themselves to posts, that demonstrations are not being held, that people are not exposing themselves to dogs and tear gas so they can go on being delivery boys forever.

And another said with wistfulness:

If you go down and say well, man, I want a job, and showed that you really want to work and were given a job, then that's hope.

The main hope, however, may be that stated by Gunnar Myrdal in his book, *The Challenge to Affluence:**

. . . at this juncture of history there is a striking convergence between the American ideals of liberty and equality of opportunity on the one hand, and of economic progress on the other. Indeed, the chief policy means of spurring economic progress will have to be huge reforms that are in the interests of social justice.

White Unions, Black Proletariat

America does not like to admit—seldom does admit—that it is divided by social and economic classes. This fantasy has persisted in large measure because of the presence of Negroes, without whom low-income and low-status whites would see they themselves have been relegated to the lower rungs of the ladder; and that for many the ladder is not a ladder at all: The presence of the Negro obscures the facts.

The white worker has felt much less a proletariat psychologically than his counterpart in Europe because of the existence of a black proletariat in subjugated status beneath him. From a psychological point of view it was correct that he should. Whites will have to risk their own status if Negroes are to be admitted into the world of work

* New York, Pantheon Books, 1963.

as peer, and the white worker has understood this instinctively. The white worker is vulnerable because he has only the reality of his wish to give some security to his assumed status. When the Negro starts moving he threatens almost total collapse of white status and of the white worker's world. This is a matter of bread and butter and self-respect to the white worker. Unlike so many who have opposed the Negro—in the churches and elsewhere—the worker is really vulnerable. He feels his own job is at stake, that his family's future is endangered, that in an automated society there will be fewer jobs for the white man as well as the black. He has no time for a stereotyped liberal response in behalf of civil rights.

Racism has been one of the persistently debilitating facts in the American labor movement. After Eugene Debs, the American labor movement was never really a solid force, a movement in which the total rights and concerns of all workingmen were protected. The American Federation of Labor's position was one of no direct involvement in politics and one of apology when it did hesitatingly enter the political arena. It refused to become a significant part or core of any labor party. The Congress of Industrial Organizations was more politically active but also uninterested in a labor party. After the initial stages the labor movement organized itself in terms of respectable nonproletarian models. As it grew strong it took on the appearance and manner of management, with large salaries, palatial offices, and privileges and prerogatives for leadership competing with the luxury symbols of management. The American labor movement is basically a vehicle by which the workingman seeks to realize his aspirations to be a boss. It is a ringing refutation of the Marxian premise of categorical cleavages between economic classes. It is inextricably bound up in the American dream of success, of upward mobility. Unions are seen as escalators to management, not just as the protector of the workingclass. The presence of Negroes on the American scene has given some objective support to this belief, for whites have moved up—in large measure—by excluding Negroes from the competition, from the unions, and hence from the better-paying jobs.

In the highest levels of labor unions, the status of Negroes is weak and almost invisible. In New York City no Negro holds a position of primary power in organized labor. Negroes have been effectively segregated in American labor, much as in American churches, with their "own" unions, such as the railroad Brotherhood of Sleeping Car Porters, for workers in jobs almost exclusively reserved for Negroes. Where Negroes are singled out as labor representatives, they hold these posts at the pleasure of white leadership. Even in unions where most workers are Negro or Puerto Rican, the actual top leadership is predominantly white and often seems responsive more to the wishes of management than to the people they allegedly serve.

A significant example of the powerlessness of the Negro worker in a major trade union with a "liberal" reputation is found in the status of Negroes in the International Ladies' Garment Workers Union in New York City. The ILGWU is unique in many respects. The ILGWU is probably the most decisive force in the ladies' garment industry in New York City because it has rationalized and stabilized industry practices and established union control over a scattered multiplicity of small, highly competitive shops. Both employers and the workers regard the union as the major power in the industry.

The ILGWU and its leaders are important politically in New York City and state through their pivotal position in the Liberal party and the role of the Liberal party in city and state democratic politics. The ILGWU is generally considered to be a major liberal social and political force. This liberal image, however justified in other respects, does not extend to the protection of the economic status of Negro and Puerto Rican workers in the garment industry. Although there are thousands of Negroes employed in garment manufacturing in New York City, they are concentrated, with few exceptions, in the low wage, unskilled classifications and with very little job mobility. For example, Negroes are concentrated in such categories as "push boys" and shipping clerks in what amounts to a segregated ILGWU "auxiliary unit" known as 60-A and which operates under the control of the predominantly white Pressers Local 60.

Herbert Hill, National Labor Secretary of the National Association for the Advancement of Colored People, in testifying before a subcommittee of the House Committee on Education and Labor on August 17, 1962, referred to 60-A as the "Jim Crow auxiliary of local 60" and stated that:

The racial practices of the ILGWU are seen most clearly in relationships to the Cutters and Pressers locals. Local 60, the Pressers local, controls jobs within its jurisdiction that on a hourly rated basis are the highest paying jobs in the entire garment industry in New York City. The average wage being almost $5.00 an hour. Local 60 has an all-white membership. On the other hand, there is 60-A which is simply an appendage to Local 60 and which has a membership which is almost entirely Negro and Puerto Rican. The members of 60-A are shipping clerks, push boys and delivery men. These workers earn in the vicnity of $50.00 per week. Yet, 60-A with twice the membership of Local 60 has never been chartered by the International as a separate local and the manager of 60, who is a presser, functions also as the manager of 60-A. One must ask, why should a local of shipping clerks and push boys, whose members are paid extremely low wages, be attached as an auxiliary unit to the pressers local whose members make the highest wages in the garment industry?

Hill has charged that:

—there is not a single Negro who is an officer of the international union;

—there is not a single Negro on the twenty-three member General Executive Board;*

—there is not a single Negro or Puerto Rican vice president of the union;

—there are no Negro or Puerto Rican local managers;

—only 11 percent of the unionized garment workers in New York earn enough to maintain a "modest but adequate" standard of living;

—the wages of workers in the New York City ladies' garment industry have declined relative to the total manufacturing average.

None of these charges was refuted by the top leadership or spokesmen of the ILGWU.

Daniel Bell, sociologist of Columbia University, said in an article in the *New Leader* (January 21, 1963):

* Until recently, there was not a Puerto Rican on the Board. In March 1964, however, as a result of exposure and pressure, a Puerto Rican was appointed to the ILGWU General Executive Board.

. . . The fact is—and this is the "bite" in Hill's charges—that the Negroes are underrepresented in the leadership of many of the unions where they form a significant proportion of the membership. In the case of these unions, what the Negroes want is "recognition" at the level of top leadership and a growing share of the spoils of office. . . . For one thing, the realistic political process in the United States, at least in the northern urban centers, has been one of ethnic groups advancing themselves precisely in this fashion; by organizing on bloc lines, electing their own kind, and using the patronage system to enhance the wealth and status of their group. . . .

Bell concludes:

. . . In economic and educational opportunity, the Negro is in a position of inequality, and the government is bound to help him move ahead. But doesn't the trade union movement have a *special* obligation to help redress the balance . . . ?

The predicament of Negroes and Puerto Ricans in the ILGWU reflects the powerlessness of their general educational, economic, political, and social status. Earlier immigrants have used labor unions, public schools, and the control of political organizations as ladders of economic and social mobility. As they became successful through the use of these institutions and instruments of power, they tended to assume leadership positions and dominate them. As the numbers of Negroes and Puerto Ricans increased in the city as a whole to a "significant proportion" of the voting strength and union membership, older ethnic groups who had already consolidated their educational, economic, and political power are reluctant to share this with Negroes and Puerto Ricans. As the sheer weight of numbers of these new minorities increases, older minorities are required to set up institutional, bureaucratic, or even moral and ideological blocks to the fulfillment of the demands of Negroes and Puerto Ricans for a share in the spoils and patronage power. Within the conflict between the past and the present lie the seeds for serious social problems and tensions of the future.*

* For a documentation of the status of nonwhite workers in the ladies garment industry in New York City and in the ILGWU see Herbert Hill, Testimony Before the House Committee on Education and Labor, 88th Congress, 1st Sess. 1569–72 (Jan. 31, 1963 Congressional Record House pp. 1496–1499); see also Hill, *The ILGWU, Fact and Fiction,* New Politics, Winter, 1963, pp. 7–27.

There are a few indications that labor unions are beginning to re-examine the role of Negroes. A. Philip Randolph, one of the AFL-CIO vice presidents, has played a crucial part in bringing the problem to the attention of labor leadership. So, too, the pressures of Hill, labor secretary of the NAACP, have been effective. The early resistance of George Meany seems to be giving way to recognition of the fact that inclusion of Negroes in the labor movement will, in fact, not be a threat but will strengthen it. If this is a new positive development in American labor it matches the recognition by leaders of business and industry that exclusion of Negroes from full participation in the economy saps the strength of the economy, artificially restricts the skilled labor supply, and thereby grants to labor unions control over that supply. The cooperation of management in the President's Committee on Equal Employment in opening job opportunities for Negroes is based on the knowledge that as one provides better jobs for Negroes one increases the number of consumers, one expands the domestic markets and the national productivity and the general level of prosperity. Labor, too, will be strengthened because as long as Negroes are kept out of labor unions they remain a vast reservoir of cheap labor which, in effect, is more of a threat to the workingman than Negro competition could be within the union. Bringing Negroes in will make the unions morally and pragmatically more powerful.

If labor unions do not fully let down the barriers of apprenticeship and membership to Negroes on an open and free competitive basis, management and ownership will have to bring pressure to bear. If management transforms its own policies, compensating for past injustice by more active hiring of Negroes at higher status levels, the labor unions themselves will heed the demands of social change. But if Negroes gain at the expense of whites, racial hostility will increase and force a regression. It is incumbent upon economic power to supply jobs for all who need and wish them. The consumer potential of the urban Negro is, in this effort, an untapped resource. The American economic society is vigorous and can respond imaginatively to threats against its own security and the stability of society itself.

The resistance of labor to automation can be tolerated up to a point, but when the economic imperatives are clear, neither management nor labor can hold the clock back in automation and in civil rights. The total economy is threatened by the decay of the heart of American cities, long the creative centers of industry, transportation, communication, and education, and by the dangers of Negro unemployment, and Negro concentration in low-status menial service jobs. No longer can the potential consuming power of one-tenth of the American people be ignored, and the power of consumption be artificially limited by the low wages of Negroes and the heavy load of Negro welfare dependency, a product of broken families caused in turn in large part by male unemployment.

The Cycle of Family Instability

One of the inevitable results of the unemployment and menial job status of urban Negroes is family instability. Family breakdown occurs among the white poor, too, but inferior racial status that makes escape seem impossible and damages the core of personality adds impetus to the problem. Once again, the Negro poor are forced to be different. As the Haryou report indicated, approximately one out of every five men in Harlem is separated from his wife, and about two out of every seven women are separated from their husbands. In the city as a whole, only one in thirty men is separated from his wife, and approximately one in sixteen women from her husband. Only about half of the children under eighteen in the Harlem community are living with both parents, compared with 83 percent in New York City as a whole. The child without a secure family life is often forced either into aggression and delinquency or into apathy and despair. As one mother said to a Haryou interviewer:

When you see an obedient child, he will come home when you tell him to be home in an hour or two. But when he comes home, the mother has the door locked and the father is gone someplace half drunk. The child can't come home like he wants to. Maybe the child wants to say something to his parents, but his parents are not home. He has no one to talk to but perhaps an older brother. When the parents are not home, the children are lost. Perhaps he's hurt. He wants to come home and talk to either his father or mother, but they are out. He can't even get in the house to use the lavatory, so they do what they have to do in the halls.

Children and young people who grow up in a community in which a large proportion of families have no father in the home, a community in which 40 percent of the men and 47 percent of the women aged 14 or over are unmarried,* find it difficult, if not almost impossible, to know what an "adequate" family is like. The cycle of family instability continues uninterrupted.

Broken families and poverty also usually mean reliance upon public assistance. In 1961, 226.5 per 1,000 Harlem youth under eighteen years of age—nearly one in four—were supported, in part, by aid-to-dependent-children (ADC) funds, three times as many as in the city as a whole (72 per 1,000). In that same year in Cleveland's Hough area, three times as many families received General Assistance and about four times as many received ADC help as for the city as a whole. Similar trends could doubtless be discovered in the other urban ghettos.

Therefore, the Negro's despair at his racial rejection is reinforced by the knowledge that he is often a heavy financial burden to himself and to the community. Fear of the poor, in turn, reinforces the white's prejudice against the Negro. Many white people have come to fear the "influx" of Negroes, from the South into Northern cities and from the large urban ghettos into smaller cities and suburbs, as a threat of social and economic dimension—the threat of higher taxes to care for the dependent, lowered property values, and the like. Few look at the causes of the vicious cycle, which lie in the white community—the low-paying menial jobs unskilled Negroes are compelled to take; the chronic rising Negro unemployment rate, the poor education of Negro children; the compulsive bargain selling of property, encouraged by "block-busters," i.e., unscrupulous real estate agents (Negro as well as white); and many other factors.

The white society which has to deal with massive social problems of poverty and despair tends to rely on the temporary expedients of counseling and emergency help rather than on direct social change.

* This statistic for Harlem is roughly the same proportion of unattached adults as obtains for the city as a whole, but in New York, especially Manhattan, a large number of single young people congregate at the start of their careers and a large number of elderly persons find living convenient—conditions not true of Harlem.

The poor, and especially the Negro poor, often seem ungrateful and resist what help is offered.

The poor, thought of as being ignorant, illiterate, and unimaginative, have developed a variety of ways of coping with the welfare worker; evasion is frequent as recipients become "welfare wise."

And so we have a typical situation of a great deal of police and control efforts on one side and a considerable amount of matching efforts at evasion on the other. The stalemate that is reached is one where frequently there is repugnance on the part of the authorities and a lack of respect on the part of the recipients.*

One family service agency director observed that the energy of "multiproblem" families of the lower socio-economic class seems directed almost entirely to giving social workers the "run-around." She felt the explanation lay in the fact that such persons are not "geared to talking," and do not know how to "make good use" of social agencies.

A young man who has, for months, sought work in vain would be expected to be pleased by the offer of a decent job or training in a desired skill. But the alienation of the Negro poor is such that the "hustler" or "bop" or unwed ADC mother, the members of the "deviant subculture," often respond with an attitude of "include me out," which reflects the cynical desire to "cash in" on a less demanding mode of adjustment. In the ghetto to "cash in" means to earn a livelihood for imaginary services, or for an outright disservice, and it means that one must establish a mutually exploitative relation with others—one must have a "hustle." "Cashing in" and the "hustle" reflect the belief that one cannot make a living through socially acceptable vocations in a complex and rejecting racist society. "Cashing in" tends to be seen as the way the world is.

Agencies that encourage their clients to accept dependency or to accept transparent "make-work" contribute to the perpetuation of the pathology of the ghetto communities. It is reasonable to assume that people who have not already been severely damaged want wholesome work. When the client cannot find such work, the professional cannot have wholesome work of his own either. This necessarily leads

* S. M. Miller, *Poverty, Race and Politics*, Syracuse University Youth Development Center, 1963.

to a mutually protective estrangement of client and worker, to the "flight from the client" illustrated by the exodus of most of the family service agencies out of Harlem. It may also increase the contempt of the "client" for all who claim to be willing to help him.

For social service and social agencies to be relevant to the pressing problems of the ghetto, those who are in control of this part of our society must have the courage to re-examine ruthlessly their present assumptions, methods, and programs and prune those postures and pretenses which reflect only traditional and bureaucratic lags or fund-raising gimmicks. To be relevant, social service agencies must above all accept and respect the humanity of those in need of help—and express this acceptance and respect through courtesy and the warmth, cleanliness, and beauty of the physical surroundings in which the help is offered. Social service cannot be relevant to the pathology of the ghetto, except to reinforce it, if it encourages even subtly the dependency of the people of the ghetto—because to encourage dependency is to rob the individual of the sense of his own dignity and to strengthen his feelings of inferiority. Relevant and human social services must dare to run the risks of being a part of a real and comprehensive program of social action and social change.

Realistic Intervention

The Haryou program was based upon the above rationale and the finding that piecemeal, isolated, and peripheral social agency programs neither helped individuals nor stemmed the tide of ghetto pathology.

To build a new culture designed to enable the ghetto to service itself would cost far less in the long run than the present list of human casualties. The ghetto needs to replace hostility and alienation with a creative, constructive culture.

Who are the most effective workers in such programs? As catalysts in this enterprise, Haryou found during its planning explorations that it could make use of artists and ex-delinquents as well as trained social workers. The advisability of recruiting large numbers of professionally trained social workers and teachers has been seriously questioned. Often it appears that professional training itself enhances the "flight from the client." Furthermore, large numbers of trained personnel are not available. The best recruits for these jobs may be residents of the community themselves who stand to benefit not only financially but also by gaining status, self-esteem and the new satisfaction of "meaningful" work. With such workers there is less of a possibility, also, that the communication barrier will be a factor, since they are literally part of the world of their clients. They will probably be more willing to endure the long hours which some of the programs require, since they have not developed a working tradition which shies away from sustained relationship with clients, from week-end and night work. They have not yet developed professional ennui.

Many of the ghetto's working mothers who now work outside the community, taking care of other people's children, could be paid instead to work within their own community as aides in preschool academies. Other potential recruits would be young mothers who have recently left school, many of whom are just beginning the aid-to-dependent-children treadmill to apathy. This plan seems more economical than the family-by-family casework approach, particularly in view of the tragic fact that many ghetto parents may be "too far gone" to be reclaimed as a wholesome influence in the lives of their children. For those persons in the community who are not yet too far gone, but who lack the personal and social skills for sound influence over their children, training may serve as a substitute for "treatment." It may be that many lower-class persons who now refuse the role of client will accept the same therapeutic help if it is offered in a course of training as part of a position as paid or volunteer trainee.

It may also prove more feasible to train sensitive lower-class persons in the necessary skills to overcome the demoralizing impact of cultural shock in middle-class workers. Most social workers and teachers are themselves middle class, some far enough removed in time and circumstance to cause an inevitable sense of strangeness between themselves and the client; others too close themselves in time and circumstance to accept without anxiety the reminders of a rejected past. The problems are not merely ones of psychological alienation between the two groups but more concrete ones of speaking different languages and responding to different standards of behavior.

In training schools and community centers in which deviant peer group codes dominate, the would-be influentials, the professionals, are often stymied by a communication barrier. The point cannot be overstressed that in Harlem, and probably elsewhere, there are people in the helping services, probation and parole officers, group workers, caseworkers, and others in presumably influential roles who have abandoned any meaningful attempt to help the people who are in need. When they show any insight into this fact, these professionals almost always explain it by pointing to some lack or deficiency in the clients whom they cannot reach or cannot help. These clients are commonly called "unreachables" or those "hard to reach." Whatever the label, it means that the professionals have abandoned hope.

Yet many of these new recruits may later decide to complete their education and qualify for professional training, and it would be one of the risks of a program of encouraging such endeavor that the workers would quickly become middle class themselves.

The problem of class and race alienation is more difficult to solve than to understand. Bureaucratic organization is such that promotion and status are related to moving up the ladder to administration, and administration in social work, in education, as in many other professions, means supervising the work of other staff personnel. It is ironic that the further "up" one goes, the further one moves from the persons for whose service the profession exists—the client in the social casework agency, the child in the classroom. Yet this movement up the ladder to status, title, and higher pay is hard to resist. Perhaps it would be important for all administrators of programs dealing with human beings to keep in touch by some degree of direct involvement—the supervisor keeping a few clients, the school principal teaching an occasional class. Yet this, too, may be impractical, for the stance of authority upon which administrative success depends is itself related to a certain distance between the "top" and "bottom" levels in the hierarchy. In any event, one must be conscious of the danger of the flight from the client and insure that personal advancement does not rest on escape from the essential service.

To insure that the ghetto gets its share of social and community services, a large group of citizens of the ghetto, both youth and adult, who are disciplined and politically sensitive, would need to be organized. Otherwise, these vast and wide-ranging programs of reform would only amount to a benevolence from outside the community, vulnerable to control and abuse, and tending to encourage further dependency.

Given a community climate of indifference and apathy, even simple services like those of the Department of Sanitation will not be efficiently performed, as Harlem's many dirty streets make obvious. That the Department of Sanitation neglects to clean Harlem's streets as frequently as it cleans the streets in other communities may be seen as a simple sin of omission. On the other hand, genuine exploitation may be at work in such neglect as when building inspectors fail to inspect, or accept bribes from landlords to overlook violations. The ghetto community fails to get necessary public services and yet, through taxation, it is also involved in subsidizing its own deterioration.

The Haryou Associates Leadership Training Workshop in the summer of 1963 combined a paid job in social service with an unpaid training period in community action projects that helped to teach Harlem youth how to insist upon and get public services their taxes had already paid for. Unfortunately, these workers often lose the very qualities for which they were recruited from the community once they are placed on the payroll and brought into contact with professional colleagues whose style they sought to imitate.

Local neighborhood boards of adults and youth who live or work in the neighborhood could help change the patterns of community immobility and impotence by defining problems and by accepting responsibility for evaluating public and private services to the community. Such neighborhood boards would have powers of patronage from the outset—recruiting staff, providing service—but if they are to become a potent voice in the local neighborhood, patronage is not enough. They must have imagination and daring, and they must assume the risk of demanding real social change.

It may well turn out that a major role in insuring that the local boards do not begin to "play it safe" could be assumed by an organization run by the youth themselves. Since young people have less to lose by a radical stance and have fewer vested interests in "the system" than most adults, hopefully they could lend the clear and fresh vision, enthusiasm, and courage of youth to the adult members of the local boards and the adult staff alongside whom they would work.

Without such grass-roots activity in the neighborhoods, no comprehensive program, no matter how imaginative, will be safe from bureaucratic dry rot and exploitation. Neighbor would be responsible for neighbor. Individuals would come to have confidence in their ability to assess conflict, incompetence, and stagnation, and their right to do so. If the youth and adults of a neighborhood cannot be brought into the actual operation of reform programs, the programs themselves, no matter how elaborately and thoroughly planned, will merely contribute to the proliferation of irrelevance.

"The resentment of the weak," writes Eric Hoffer in *The Ordeal of Change,** does not spring from any injustice done to them, but from the sense of their inadequacy and impotence. Our healing gift to the weak is the capacity for self-help. We must learn to impart to them the technical, social and political skills which would enable them to get bread, human dignity, freedom and strength by their own efforts."

There is harnessable power to effect profound social change in the generally repressed rage of the alienated. There is much energy and imagination in the deviant subcultural forms in which this rage presently finds expression. Initially operating as close to the marginal world as is possible, a successful program of social rehabilitation must help the poor and the delinquent rehabilitate others like themselves and, in the process, effect their own salvation. This is one of the hopes for the ghetto. But if it is to work, the people of the ghetto must be respected and must learn to respect themselves through evidence of actual success in attempts at improving their condition. They cannot

* New York, Harper & Row, 1963.

have this opportunity without serious risks and the many forms of turbulence inevitably associated with genuine social change.

Black Social Mobility

In response to white society's criticism of Negro family instability and the patterns of poverty, many middle-class Negroes have tended to accept the judgment of many whites that they are responsible for their own troubles, that economic dependency is related directly to immorality. As one Negro woman put it:

Whenever a woman has a child of course she will do anything to provide for it, even to accepting welfare, but family breakdown and the moral state that we find ourselves in as a people has accounted for this development of the welfare programs.

Now we could develop ourselves morally, perhaps, and this can only come about through an economic development. If we had some of the better things in life, that is, if we had the necessary leisure to develop ourselves intellectually, or if we had enough money to provide for ourselves and enjoy life, and to be happy, then the family would become stronger, and the moral development of the people would increase, and these welfare programs would be done away with.

The middle-class prisoners of the ghetto are ashamed of these elements in the community which bring disgrace to that community. They view themselves as an example of respectability and are viewed by others in the same way. After the summer revolts of 1964, it was they who called for counterrallies of religious commitment to show the world "the other Harlem." They often preach that if the lower class would work hard and clean up their homes and not litter their streets and show more interest in their children, the Negro predicament would be solved.

One such rather influential woman leader, in a talk to a Negro church in Harlem, urged Negro women to organize for community reform. On every block in Harlem, she said, a committee should be rallied to buy brooms; squads of women and children would be recruited to sweep the streets. She argued that people who live on dirty streets could not hope to gain the respect of others. Negro children, she said, should be taught to respect cleanliness and this would in turn give them pride in their parents and in themselves.

She did not understand that it is not the job of the people to sweep the streets; it is the job of the Department of Sanitation. It had not occurred to her to advise these women to organize to gain these services to which they were entitled. In a middle-class neighborhood, the people see to it that government does provide services. To lecture the miserable inhabitants of the ghetto to sweep their own streets is to urge them to accept the fact that the government is not expected to serve them. But to force the government to provide sanitation and care is an effort beyond their capacity for, in such ghettos, people are so defeated that their sense of powerlessness becomes a reality. They are immobilized against action even in their own behalf.

Most disturbing of the implications of her advice was that Negroes are responsible for their own condition, that dirt reflects defects in the inhabitants. She was buying the position of many middle-class whites that social victims are responsible for their plight. She was in error, but even more important was the fact that she was, in effect, presenting an apology for oppression.

Ghetto residents, particularly members of the middle class, are often obsessed with what they feel to be a lack of initiative and moral fiber on the part of other Negroes. In a ghetto each member identifies, to some degree, with the other, and feels shame at the other's plight as though a member of the family had gone wrong. Often he resents the troublesome lower-class Negro, and then responds to this dislike by a pervasive sense of guilt—particularly when he finds there is no escape, after all. Although in the days of extensive European immigration, the second generation often felt guilt at its wish to escape the language and habits of their parents' "old country," a white person who moves into the middle class or upper class today can afford to forget his origins; he no longer needs to identify with those he has left behind. But in a society where wealth, aristocratic bearing, and talent are insufficient to overcome the stigma of the color of one's skin, there is no such escape for any generation. While this sense of relatedness may have its points, it also imposes a heavy psychological burden upon people whose own lives are hard enough to bear without the additional shame they feel the white community asks them to feel for their neigh-bors. Shame and despair, unlike anger, seldom lead to effective social or personal reform.

There are few middle-class sections in the central urban ghetto of Harlem. One of them is the Riverton Development and its residents are proud of the fact that it is an oasis in the slums in an area that was once one of the worst slum neighborhoods in the city. The middle-class Negro points with pride to the fact that the grounds are well kept, that the halls are scrupulously clean, that the elevators are in working order. Neighbor vies with neighbor in Riverton for the most luxuriously furnished apartment. As a consequence, James Baldwin's article in *Esquire* about Riverton outraged most of Harlem's middle-class residents.* Actually Riverton is not a slum, but James Baldwin was right that in an important sense it *is*. It is a spiritual slum, a paradoxical symbol of the phenomenon it seeks to deny, a symbol of Jim Crow. Riverton exists because at one time the Metro-politan Life Insurance Company's policy excluded Negroes from Stuyvesant Town on Manhattan's East Side, containing them in the ghetto. Today there are only a token number of Negroes in Stuyvesant Town, and there are no white families in Riverton. Thus, residents of Riverton are as much prisoners of the ghetto as their neighbors in rat-infested tenements across the street or in the low-income public housing on the other side. Their very attempt to exist in isolated defiance inevitably involves them in the total system of the ghetto. They constantly fight the slum but can never be victorious. The ghetto is all-encompassing, a psychological as well as a physical reality. It consumes all its residents.

Yet the struggle of the middle-class Negro against the ghetto can-not be cynically dismissed. It is from this group of upwardly mobile Negroes that outstanding Negroes come. These are the young people who are stimulated by the desire and determination for personal success in spite of or because of the handicaps of rejected racial status. If they succeed, many whites nod approvingly: "I said so all along; American racial oppression is not unbearable; it can be overcome." The masses of lower-class Negroes regard this movement

* "Fifth Avenue Uptown," *Esquire*, 1960, Vol. 54, p. 70.

up the ladder with mixed feelings, both proud and resentful of the success of "one of their own."

Such middle-class Negro youth spend a considerable amount of their human energy seeking to mold their lives in rigid conformity to the prevailing middle-class values and standards. They are clean, they dress well, they speak well, they strive very hard to make good grades in school and to get a good education. They dedicate their lives to the task of becoming walking refutations of negative racial stereotypes. They are the opposite of the flamboyantly rebellious ghetto youth, more likely to withdraw passively and seek to repress any sign of hostility. Many express a subtle form of self and group hatred by denying awareness of any racial problems, or even by interpreting racial discrimination as an understandable response to the uncouth "lower-class" street Negro.

One poignant example was reflected in the response of a Negro undergraduate at Columbia College. An interview in the college magazine described and quoted him, as follows:

A sophomore who was raised in Harlem, Henry graduated third in his class of 400 ("beaten by two girls, as you might suspect") from Benjamin Franklin High School, which is 90 per cent Negro and Puerto Rican. His parents migrated from South Carolina; his father is a power press operator. Although his high school had no football team, he is out for the lightweight football squad. He lives in a single room in John Jay. Henry shuns demonstrative protests, preferring to participate in such projects as SEER, a Columbia College–initiated national program to help prepare Negro students for college during the summers. He likes social studies, but is toying with the idea of becoming a physician.

"Most people in Harlem, and, I suspect, other Negroes, feel very discouraged and are full of resentment against whites—too much so, I think. Negroes have to stop feeling so sorry for themselves and start trying to help themselves. Harlem could actually be a nice place to live. My parents have taught me not to expect to have things handed to me, but to work hard and get what I wanted. My teachers have encouraged me in the same way. But maybe if I had different parents and teachers I would feel trapped and bitter too. I really like Columbia, but I sometimes wish it had a lake."*

* Negroes and the College. *Columbia College Today.* New York: Columbia College, Columbia University, Vol. 12, No. 1, Fall 1964, p. 32.

As adults they embark on the competitive cycle of conspicuous consumption and seek to share the good life of American middle-class suburbia. Some struggle to break through into nonsegregated communities in order to escape the ghetto, prepared to run the risks of overt hostility or even of violence. Others accept the easier escape to one of the middle-class suburban Negro ghettos. On the surface, the ghetto population in New York—unlike that in other cities—seems to be declining. (Harlem's population has decreased by 27,000 between 1950 and 1960, roughly a 10 percent loss despite the high birth rate.) But the fact is that Harlem's Negroes are merely shifting to other ghetto pockets in the city—Brooklyn's Bedford-Stuyvesant, the Lower Bronx, or Queens, or to suburban ghettos, such as those in Englewood, New Rochelle, Mount Vernon, and elsewhere. Many of those who move away from the central city are young couples—another drain on the ghetto's sources of energy and leadership.

Middle-class Negroes do not generally react with the overt, active hostility prevalent in many members of the "working class," but they, too, are often hostile, in ways similar to the larger pattern of white middle-class competitiveness, yet complicated by the persistent problems of racial anxiety, hypersensitivity, and defensiveness.

Negroes who do succeed in reaching the point of real competition with whites and who are rewarded with high-status jobs do not find that they have thereby resolved the problem of being Negro in a white society. Negroes brought into high-status jobs must be significantly above the norm, but feel they must adopt a style of compensatory gentility, allowing the whites to feel less threatened and even causing many to assume a protective role toward them. Negroes who do take this precautionary step must be certain that it is appropriate to the nature of the job itself, for a "show Negro" cannot afford to play, in an executive management job, a comic or subservient role. He needs an air of authority or he will lose status. If he adopts a stance or role of subtle deference, he will also be successful in protecting himself by assuaging the fears of whites. He must be constantly careful not to make his white colleagues uncomfortable, either by apparent arrogance or inappropriate obsequiousness.

Other Negroes in status jobs choose to protect themselves by keeping a careful distance between themselves and others, by neither asking for nor granting favors, by remaining aloof so that no one can be effectively patronizing. This pattern of overcompensation often leads to great productivity and intense concentration on the job. Less time and energy are available for socializing with others. Both closeness and acceptance are feared. Cliques are avoided as risky involvement. Friendship—with its danger of rejection—is not sought. When solicitousness is offered, it is regarded with disdain. The reputation sought is one of remoteness, single-minded dedication to the job, unremitting self-respect. If the Negro seems also to be cold and to lack concern for persons, he will accept this as evidence that his stance of invulnerability is effective. Colleagues are expected to be sophisticated enough not to intrude beyond the limits the Negro has set. If one sets the boundaries oneself, excluding others, one cannot oneself be excluded.

These protective devices to which high-status Negroes often resort are evidence of the depth of damage which racism has done. Such defenses must be seen for what they are—a response to fear of rejection and the anticipation of pain.

The middle-class Negro is demanding the right to share in the status symbols of personal success—quality education for his children; white-collar, managerial, or executive jobs; a fine home in one of the better neighborhoods. Having accepted the same value system which the middle-class whites live by, middle-class Negroes are forced to compete with them even at the risk of conflict. The demand for nonsegregated public schools comes largely from upwardly mobile middle-class Negroes; the demands for better white-collar, managerial, and executive jobs and for better nonsegregated housing come from the more successful and stable middle-class Negroes. If whites respond without mere grudging tokenism—"We already have a Negro in our firm (in our block) (in our school) (in our church)"—the masses of workingclass and lower middle-class Negroes will benefit. Other Negroes, too, will come to believe that the average Negro can win rewards through persistence, hard work, thrift, and character.

The competitive demands of the growing Negro middle class, if successful, would open more doors for all Negroes. A Negro in a managerial or executive position tends, also, to reduce the novelty of a Negro foreman or Negro salesman. A Negro professor might increase the employment chances for Negro secretaries on a college payroll. The tendency of white Americans to lump all Negroes together could lead ironically to major social advances, as Negroes in high-status jobs prepare the way for gradual acceptance of all Negroes. Still, whites who otherwise generalize about Negro racial traits ("All Negroes look alike to me") are often inconsistent when confronted with a Negro in a high-status post, viewing him as an exception to the rule.

To leave the heart of the ghetto is the goal of the average young educated Negro. The retreat of young professional Negro men and women—doctors, nurses, lawyers, engineers, teachers—from the central ghetto to the opening suburbs imposes a burden of decay of leadership upon the central city; yet the psychological stability of these families often seems to depend upon just such flight. The reminders of the ghetto, however, are never far away, for as Negroes—educated, clean, dignified, self-respecting families, the elite of Negro society—come to a formerly white community where whites had earlier retreated, white families often flee before them as though they were the carriers of a dread disease. The only contagion they carry is freedom, but what could be more dangerous than freedom to those who themselves live insecure, unhappy lives bound to frequently abhorred routines of family duty, unfulfilling job, and status-seeking? The insecure try to enhance their own personal status by denying others the very security and status which they seek for themselves.

This flight of the middle-class white to suburban, presently all-white communities, is a temporary stopgap only, unrealistic in view of the constant pressure of middle-class minority group members to escape the ghetto's deterioration and distress. Suburban communities can only be temporary havens for whites who desire racial homogeneity. The pressure for open occupancy in the suburbs will increase in the next decade with rising momentum. The pressure for integrated suburban schools will follow, as the struggle to abolish *de facto* school segregation in Orange, Englewood, and Teaneck, New Jersey, and in New Rochelle, White Plains, Manhasset, and

Malverne, in New York, already demonstrate. It would indeed be a pathetic repetition of social, economic, and political folly if whites respond by techniques of exclusion that "worked" in the past, by developing suburban ghettos. But such a routine, unimaginative, and fearful response is all too likely—people tend to follow familiar patterns of behavior unless interrupted. An immediate systematic plan is needed to introduce minority group members into the suburbs without, at the same time, building new suburban ghetto substitutes. Such a plan could "interrupt" accustomed patterns of response to anxiety and break the cycle.

But though many middle-class residents of the ghetto do have a constant wish for physical and psychological escape, the ghetto has a devouring quality and to leave provokes a curious struggle. In an important sense no one can ever leave. Those who do not try feel that those who *do* try should have some feeling of guilt and a sense of betrayal. They demand allegiance to the pathology of the ghetto. The ghetto develops the sinister power to perpetuate its own pathology, to demand conformity to its norms; it ridicules, drives out, or isolates those who seek to resist those norms or even to transform them. This is an almost irresistible social Gresham's Law that none is allowed to escape with impunity.

That Negroes continue to seek to imitate the patterns of middle-class whites is a compliment, not the threat it may seem, but a compliment in large part undeserved, and the scars inflicted upon Negroes who are constantly confronted by the flight of those they encounter are deep and permanent. The wounded appear to eschew bitterness and hatred, but not far below the often genial, courteous surface lies a contempt that cannot easily be disguised.

4

THE PSYCHOLOGY OF THE GHETTO

It is now generally understood that chronic and remediable social injustices corrode and damage the human personality, thereby robbing it of its effectiveness, of its creativity, if not its actual humanity. No matter how desperately one seeks to deny it, this simple fact persists and intrudes itself. It is the fuel of protests and revolts. Racial segregation, like all other forms of cruelty and tyranny, debases all human beings—those who are its victims, those who victimize, and in quite subtle ways those who are merely accessories.

This human debasement can only be comprehended as a consequence of the society which spawns it. The victims of segregation do not initially desire to be segregated, they do not "prefer to be with their own people," in spite of the fact that this belief is commonly stated by those who are not themselves segregated. A most cruel and psychologically oppressive aspect and consequence of enforced segregation is that its victims can be made to accommodate to their victimized status and under certain circumstances to state that it *is* their desire to be set apart, or to agree that subjugation is not really detrimental but beneficial. The fact remains that exclusion, rejection, and a stigmatized status are not desired and are not voluntary states. Segregation is neither sought nor imposed by healthy or potentially healthy human beings.

Human beings who are forced to live under ghetto conditions and whose daily experience tells them that almost nowhere in society are they respected and granted the ordinary dignity and courtesy accorded to others will, as a matter of course, begin to doubt their own worth. Since every human being depends upon his cumulative experiences with others for clues as to how he should view and value himself, children who are consistently rejected understandably begin to question and doubt whether they, their family, and their group really deserve no more respect from the larger society than they receive. These doubts become the seeds of a pernicious self- and group-hatred, the Negro's complex and debilitating prejudice against himself.

The preoccupation of many Negroes with hair straighteners, skin bleachers, and the like illustrates this tragic aspect of American racial prejudice—Negroes have come to believe in their own inferiority. In recent years Negro men and women have rebelled against the constant struggle to become white and have given special emphasis to their "Negroid" features and hair textures in a self-conscious acceptance of "negritude"—a wholehearted embracing of the African heritage. But whether a Negro woman uses hair straightener or whether she highlights her natural hair texture by flaunting *au naturel* styles, whether a Negro man hides behind a neat Ivy League suit or wears blue jeans defiantly in the manner of the Student Nonviolent Coordinating Committee (SNCC), each is still reacting primarily to the pervasive factor of race and still not free to take himself for granted or to judge himself by the usual standards of personal success and character. It is still the white man's society that governs the Negro's image of himself.

Fantasy Protections

Many Negroes live sporadically in a world of fantasy, and fantasy takes different forms at different ages. In childhood the delusion is a simple one—the child may pretend that he is really white. When Negro children as young as three years old are shown white- and Negro-appearing dolls or asked to color pictures of children to look like themselves, many of them tend to reject the dark-skinned dolls as "dirty" and "bad" or to color the picture of themselves a light color or a bizarre shade like purple. But the fantasy is not complete, for when asked to identify which doll is like themselves, some Negro children, particularly in the North, will refuse, burst into tears, and run away. By the age of seven most Negro children have accepted the reality that they are, after all, dark skinned. But the stigma remains; they have been forced to recognize themselves as inferior. Few if any Negroes ever fully lose that sense of shame and self-hatred.

To the Negro child the most serious injury seems to be in the concept of self-worth related directly to skin color itself. Because school is a central activity at this age, his sense of inferiority is revealed most acutely in his lack of confidence in himself as a student, lack of motivation to learn, and in problems of behavior—a gradual withdrawal or a growing rebellion. The effects of this early damage are difficult to overcome, for the child who never learns to read cannot become a success at a job or in a society where education and culture are necessary. In addition, there is the possibility that poor teaching, generally characteristic of the ghetto schools, tends to reinforce this sense of inferiority and to give it substance in the experience of inferior achievement. The cycle that leads to menial jobs and to broken homes has then begun; only the most drastic efforts at rehabilitation can break that cycle.

The obsession with whiteness continues past childhood and into adulthood. It stays with the Negro all his life. Haryou recorded a conversation between teen-age boys about their hair styles that reflected this obsession.

You know, if he go in there with his hair slick up like white, they might go for him better, you know.
They might use him for a broom or a mop.
Well, why do you wear "brushes?"
Why do I wear "brushes?" It's a blind, a front. Are you saying that I'm ignorant?
He's a playboy. He like to do his hair like that. He's ashamed of his own hair, you know. He feels bad that he's black and now he wants to be half and half. He wants to be a half-breed.
When your great granmammy was taken advantage of in the fields,

what was happening then? Have you ever seen a light-skinned African? Have you ever seen an African your color?

No.

All right then; two bird dogs don't make nothing but a bird dog.

You don't have to go all the way, getting your hair slicked.

I don't have to go all the way black either, do I?

What are you going to do? You can't go all the way white.

Teen-age Negroes often cope with the ghetto's frustrations by retreating into fantasies related chiefly to their role in society. There is, for example, a fantasy employed by many marginal and antisocial teen-agers, to pretend to knowledge about illicit activities and to a sexual urbanity that they do not, really, have. They use as their models the petty criminals of the ghetto, whose colorful, swaggering style of cool bravado poses a peculiar fascination. Some pretend falsely to be pimps, some to have contacts with numbers runners. Their apparent admiration of these models is not total but reflects a curious combination of respect, of contempt, and, fundamentally, of despair. Social scientists who rely on questionnaires and superficial interviews must find a way to unravel this tangled web of pretense if their conclusions are to be relevant.

Among the young men observed at Haryou, fantasy played a major role. Many of these marginal, upward-striving teen-agers allowed others to believe that they were college students. One young man told his friends that he was a major in psychology. He had enrolled in the classes of a Negro professor with whom he identified, and he described those lectures in detail to his friends. The fact is that he was a dropout from high school. Others dressed like college students and went to college campuses where they walked among the students, attempting to feel a part of a life they longed for and could not attain. Some carried attaché cases wherever they went—often literally empty. One carried ordinary books camouflaged by college bookcovers and pretended to "study" in the presence of friends. Most of these young men were academically at the fifth- or sixth-grade reading level; none was in college. Another youngster who said he was in college planned to become a nuclear physicist. He spoke most convincingly about his physics and math courses and discussed the importance of Negroes' going into the field. Within a year, however, he had been dropped for nonattendance from the evening session of the municipal college at which he was enrolled. He had not taken even a first course in physics and had not been able to pass the elementary course in mathematics. He explained this failure in a complicated story and reported that he now intended to get a job. Later he described his new job in the executive training program of a high-status department store downtown. He was saving for college where he would continue with nuclear physics. He carried an attaché case to work each day. But the truth was that he was not in an executive training program at all; he had a job as a stock clerk. Yet the fantasy was one of performance; there was truth in his dreams, for if he had been caught in time he might have become a scientist. He did have the intellectual potential. But as a Negro, he had been damaged so early in the educational process that not even the surge of motivation and his basic intelligence could now make his dreams effective. His motivation was sporadic and largely verbal; his plans were in the realm of delusion. To some, this form of social schizophrenia might seem comic, but a more appropriate response is tears, not laughter.

Sex and Status

In Negro adults the sense of inadequate self-worth shows up in lack of motivation to rise in their jobs or fear of competition with whites; in a sense of impotence in civic affairs demonstrated in lethargy toward voting, or community participation, or responsibility for others; in family instability and the irresponsibility rooted in hopelessness.

But, because, in American life, sex is, like business advancement, a prime criterion of success and hence of personal worth, it is in sexual behavior that the damage to Negro adults shows up in especially poignant and tragic clarity. The inconsistency between the white society's view of the Negro as inferior and its sexual exploitation of Negroes has seemed to its victims a degrading hypocrisy. Negroes observe that ever since slavery white men have regarded Negroes as inferior and have condemned interracial marriage while considering illicit sexual relationships with Negro women appropriate to their own higher status. The white man in America has, historically, arranged to have both white and Negro women available to him; he has claimed sexual priority with both and, in the process, he has sought to emasculate Negro men. Negro males could not hold their women, nor could they defend them. The white male tried to justify this restriction of meaningful competition with the paradoxical claim that Negro males were animal-like and brutish in their appetites and hence to be feared and shunned by white women. The ironic fact has been that, given the inferiority of their racial status, Negro males have had to struggle simply to believe themselves men. It has long been an "inside" bit of bitter humor among Negroes to say that Negro men should bribe their wives to silence.

Certain Negro women of status who have married white men report that their choice was related to their discovery that the Negro men they knew were inferior in status, interests, and sophistication and hence unsuitable as partners. Many problems of race and sex seem to follow this principle of the self-fulfilling prophecy. The Negro woman of status may see the Negro male as undesirable as a sexual partner precisely because of his low status in the eyes of whites. Unlike a white female who may reassure herself that the lower the status of the male, the more satisfying he is as a sexual partner, the upper-class Negro female tends to tie sexual desirability to status and exclude many Negro males as undesirable just because their status is inferior. It is a real question whether this "discovery" is based on fact or whether these women are not accepting the white society's assumption of the low status of Negro men and therefore expecting them to be weak. On the other hand, frustrated, thrill-seeking white males or females who have been told all their lives that Negroes are primitive and uninhibited may seek and find sexual fulfillment among the same Negroes who are cool, distant, or hostile in their relationship to other Negroes. In sexual matters it appears that those who expect weakness or gratification often find what they expect.

As Negro male self-esteem rises in the wake of the civil rights movement, one interesting incidental fact is that any Negro woman who is known to be the mistress of a white public official—and par-

THE PSYCHOLOGY OF THE GHETTO 69

ticularly any mistress of a segregationist—has been put under a growing pressure to break that relationship. In the past, Negroes tended to suppress their bitterness about such illicit relationships, accepting the white male's evaluation of himself and of them, and in a sense forgiving the Negro woman for submitting to the temptation of protection and economic gain. In the last decade, however, Negro mistresses of white officials are more openly rejected and are regarded as one of the "enemy."

White men were accustomed to possessing Negro women without marriage, but today the fact that a number of white men are married to Negro women of status, particularly those who are well known in the theatrical world, indicates that Negro women are placing higher value upon their own dignity than many other Negro women were permitted to in the past—and so are the white men who marry them. But, though a Negro woman may gain status by marrying into the white community, Negro men, even in the North, remain vulnerable if they seek to cross racial lines and to break this most fearsome of social taboos. When they have done so they have paid a tremendous price—lynching, murder, or a prison sentence in the South, social condemnation in the North—but, above all, the price of their own self-doubt and anxiety. The full complexity of social disapproval and personal doubt is difficult to resist psychologically even when the law allows and protects such nonconformist behavior.

The emerging, more affirmative sexual pride among Negro males may have as one of its consequences an increasing trend toward more open competition between white and Negro males for both white and Negro females. One of the further consequences would probably be an intensification of hostility of white males toward interracial couples and toward the white female participants, reflecting the desire on the part of the white male to preserve his own competitive advantage. One would expect him then to employ his economic and political power—without suspecting the fundamental basis of his antagonism —to maintain the inferior status of the Negro male for as long as possible. An important level of racial progress will have been reached when Negro and white men and women may marry anyone they choose, without punishment, ostracism, ridicule, or guilt.

The Negro Matriarchy and the Distorted Masculine Image

Sexual hierarchy has played a crucial role in the structure and pathology of the Negro family. Because of the system of slavery in which the Negro male was systematically used as a stud and the Negro female used primarily for purposes of breeding or for the gratification of the white male, the only source of family continuity was through the female, the dependence of the child on his mother. This pattern, together with the continued post-slavery relegation of the Negro male to menial and subservient status, has made the female the dominant person in the Negro family. Psychologically, the Negro male could not support his normal desire for dominance. For the most part he was not allowed to be a consistent wage earner; he could not present himself to his wife and children as a person who had the opportunity or the ability to compete successfully in politics, business, and industry. His doubts concerning his personal adequacy were therefore reinforced. He was compelled to base his self-esteem instead on a kind of behavior that tended to support a stereotyped picture of the Negro male—sexual impulsiveness, irresponsibility, verbal bombast, posturing, and compensatory achievement in entertainment and athletics, particularly in sports like boxing in which athletic prowess could be exploited for the gain of others. The Negro male was, therefore, driven to seek status in ways which seemed either antisocial, escapist, socially irresponsible. The pressure to find relief from his intolerable psychological position seems directly related to the continued high incidence of desertions and broken homes in Negro ghettos.

The Negro woman has, in turn, been required to hold the family together; to set the goals, to stimulate, encourage, and to protect both boys and girls. Her compensatory strength tended to perpetuate the weaker role of the Negro male. Negro boys had the additional problem of finding no strong male father figure upon which to model their own behavior, perhaps one of the reasons for the prevalent idea among marginal Negroes that it is not masculine to sustain a stable father or husband relationship with a woman. Many young men establish temporary liaisons with a number of different women with no responsibility toward any. Among Negro teen-agers the cult of going steady has never had the vogue it seems to have among white teen-agers; security for Negroes is found not in a relationship modeled after a stable family—for they have seen little of this in their own lives—but upon the relationship they observed in their own home: unstable and temporary liaisons. The marginal young Negro male tends to identify his masculinity with the number of girls he can attract. The high incidence of illegitimacy among Negro young people reflects this pervasive fact. In this compensatory distortion of the male image, masculinity is, therefore, equated with alleged sexual prowess.

The middle-class white and Negro male often separates women into two categories, good women with whom he will go steady and marry, and others with whom he has and will continue to have sexual relations alone. The lower-class Negro is, in a way, more sophisticated than either in his refusal to make undemocratic distinctions between "good girls" and "others." The consistently higher illegitimacy rate among Negroes is not a reflection of less virtue or greater promiscuity, but rather of the fact that the middle-class teenagers are taught the use of contraceptives and learn how to protect themselves from the hazards of premarital and illicit sexual contacts. The middle-class girl is able to resort to abortions, or she gives birth secretly, surrendering the child for adoption. In the case of marginal young people, or the upwardly mobile Negro, what contraceptive ideas he has are unreliable; and rarely does the girl participate in protection, in part because it is taken as a sign of masculinity for the male to supervise such matters. Illegitimacy among these groups, therefore, is a consequence, in large part, of poverty and ignorance.

Among Negro middle-class families the attitude toward sex is vastly different from that among marginal and lower-class Negro groups. The middle-class Negro fears he will be identified with the Negro masses from whom he has escaped or tried to escape, and sex is a focal point of anxiety. The middle-class girl is often so rigidly protected that normal sexual behavior is inhibited, or she learns to be sophisticated about the use of contraceptives. For her, as for white middle-class girls, sex is tied to status and aspirations. She wants to make a good marriage—marriage to a white man might even be available—and the motivation to avoid illegitimate pregnancy is great.

The marginal young people in the ghetto, through their tentative and sporadic relationships, are seeking love, affection, and acceptance perhaps more desperately than young people elsewhere. Person-to-person relationships are, for many, a compensation for society's rejection. They are, in a sense, forced to be quite elemental in their demands, and sex becomes more important for them than even they realize. They act in a cavalier fashion about their affairs, trying to seem casual and cool, but it is clear nonetheless that they are dominated by the complexity of their needs.

The girl, like the boy, has no illusions. Unlike the middle-class girl who believes—or demands—that each relationship should be forever, and who tries to hold on to the boy, the marginal Negro lower-class girl is realistic about the facts of the situation. Nor does she expect to hold the boy. Sex is important to her, but it is not, as in middle-class society, a symbol of status, to be used to rise into a better family or a higher income bracket. The marginal Negro female uses her sex, instead, to gain personal affirmation. She is desired, and that is almost enough. The relationship, whatever its social and psychological limitations, is pure in the same sense as innocence—that is, it is not contaminated by other goals. For her and for the boy, sex is time-contained, with its own intrinsic worth and value, not animal in its expression, but related to the urgent human need for acceptance; it is sophisticated, not primitive.

This innocent sophistication includes the total acceptance of the child if a child comes. In the ghetto, the meaning of the illegitimate child is not ultimate disgrace. There is not the demand for abortion or for surrender of the child that one finds in more privileged communities. In the middle class, the disgrace of illegitimacy is tied to personal and family aspirations. In lower-class families, on the other hand, the girl loses only some of her already limited options by having an illegitimate child; she is not going to make a "better marriage" or improve her economic and social status either way. On the contrary, a child is a symbol of the fact that she is a woman, and she may gain from having something of her own. Nor is the boy who fathers an illegitimate child going to lose, for where is he going? The path to any higher status seems closed to him in any case.

Illegitimacy in the ghetto cannot be understood or dealt with in terms of punitive hostility, as in the suggestion that unwed mothers be denied welfare if illegitimacy is repeated. Such approaches obscure, with empty and at times hypocritical moralizing, the desperate yearning of the young for acceptance and identity, the need to be meaningful to some one else even for a moment without implication of a pledge of undying fealty and foreverness. If, when the girl becomes pregnant, the boy deserts or refuses to marry her, it is often because neither can sustain an intimate relationship; both seem incapable of the tenderness that continues beyond immediate gratification. Both may have a realistic, if unconscious, acceptance of the fact that nothing else is possible; to expect—to ask—for more would be to open oneself to the inevitable rejections, hurts, and frustrations. The persistent experience of rejection spills over into the anticipation and acceptance of rejection in a love relationship. This lack of illusion stems from the fact that there can be no illusion in any other area of life. To expose oneself further to the chances of failure in a sustained and faithful relationship is too large to risk. The intrinsic value of the relationship is the only value because there can be no other.

Among most lower-class Negroes, competition in sex is predominantly heterosexual and free. In the Negro middle class sexual freedom and expression are often identified with lower-class status, and many men and women are therefore governed chiefly by their inhibitions and cannot act freely in matters of sex. The men may be impotent, the women frigid, and both afflicted with guilt. Some compensate for the restraints on sexual adequacy and fulfillment through fantasies and boasting about a false prowess. Other middle-class Negro men retreat into noncommittal peripheral relationships with women, avoiding all alternatives—homosexuality, heterosexuality, or verbal bombasts—as risks requiring more ego strength than their resources permit. Instead, a blank and apathetic sexlessness dominates their lives. They withdraw from all commitment to another person seeking refuge from the dangers of personal vulnerability.

Considering the depth and the complexity of the need, aggressive sexual behavior may, for many of the racially damaged, make the difference between personal stability and instability. Until the lower-class Negro is free to compete for and to win the socially acceptable rewards of middle-class society, the ghetto's pattern of venereal disease, illegitimacy, and family instability will remain unbroken. But when that time comes, no one can expect destructive sexual activity to cease abruptly. What is more likely is a shift to another, some would say "higher," level of behavior; then the Negro's sexual "misbehavior" will be indistinguishable in all respects from that of the respectables—with full participation in divorce, abortions, adultery, and the various forms of jaded and fashionable middle- and upper-class sexual explorations. There might even be the possibility of sexual fulfillment and health.

White Rationalizations

It is now rare even for the most ardent apologist for the *status quo* seriously to assert that the American pattern of segregation has beneficial consequences. Some do, however, continue to argue that the Negro's inferiority and inherent character defects demand that he be segregated. Others suggest that the chances of his developing those traits and characteristics which would make him more acceptable to the white community would be greater if he would function within his own community until he demonstrates that he is worthy of associating with others. Among the questions which remain unanswered by this type of argument are: Under what circumstances is the Negro ever adjudged worthy or deserving of association with others, and how can he be expected to develop these traits of "worthiness" under conditions which tend to perpetuate characteristics of unworthiness as described by the proponents of this position themselves? In the belief no doubt that this was a statement of compassion, one white opponent of New York's school integration plan said: "If I were God, what would I do to improve the lot of the Negro? If I were God, I'd make everybody white."* To sensitive Negroes, this betrays the ultimate condescension—the belief that to *be* Negro means irrevocable rejection.

Even this point of view is not logically consistent, since the same individuals who reject Negroes as offensive have no difficulty, as we have noted above, in accepting Negroes in close and at times intimate

* *New York Times Magazine,* September 20, 1964, p. 122.

association and relationship, for example, as servants or menials or mistresses, as long as the inferior position of the Negro and the dominant position of the white is clearly perceived and accepted by both.

The answers to these questions cannot be found in any single devil —but must be sought in the compliant or accessory role of many in society. However, more privileged individuals understandably may need to shield themselves from the inevitable conflict and pain which would result from their acceptance of the fact that they *are* accessories to profound injustice. The tendency to discuss disturbing social issues such as racial discrimination, segregation, and economic exploitation in detached, legal, political, socio-economic, or psychological terms as if these persistent problems did not involve the suffering of actual human beings is so contrary to empirical evidence that it must be interpreted as a protective device. After World War II, the bulk of the German people *could not know* what was going on in the death camps. The people of Mississippi *had to believe* in 1964 that the disappearance and death of the three civil rights workers in that state was a diversionary strategy plotted by civil rights groups. Negroes generally expected that a grand jury in New York City *would have found* that it was justifiable homicide performed in the line of duty for a white policeman to kill a fifteen-year-old Negro boy who was "attacking him with a penknife." Insensitivity is a protective device. Among its more primitive examples are: The prevalent beliefs that the predicament of the masses of Negroes reflects their inherent racial inferiority; that the poor are to blame for the squalor and despair of the slums; that the victims of social injustice are somehow subhuman persons who cause and perpetuate their own difficulties; that the more responsible and superior people of the society not only have no obligation for the "irresponsibles" but must be vigilant to see that all of the power of government is used to protect them and their children from them; and that any contrary or compassionate interpretation of the plight of the poor or the rejected is merely the sentimental and naive expression of impractical do-gooders or "bleeding hearts."

More subtle and obscure forms of protection against facing the consequences of social injustice are to be found among those social scientists who cultivate that degree of academic detachment which blocks meaningful or insightful study of human affairs. The preoccupation with trivia—as if this were the ultimate scientific virtue and goal—leads to the irrelevance of much social science research. It is interesting to speculate on the significance of the fact that during the ten years after the U.S. Supreme Court school desegregation decision, an increasing number of social scientists have raised questions concerning the "scientific validity" of the psychological and sociological data cited by the Court as evidence of the damage which segregation inflicts upon personality. Not one of these critics had questioned these data and their interpretations prior to the Court's decision, although the studies on which they were based had been published and available for critical reactions for many years prior to their use in the historic decision.

Certain students of jurisprudence have also criticized the Court's decision on the grounds that the Brown decision, which ruled that state laws requiring or permitting racial segregation in public schools violated the equal protection clause of the Fourteenth Amendment, was based upon flimsy sociological and psychological data rather than upon more stable and heretofore determining legal grounds. This, too, is a purist approach rooted in the belief that detachment or enforced distance from the human consequences of persistent injustice is objectively desirable. It may rather be of service primarily as a subconscious protection against personal pain and direct involvement in moral controversies.

The language and the emphasis of the Court's decision made any such evasion of the human costs of racial segregation quite difficult. The Court insisted upon a simple and direct statement of the reality:*

To separate them from others of similar age and qualifications solely because of their race generates a feeling of inferiority as to their status in the community that may affect their hearts and minds in a way unlikely ever to be undone. The effect of this separation on their educational opportunities was well stated by a finding in the Kansas case by a court which nevertheless felt compelled to rule against the Negro plaintiffs:

* *Brown v. Board of Education,* 347 U.S. 483 (1954).

Segregation of white and colored children in public schools has a detrimental effect upon the colored children. The impact is greater when it has the sanction of the law: for the policy of separating the races is usually interpreted as denoting the inferiority of the Negro group. A sense of inferiority affects the motivation of a child to learn. Segregation with the sanction of the law, therefore, has a tendency to retard the educational and mental development of Negro children and to deprive them of some of the benefits they would receive in a racially integrated school system.

The obscuring function of legal technicalities and the equivocations of social science jargon were rejected and in their place was offered an understandable statement of the inevitable anguish of rejected and stigmatized human beings.

The pervasive need to turn one's back on any clear evidence of man's inhumanity to man exemplified in the cool objective approach is probably most clearly seen, though in a more subtle form, in the detached "professionalism" of many social workers and in the selective isolation of many psychiatrists and clinical psychologists. Some members of these "helping fields," too, have often defended as objectivity what, to the client, feels more like insensitivity. Furthermore, in their preoccupation with the problem of the individual and their insistence upon reducing him to a manageable system of assumptions, the disturbing and dehumanizing social realities behind his personal agony may be avoided. With the professional perspective which constricts social vision to the impulses, strengths, and weaknesses of the individual "client" as if these can be isolated from the injustices and pathologies of his life, these professionals need not confront the difficult problems of the nature and origin of the social injustices nor run the risks of conflict with the many vested interests which tend to perpetuate the problems of the poor and the rejected. This posture is built into the nature of their training and reinforced by their complex role as agents of the more privileged classes and the admitted and irrevocable fact of their identification with the middle classes. The professionals themselves would point out, also, that the routinizing pressure of bureaucratic procedures, and a heavy case load of human suffering dull the edge of concern and that the most sensitive among them feel, within the structure, uncertain and helpless as to how to address themselves to the problem of social change. It is not surprising, altogether, that compassion is usually sooner or later subordinated to accommodation; yet it is hard for many to understand why they are irrelevant to the root problems of the poor.

Some theorists and practitioners maintain that it is not within their power or training to attempt to help workingclass and low-status people because the problems of these people are psychosocial and, since they cannot be "reached," are not amenable to the psychotherapeutic and casework techniques thought to be helpful in working with middle-class individuals. Some professionals tend to limit their role to that of models or interpreters of the middle-class norms of speech, behavior, dress, values, and ways of handling problems and feelings. In view of their status and psychological distance, the social worker's concern to "relate to" the "client" seems pathetic in its failure of elemental empathy. The stated or unstated goal of this type of "therapeutic" relationship must then become that of helping the client "adjust" to his life realities, i.e., to keep him from "acting out" his rebellion in antisocial or self-destructive ways and thereby to function more effectively *within* the continuing pathology of his society. These goals are consistent with the *status quo* convenience of the middle class. They are consistent with the benign artificiality of response from these professionals which repels the members of the working class, for whom the immediate and pressing realities of their daily lives alone seem relevant. That middle-class individuals are not equally repelled may be an indication of the extent to which pretenses and protective detachment have become norms of middle-class adjustment—particularly in a society of accepted injustice. This is not to say that individual therapy is not needed and cannot be effective. It is to say that such procedures are not effective where social pathology is at the root of the individual's maladjustment. It is a real question whether adjustment or indifference to the reality of injustice is not the real neurosis, and rebellion the evidence of health.

Moral Objectivity

Objectivity, without question essential to the scientific perspective when it warns of the dangers of bias and prejudgment in interfering with the search for truth and in contaminating the understanding of truth, too often becomes a kind of a fetish which serves to block the view of truth itself, particularly when painful and difficult moral insights are involved. The question of the nature of objectivity in law, in science, in human relationships, is complex and cannot be resolved by attempts to make it synonymous with the exclusion of feeling and value. Objectivity that implies detachment or escape from psychological reality decreases understanding and can be used merely to avoid the problem. In the social sciences, the cult of objectivity seems often to be associated with "not taking sides." When carried to its extreme, this type of objectivity could be equated with ignorance. When the social psychology department of an outstanding Eastern university received a substantial grant to endow a chair in the field of race relations, the responsible officials of that department decided that, in order to obtain the most objective person, they should consider no one who had worked extensively in the field of race relations. Indeed, they decided to appoint someone who had had no experience in this field at all, and chose a man whose major contribution to psychology was rather in the field of the experimental psychology of visual discrimination. Perhaps the guiding assumption was that the problem of American race relations was to be understood in the most fundamental terms of the capacity of the rods and cones of the human retina to differentiate color! Imagine, however, if, a chair in nuclear science were to be filled in any university, how transparently absurd it would seem to choose a man with no experience in the field, on the grounds that he thereby would be more objective! The fact that this did not seem absurd to scholars in the case of race relations is a revealing commentary. It may be that where essential human psychological and moral issues are at stake, noninvolvement and noncommitment and the exclusion of feeling are neither sophisticated nor objective, but naive and violative of the scientific spirit at its best. Where human feelings are part of the evidence, they cannot be ignored. Where anger is the appropriate response, to exclude the recognition and acceptance of anger, and even to avoid the feeling itself as if it were an inevitable contamination, is to set boundaries upon truth itself. If a scholar who studied Nazi concentration camps did not feel revolted by the evidence no one would say he was unobjective, but rather fear for his sanity and moral sensitivity. Feeling may twist judgment, but the lack of feeling may twist it even more. And to insist on quantitative measurement and analysis of certain phenomena, of, for example, love or friendship, is to distort the nature of the phenomenon itself. It is not to enlarge truth, but to constrict it.

Even to pose an hypothesis is to move away from literal objectivity, *if* objectivity is to be defined as total openmindedness. Objectivity should play a role not in the refusal to make hypotheses, but in the rigorous assessment of the evidence accumulated for that hypothesis, so as to guard, as far as possible, against any distortion of these facts. When one cares deeply what the answer to a question is, one must exercise even greater care to examine the evidence than if the answer is of no personal consequence. To refuse science the right to deal with such phenomena is to set intolerable limits, for moral decisions, like all others, should be based on fact. Responsible objectivity includes the totality of reality, not a part alone.

5

THE PATHOLOGY OF THE GHETTO

The dark ghetto is institutionalized pathology; it is chronic, self-perpetuating pathology; and it is the futile attempt by those with power to confine that pathology so as to prevent the spread of its contagion to the "larger community."

It would follow that one would find in the ghetto such symptoms of social disorganization and disease as high rates of juvenile delinquency, venereal disease among young people, narcotic addiction, illegitimacy, homicide, and suicide. All of these forms of social pathology do thrive in the ghettos, except suicide; only in suicide statistics does Harlem fall below the norms of New York City as a whole.

Not only is the pathology of the ghetto self-perpetuating, but one kind of pathology breeds another. The child born in the ghetto is more likely to come into a world of broken homes and illegitimacy; and this family and social instability is conducive to delinquency, drug addiction, and criminal violence. Neither instability nor crime can be controlled by police vigilance or by reliance on the alleged deterring forces of legal punishment, for the individual crimes are to be understood more as symptoms of the contagious sickness of the community itself than as the result of inherent criminal or deliberate viciousness.

Emotional Illness

The emotional ill health of the dark ghetto is a continuum ranging from the anxious but "normal" individual to the criminally psychotic. The harmful effects of American racism on personality development and psychological balance are unmistakable. Still, it is one thing to show that prejudice damages individuals and another to show that the emotional illness of a particular individual has been caused by prejudice and its social consequences. The link between the phenomenon of the dark ghetto and individual destructiveness and withdrawal seems clear in many cases; in others the relationship is less sharply drawn.

The evidence concerning the nature and extent of individual psychoses and neuroses in the ghetto is far less available and not easy to interpret. There are comparatively few Negro or white psychiatrists in the ghettos; and psychotherapy has not had the vogue among Negroes that it has in white middle- and upper-class urban communities in large part because the middle class is the central group in the white community and it is not in the Negro community. Individual psychotherapy tends either to be restricted to those sufficiently and destructively ill enough to require the intervention of society—and here it is largely custodial in nature—or to those less seriously damaged who have the funds and the inclination to seek help for themselves. It would be, in fact, surprising to find many Negro patients receiving extensive voluntary personal treatment, though the number doubtless will rise as Negroes move into more high-status jobs, thereby gaining both the money to pay the high cost of prolonged therapy and the psychological orientation to accept it.

One would expect, however, given the pathology of the dark ghetto, to find a high rate of admission of Negro patients to the state and city psychiatric wards. Harlem has the highest rate of admission to state mental hospitals of any area in New York City. The crude rate per 10,000 population is 38.5 for Harlem compared to a mean rate for the rest of the city of 13 per 10,000. According to the Research and Planning Division of the New York City

Community Mental Health Board, in 1961, "Three percent of the total population of New York City lived in Central Harlem, which ranked first in rates of admissions to state hospitals, contributing 6.5 percent of all New York City admission."* But admission to state hospitals is only one index of mental illness, and if statistics for patients in private hospitals and under home or office therapy were known, the ghetto's rate of treated illness would significantly decline in comparison with that of the white community. There are, of course, no statistics for untreated or undiagnosed illness.

In the absence of adequate and urgently needed research into the degree of actual prevalence of emotional illness in Negro urban communities, one can do little more than speculate. Is the pathology of the dark ghetto so pervasive that mental disturbance does not stand out as clearly as it does elsewhere? Is the city government less observant of deviant behavior in the ghetto because it is subconsciously less concerned to protect the community from threat? Is less illness reported—or even recognized *as* illness—by ghetto families and friends? Are persons who are emotionally disturbed already institutionalized for other pathologies—drug addiction, delinquency, homicide—and hence not diagnosed or treated as ill? Does the pattern of violence in the ghetto provide an outlet for emotional release that would in another culture be turned inward into phobias and depression? Do ghetto residents feel too alienated from the clinics and social agencies to seek help? Do the agencies tend to prefer as clients those who are "reachable" and hence indirectly weed out prospective Negro patients? The report on urban mental illness based on a neighborhood study conducted in mid-Manhattan and reported publicly in 1962 concluded that one in three in the area was, in some degree, emotionally disturbed.† What would such a study in a Negro ghetto show? And, in the absence of such a

* From unpublished information, New York State Department of Mental Hygiene, year ended March 31, 1961, as cited by Research and Planning Division, New York City Community Health Board, pp. 21–22, Unpublished Report 764.

† Leo Srole, Thomas S. Langner, Stanley P. Michael, Marvin K. Opler, Thomas A. C. Rennie, *Mental Health in the Metropolis, The Midtown Manhattan Study*, Vol. 1, New York, McGraw-Hill, 1962.

study, are the figures on admission to mental hospitals other than suggestive? Or are the problems to be dealt with in the nation's dark ghettos so demanding of individual energies that there is not even the strength for emotional illness? Is mental illness—other than the starkly and destructively psychotic—itself a luxury of the middle and upper classes?

Whatever the facts about the incidence and the causes of emotional illness in the Negro ghetto, it is clear that facilities for treatment are inadequate. In Harlem, for example, there are four services for emotionally disturbed children, two of them public, and two private. According to data supplied by three of these agencies, they serve 560 young people under twenty-four.* But if one in ten of the general population is emotionally disturbed, as the National Association for Mental Health estimates, more than twelve times this number of young people alone in Harlem need help, not counting the adults.

Homicide and Suicide

The homicide rate for ghetto areas, like the delinquency rate, is startling. In Harlem it is nearly six times the rate for New York City.† In one area of about fourteen square blocks in New York the rate is fifteen times that of the city as a whole. In that neighborhood, between Fifth and Lenox avenues from 126 to 140 Streets, the ghetto's physical and human blight is at its worst. But in that neighborhood, with its 17,089 residents, are some of Harlem's best and newest middle-class housing projects designed to combat the decline of the area. In 1961, thirteen people were killed in that neighborhood.

The rate of suicide for the ghetto is, on the other hand, lower than the city average. For Harlem the rate is 8.2 per 100,000 population compared to the city rate of 9.7. Throughout the country Ne-

---

* Data are available only for the two private agencies within the community and one additional agency located outside the community but drawing 90 percent of its caseload from the Harlem area.

† In the 1961 St. Louis survey of a ghetto area two-thirds Negro, the homicide rate was more than double the city's, but there is no breakdown for the Negro population alone.

groes, and communities with a high proportion of Negroes, ordinarily have lower suicide rates. The meaning of this consistent finding is still subject to dispute. One current view holds that low suicide rates mirror high social homogeneity. Another view holds that high suicide rates accompany the "middle-class rat race." From this viewpoint, Harlem in 1961 needed only four more suicides in order to be considered a full participant in the mainstream of American life. In three areas of Harlem, however, the suicide rate is almost twice as high as for the city as a whole. The highest suicide rate in Harlem (21 per 100,000 for 1961, the most recent year for which figures are available) is on the western periphery of Harlem bordering the socially and economically more viable Columbia University–Morningside Heights area, where the homicide rate is, for the ghetto, lower than average. The second highest (18 per 100,000) also has a below-normal homicide rate; it contains the last vestige of stable middle-class, even elite, families left in Harlem. Here, at 138 and 139 Streets, are found the old brownstone homes designed by Stanford White for the white upper class at the turn of the century. In the 1920s and 1930s, the neighborhood became known as Strivers' Row, symbolizing the status-seeking of the new Negro residents. Some of Harlem's best-known physicians and dentists have their offices on these streets, and some continue to live there. Many of these old families have stayed, in a desperate attempt to stem the creeping ghetto blight, an attempt not always successful in an area where slowly the old brownstones are becoming converted into rooming houses.

Like suicide rates elsewhere, therefore, the incidence in Harlem seems to be related to higher status and its concomitant anxieties; and, where suicide does occur in the Harlem ghetto, it appears to occur with the intensity and frequency of homicide.

It is interesting to speculate upon the comparative difference between the rates of homicide and suicide for Harlem. Suicide may be conceived of as aggresssion turned inward. In this, Harlem, except for a few areas, is low. Homicide, on the other hand, is the ultimate aggression turned outward. In this, Harlem ranks high. Furthermore, the victims in homicide cases in the ghetto and elsewhere are for the most part friends and relatives, and not the feared and hated "Whitey." A tantalizing deduction about the social pathology of the community, therefore, is that it is primarily manifested in aggression directed toward intimates and fellow victims of the ghetto. This may mean that the victim of oppression is more prone to attack his fellow victim than to risk aggression against the feared oppressor.

Other factors which may be related to the high intra-ghetto homicide rate are the sheer social abrasiveness of population density, the general purposelessness and irrelevance of constricted lives, and the fact that aggressions of Negroes against whites are more likely to be punished severely than similar aggressions against other Negroes. In a disturbing sense, there remains the possibility that homicide in the ghetto is consistently high because it is not controlled, if not encouraged, as an aspect of the total network of the human exploitation of the ghetto. The unstated and sometimes stated acceptance of crime and violence as normal for a ghetto community is associated with a lowering of police vigilance and efficiency when the victims are also lower-status people. This is another example of the denial of a governmental service—the right of adequate protection—which is endured by the powerless ghetto.

As for suicide, one would expect its incidence to increase rather than decline as the members of the ghetto are admitted into the mainstream of American society. There is no human society where total happiness can be reliably found, as the national suicide rate affirms, but the American Negro is determined to share the total American culture with all its tension and trouble.

Delinquency

The problems of delinquency, drug addiction, and crime are severe in the dark ghettos everywhere. In St. Louis, a 1961 study of a ghetto area, 60 percent Negro, showed a delinquency rate three times that of the rest of the city. Another, conducted in the Greater Boston area in 1963 in a ghetto region one-quarter Negro, where almost all of Boston's Negroes live, showed four times the delinquency rate for Boston as a whole. In a Minneapolis ghetto area, in

1960, the delinquency rate was more than double that in the rest of the city. So was it in Cleveland's Hough Area, predominantly Negro, as reported in 1961. In Syracuse, in 1962, in a ghetto community 80 percent Negro, the delinquency rate was also double. In 1962, the delinquency rate in Harlem was 109.3 per 1,000 population between the ages of seven and twenty, while in New York City as a whole for that same year the rate was 46.5. Consistently, for the previous ten years, the rate in Harlem was more than twice as high as that of the rest of the city.

One of the paradoxes in attempting to understand the problem of juvenile delinquency in a ghetto is not so much the obvious facts of the disproportionately high rate when compared with the rest of a city, but that even in a community of such obvious pathology, so many—more than 90 percent of the youth population in most ghettos—do *not* come in direct conflict with the law. This is important in any real understanding of the power of human resiliency. One must question, however, whether any society can afford the wastage of human resources implied in the fact that 10 percent of its young people are adjudged as delinquents. No one knows, in addition, from delinquency statistics alone—with which society is often preoccupied—how many other ghetto youths lead lives caught up in a tangle of antisocial activity dominated by apathy and despair. Delinquency statistics may obscure rather than clarify, not only because of their unreliability in terms of sources and definitions and the extent to which their meaning is contaminated by such tangential problems as neglect and abandonment of children, but also because they only hint at the real problem.

The high rate of venereal disease in the ghetto among Harlem youth, for example—six times as high as the city rate, 110.3 for 10,000 Harlem youth under 21 compared to 17.2 for the city as a whole*—is directly related to the patterns of family instability in the lower-class Negro community, the systematic vocational and

* In Minneapolis, a study of an area in which Negroes were concentrated showed a rate of venereal disease more than double that for the city as a whole. ("Youth Development Demonstration Project," submitted to the President's Committee on Juvenile Delinquency and Youth Crime by the Community Health and Welfare Council of Hennepin County, Inc., Minneapolis, April 1964, p. 312.)

psychological emasculation of the Negro male, and the reflection of these in a lower level of personal hygienic standards. The same can be said of the high incidence of illegitimacy in Harlem reflected to some extent in ADC statistics and of the relatively low rate of abortions. Figures are only available, of course, for legal abortions, but cf such therapeutic abortions in New York City, most are sought by upper- and upper-middle-class white women.*

The possibility that a young person may act out his frustrations in ways inconvenient to more privileged persons outside of the ghetto —through thefts to support the drug habit, through vandalism and muggings in subways and busses, through the stoning of trains— arouses retaliatory concern from the larger threatened society. The Negro delinquent, therefore, calls attention to the quiet pathology of the ghetto which he only indirectly reflects. In a very curious way the delinquent's behavior is healthy; for, at the least, it asserts that he still has sufficient strength to rebel and has not yet given in to defeat. One may speculate that as social reforms shore up the ego structure of ghetto residents, there could be a temporary increase in the amount of overt rebellion which the larger society would classify as delinquent. This would be a stage intermediate between complete oppression and social justice. Evidence for this is to be found in the finding that delinquency is low among Puerto Ricans in Puerto Rico and comparatively high among Puerto Ricans who migrate to New York City. It would appear to be a paradox that those who live in relatively greater squalor in Puerto Rico are not delinquent while those who are living in better conditions in New York City are more likely to be. In a sense, delinquency statistics show that a group is in ferment, in the process of rejecting an earlier inferior status and moving to a higher level. Delinquency has the further social "advantage" of bringing greater police vigilance to a neglected community, and in stimulating greater public sensitivity to the problems of a population seeking to break its ghetto boundaries.

---

* Nine out of every ten legal abortions in New York are sought by white women, most of them "private service" patients in the city's more expensive hospitals. See "Therapeutic Abortions in New York City: A 20 Year Review," a study by Dr. Edwin M. Gold, Dr. Carl L. Erhardt, Dr. Harold Jacobziner, and Frieda G. Nelson, unpublished manuscript, 1964.

There was a time when it appeared that Harlem was dominated by almost countless adolescent gangs. Every youngster seemed required to belong to one in order to be able even to attend school without being molested. In 1948, the time when gangs were most dominant, as the Haryou report relates, there were about forty different fighting gangs in Harlem, and the ghetto was divided into "turfs," each with its own gang lord and his lieutenants. Primarily because of more effective police action— the ability to concentrate a sufficient number of radio police cars at any point of impending gang activity—many of these fighting gangs no longer exist. The last gang "war," according to police records, was in early 1963, but, according to 1961 figures, Harlem still has more gangs and more youth gang members than any other part of Manhattan. Fourteen of the groups now operating are still classified as fighting gangs, but their activities are "antisocial" in many ways—sexual promiscuity, glue sniffing, alcohol, marijuana, and sometimes heroin. Most are teen-agers, but children ten years or even younger are admitted.

But curiously the present relationship between gangs and delinquency is unclear. There is evidence to suggest that the known presence or absence of a gang does not affect the rate of delinquency in a neighborhood. The region between 118 and 126 Streets, from Fifth to Eighth Avenues, which has the second highest rate of delinquency in Harlem, has no known juvenile gangs. Social workers contend that the delinquency there is primarily general vandalism and the use of narcotics. In contrast to the 1950s and earlier when organized gangs operated in hostile campaigns, the delinquency of the 1960s seems to consist primarily of a general "nothingness," without style or meaning.

A boy of 19 had a conversation with a Haryou worker that revealed the prevalent mood:

How do you feel about the conditions here?
I don't know.
What do you mean, you don't know? You're out here every day.
As long as I can survive, I don't care about nobody else, man.

Is it rough out here in the streets, trying to survive?
Yes, if you don't put your mind to it, you know, to do something to survive by, it's rough.

Drug Addiction

As gangs declined, the more menacing and insidious problem of drug addiction increased—at least in the Harlem ghetto. The best estimates are that something between 40 and 60 percent of the 60,000 addicts in the United States—or about 25,000 to 36,000—live in the city, and that a large number of them are Negro. Drug addiction does not, on the basis of the available data, appear to be a significant problem in other urban ghettos.

The rate of narcotic use in Harlem from 1955 through 1961 is consistently almost ten times as high as for the city as a whole. The trend for Harlem has followed that for New York City as a whole, a decline from 1955 to 1957, with a steady increase since 1957, and dramatic leaps for the years 1959 to 1960 and 1960 to 1961. It is not certain, however, whether the sharp rise in reported cases of narcotic use reflects a real increase or fuller reporting of cases. For unknown reasons the rise in reported narcotic cases in Harlem is much less sharp than for several other parts of the city.

The statistics on addiction are unreliable. Probably the most important reason for their unreliability is that the use of narcotics is, under present American governmental policy, considered to be illegal and a criminal act. This policy demands that narcotic users blend with the more furtive, illicit, and criminal elements and style of the ghetto. The fact that those who use marijuana, a nonaddictive stimulant, are also required to see themselves as furtive criminals could in some part account for the presumed tendency of the majority of, if not all, drug addicts to start out by using marijuana. It is a reasonable hypothesis that the movement from the nonaddictive drugs or stimulants to the addictive is made more natural and likely because both are forced to belong to the same marginal, quasicriminal culture.

Harlem is the home of many addicts; but as a main center for the distribution of heroin, it attracts many transients, who, when the "panic is on, cannot buy drugs at home. The social as well as the personal price of the drug industry is immense, for though addicts are victims of the system so, too, are nonaddicts: Many addicts resort to crime in their desperate need for money to feed the expensive habit. Most Harlem residents cannot afford or cannot obtain insurance against prevalent burglary of their apartments, but the addicts do not steal only in Harlem, moving into the white community as well.

Narcotic addiction is chiefly an economic and class problem in any ghetto. Addicts who have the funds do not have to steal to buy drugs. The affluent addict can be reasonably sure of the quality of his heroin; the poor addict has no choice and may find he has bought milk sugar or too strong a dose. The addict of the ghetto shares with others of his community the fact that they are all powerless to protect themselves from a complex and interrelated pattern of multiple exploitation.

For many ghetto young people, narcotics offer a life of glamour and escape, or the illusion of personal importance or even success. Various programs have been periodically announced to stamp out this notorious traffic, but so far Harlem has had no successful program for prevention or treatment. The possibility of an effective solution through the treatment of adolescent addicts seems remote. As the Reverend Norman C. Eddy, director of the Narcotics Committee, East Harlem Protestant Parish, Inc., says: "The young boys and girls who use heroin love it, and they don't want, really, to give it up."*

In group discussions and street corner interviews Haryou documented this mysterious appeal of the drug life. Mr. Eddy reports:

We have over the years in the East Harlem Protestant Parish, where our Narcotics Committee is centered, had a certain amount of experience with addicted adolescents. The tragedy of it is that you start working with adolescents as we did back in 1951 and they grow up and they're still addicted and you find yourself no longer working with adolescents, you're

* "Narcotics—the Dilemma," transcript of a forum sponsored by the Federation of Protestant Welfare Agencies, Inc., February 26, 1963, mimeo.

working with adults and then you have to look again and see the tragic fact that another crop of adolescents is coming up that needs to be helped.*

Since the ineffectiveness of treatment is admitted, it is puzzling why medical certification of addicted persons and the legalization of their use of drugs is not seriously considered. If heroin and morphine were no more glamorous than insulin, the psychological need for them might decline. A possible answer for the failure even to experiment with such a plan is that many are profiting from the drug traffic. Who will speak for the victims? The criminal base of the drug traffic supports a pyramid of other crime—from the crime of a "fence" who accepts stolen goods to that of the policeman who takes a bribe not to see a "pusher" at work.

Dr. Alfred R. Lindesmith of Indiana University has written:

It is impossible to interpret the effects of a drug habit upon a person's social life or his character in terms of organic deterioration or alleged "toxic effect" . . . there are no demonstrable major effects that necessarily follow the use of opiate drugs—addicts escape most of the alleged degenerative results of the drug if they are sufficiently well-to-do, and many addicts suffer serious "character deterioration" only after the narcotic agents catch up with them. In other countries about which we have excellent information . . . addicts do not suffer the evil effects that are forced upon American users. They do not steal, lie, engage in prostitution, or become derelicts to the extent that our addicts do.†

Will Sparks, who quotes Lindesmith's statement in an article, "Narcotics and the Law," goes on to comment:

It seems quite clear that American opiate addicts steal or engage in prostitution not from the effects of the drug but from the effects of the laws, laws which transform a cheap and common chemical into a priceless commodity able to support a vast criminal drug traffic. Having created the economic basis for this traffic with the passage of the Harrison Narcotics Act of 1914, our lawmakers have for forty-seven long years been unable to eradicate it. In the meanwhile, unnecessary human misery, the civic corruption which accompanies opiate prohibition no less than alcohol prohibition, remain the hallmarks of U.S. drug control policies. There is no excuse for this.‡

* *Ibid.*
† *Commonweal,* August 25, 1961, p. 468.
‡ *Ibid.*

Haryou workers interviewed many drug addicts and tape recorded their responses—the plaintive stories that follow, drawn from *Youth in the Ghetto,* need no embellishment.

My first bit—I did five years, and I feel that was unjustified because I feel that if they had given me some kind of break from the jump— probation—then I might have done something for myself. I would have been, you know, still in the street, but under their supervision. But they didn't do that. What they did was just send me upstate, and I stayed up there six or seven months before I saw the streets again. I was eighteen years old when I went up there, and it was the first time I had even been arrested in my life. I think it was wrong. If they had given me some probation, like they are giving the white kids, understand, I might have been able to have the same advantages that he did. Maybe I would have gone out and got a job, and I would have worked from then until now, you know. But I wasn't given that chance. I was black, so I was sent away. And I was told it was for my good. I was sent away for six or seven months for *my* good. I was sent to a place where there was only criminals, and the only thing I could learn up there was how to be a better criminal than I was. You know, they haven't done anything for me. All they did for me was tell me I was a slave. That's the best way I could put it, brother.

—Drug addict, male, age 26

All you have to do is to stop that white man from selling us the drug, like that. Then you won't have any drug addiction. We don't have any connection for getting drugs, we don't produce them or process them, we don't have anything to bring them into Harlem, or any place, with. So the real crime rate in drugs doesn't stem from us. You have to get to the hoard where it really comes from in the beginning. When you stop that, when you find that, you have your answer right there. You can't blame it on us. We couldn't find it, we couldn't touch it, if it wasn't for him.

Besides, most of us don't know anything about drugs, or anything else, until we meet one of these types of people, and they introduce us to it— telling us about a way to make a dollar. That way we are deteriorating our race, by listening to them and by participating. But we don't have jobs, what can we do? We all need a dollar. We have to eat—we have to raise our families.

The Man, he wants these things to exist in Harlem. Everything that exists in Harlem the government wants it to exist. If they didn't want it, they would stop it.

—Man, age about 30

You have to survive . . . if you don't have the proper education that you should have, and you go *downtown* and work, they don't pay you any money worthwhile. You can work all your life and never have anything, and you will always be in debt. So you take to the streets, you understand? You take to the streets and try to make it in the street, you know what you have out here in the street you try to make it. Being out in the street takes your mind off all these problems. You have no time to think about things because you're trying to make some money . . . I've been trying to make it so hard and trying to keep a piece of money. I'm trying not to work like a dog to get it, and being treated any sort of way to get it. How to make another buck enters your mind. As far as bettering the community, this never enters your mind because it seems to me, well, I'm using my opinions—to me the white man has it locked up. The black man is progressing, but slowly. The only solution I see to it, I mean, if you are actually going to be here awhile, you have to stay healthy and not die, for one thing. The other thing is while you're here you want to live the best you can. And since Whitey has all the luxuries, I mean, he has it all locked up, you want to get a piece of it, so you have to make some kind of money so you can get it. You can't get what he's got, definitely, but you can get enough to make you feel comfortable. So you're always scheming how to, you know, how to make some money.

—Drug addict, male, age about 37

I took one cure down to Manhattan General, if you want to call that a cure. I went in there for about three, two and a half weeks. And all the other cures were in jail—in and out of jail.

So, why is it, when you get the cure and come out, that you go back to it?

I wish I could answer that for you. I really wish I could. I don't know. I couldn't give you a good answer to it.

Do you have any skills?

In the trade or working? Yes, I have them. I've been working in the garment center. I've worked on trucks. I've worked as a dishwasher, you know, all those things. But my only skill is pressing.

If you could get a job, what type of a job would you like to get?

Any kind—any kind. If I can get work—any kind to start me working, you know, to get in the bracket of a clean life, a working life. For frankly, I haven't done that type of thing in quite a few years; it's not easy to get back into it. People think it is, but to me it is not. I haven't been able to, and I have put forth, you know, I have put forth an effort to try to get it. I have, but most people don't think so. I know within myself. I've been down to the Department. I've been down to the employment agency, I've been in the penitentiary and out for about three weeks now, and I've been down to the employment agency four days, four times. Each time when I go down there, well, I sit down there all day and they tell me, well maybe tomorrow they'll have something.

I've asked for truck driving, I've asked for dishwashing, and I've asked to work in the hospital—anything. But . . . when they mention anything about a previous job, I haven't worked in so long, you know, and tell them about things I've been in and out—if I mention the penitentiary I'm always the last one. And you know how many there are before—they have clean records. You know they will come before me. And if I mention anything about dope, that's out. You know that.

—Drug addict, male, age 34

And if you're just filling up, being bored, it's a hell of a thing being bored and lonely in the midst of millions of people.

—Drug addict, male, age 30

I was just born black, poor and uneducated. And you only need three strikes all over the world to be out, and I have nothing to live for but this shot of dope.

I have nothing to shoot at. All I have to look forward to is a thrill and it's in a bag, and they run me up on the roof to get that. I don't have any place to turn, but I imagine you have. I'm poor and all I can look forward to is what I can get out of this bag. That's the only thrill in life for me, you know. I've never had anything, no opportunity, you know, to get any money, no nothing. All I can look forward to is what I can get out of this bag, and that's nothing really.

When I started I was fourteen years old, and that's twelve years ago. Drugs were much different then. For a dollar a cap poor people got rich. I started back where a man could shoot dope—hey cook that up for me, Eddie. Can you cook? Okay, hit me, man. I started back when I was fourteen years old in 1951, you understand, and I've been using dope ever since, except for the time I spent in the penitentiary. I figure if Whitey gives me half a chance, you know, when I came through school, I could have done something more than this, you know. I know it. But I didn't have the chance because, like I say, I had those three strikes against me.

I'm not really blaming him, you know, the younger ones, but all Whiteys are associated with their race, and I blame them all because there isn't anything else I can do, you know, but shoot dope.

Well, I don't think anything can be done to correct it. Me, because I'm too far gone on it, you know. But, I mean, for my brothers and sisters, you know, people that are coming up younger than I, you know, they can do something. Give them a better education and better job opportunities.

Because I've been in this so long, this is part of my life. I'm sick now, I'm supposed to be in a hospital. They tried to admit me into the hospital three days ago, but knowing that it will be detrimental for me to stay out here, I stayed anyway because I'd rather have this shot of dope than go into anyone's hospital.

Like I say, it's only natural. It's part of my life after twelve years. I never come out of jail and try to do something else but go to this cooker. So, like I say, this is all that's left to me. Look, I started when I was fourteen. I'm not going to say that I never tried to get a job. I tried to get a job, but what references can I give. When I go to State Employment Agency, and they ask where have you been working for the last—since 1952, and I tell them, well, I've been in jail—that's no reference. They won't give me a job. Or, if I get a job you tell them I've been in jail, they turn me loose anyway, you know.

There's nothing I can do, you know. What the hell else can I do? I can't get a legitimate job, but anything else I do they say is against the law. And as long as I stay in this, I'm going to stay in dope, because everyone that's doing something against the law is in dope.

Your environment, I read somewhere, is just a mirror of yourself, you know. So what can I do?

I mean, I have to get my thrills from life someway. I can't lay back. I think I can enjoy working, and raising a family, like the next man, but this is all they left me. I can't work, so I must steal. And mostly the women who will accept me are thieves, or in the trade. And I mean, they're not thinking about raising a family. I mean, they think about what would be good for them, you know. The relief won't take them, so if I had a woman she would have to go out and turn tricks. I have to go out and steal to support my habit. So what can we do but shoot dope for enjoyment. They have left us nothing else.

Work, work, some kind of work program setup where a man can work and get ahead and support himself. Then he can go to some type of school at night, you know, to learn some type of trade, because in jail you can't learn a trade. You know, they tell you that you can, but you can't. If you go there, it's just a house of brutality, you know, that's all I've ever found. A bunch of people—I don't know how the administration thinks, but I know the guards that are head over you all the fellows are interested in are confining you there, working you, making sure you obey, not the administration's orders, but their orders, you know.

So you can't learn anything in jail, you know. All you can do there is learn to hate more. You can't learn a trade or anything. All you learn there is how to stay out of the police's way as much as possible, even if it means ducking work. You duck work—you stay away from the law, because you know the more that you stay around them, the more they see you, the more they want to whip you. I know that, because I started going to jail when I was a kid.

I don't think I could be rehabilitated, you know, not now, in this society. Maybe if I see something better offered. But I hope that in the future they offer kids, or my sister's kids, or someone's kids, a better opportunity than they offered me, because they didn't offer me anything. I either accepted a porter job for the rest of my life regardless of how much education I had, or went to jail. In fact, I think jails were built for black men. You understand? If you look at the population up there, the black man is more popular in jail than the white man. The black man makes parole less frequently than the white man; the black man gets more time than the white man; and the black man goes to the chair more often than the white man. Whitey gets all the breaks in this world.

—Drug addict, male, age 26

The fact that the kind of creative sensitivity reflected in these testimonies has been made alien to the larger society is one of the major tragedies of the ghetto and the society as a whole.

Prevention and Rehabilitation

The desperate quest of many children and youth of the dark ghettos for a way of life of purpose and worth is indicated by the zest and dedication with which many adopt the styles of the delinquent or marginal subcultures, from the extremely violent "bopping gang" member (the antisocial pattern on the wane in Harlem) to the "cool" drug-using "hipster" or the "hustler" out to "run his game" for a quick and easy dollar.

To redirect these energies into more personally and socially constructive channels is a major task. The special programs proposed by the Haryou research and planning staff were designed primarily for children from family situations of marked instability, neglect, and rejection. Such proposed programs as the Cadet Corps and the Junior and Senior Academies were intended to compensate for the chaotic lives of these children. It was *not* the primary objective of these programs to bring these youngsters into a "helping" relationship with a case worker, group worker, or remedial specialist, but rather to provide a new subculture equipped with the symbols of culture—insignia, slogans, rituals, rules—designed to build an *esprit de corps* and a tradition of effective social participation leading toward constructive rather than self-destructive ego satisfaction. In these programs the impetus to achievement, both personal and collective, would be primarily the demands and pressures of one's peers rather than that of a remedial teacher or social worker. The Haryou's program planning placed its stress upon a restructured *culture,* or a new way of life, rather than upon a therapy.

Such culture building as a stratagem differs from remedial methods of less ambitious scope in that it gives more immediate and more vivid rewards for behavior that ordinarily does not offer intrinsic gratification, e.g., studying one's lessons. Moreover, it provides an acceptable environment also for casework, remedial tutoring, clinical group work, and other forms of help. These helping methods are now often spurned by the majority of the ghetto youth who need them when they are offered in isolation or on terms which emphasize for the individual the fact of his dependency and inadequacy.

An attractive and imaginative subculture enables a teen-ager to begin to think about a career and advancement. This is certainly true of delinquent cultures, as the Haryou document pointed out. In the bopping gangs some years ago, a member of the Tiny Tots division could dream of becoming the War Counselor of the Seniors and therefore could accept the tests and trials that would lead him there. So, too, it is possible that in a constructive culture, a boy might willingly undergo the rigors of coffee shop management training, with its arduous business arithmetic, secure in the knowledge that at the end of his course a "prestige" job would be available.

The human casualties of discrimination and neglect can be salvaged not by programs alone but by what is even more important, evidence that some one cares enough and consistently enough really to help them. Their experiences, their lives, give substance to a persistent doubt that this is so. The ironic status of the present continued neglect of ghetto children is found in the nonrelevance of community programs designed to prevent delinquents and is made even clearer by the fact that those who are judged as delinquents are seldom rehabilitated by society. Available data suggest that nine out of ten go back to the ghetto without any change in the conditions that sent them into rebellious antisocial behavior in the first place.

Eighty-six social service organizations in Harlem that have tried to deal with the problem of delinquency reported in 1963 that recreation and vacation programs were their most prevalent activity— a trend that holds in other urban ghettos. According to an inventory of the Community Council of Greater New York, Harlem has twenty-seven playgrounds and playing fields, twenty part-time afternoon and evening centers, and eighteen public and voluntary full-time centers.* In its deliberations, the Social Agencies Committee associated with the Haryou planning stage felt that, except for the area below 120 Street, west of Lenox Avenue, the Harlem community is adequately serviced by group work and recreational agencies at the present time. For the city as a whole, Harlem is above the norm. In recreational facilities Harlem ranks sixth highest out of the seventy-four neighborhoods defined by the Community Council. The youth in the community do use these services, as a recent study showed. Incidentally, relatively few of Harlem's youth participate in scouting, in keeping with a strong tendency everywhere for scouting to be peripheral in communities of low socio-economic standing. In the Community Council study, for example, in thirty-seven communities which were below average in median family income only one was above average in scouting participation.

The common urban emphasis upon recreational and leisure time pursuits to keep youth out of trouble is typical of most communities. The need for such services cannot be denied, and it may be presumed that they bring some measure of gratification and pleasure to the lives of youth in the ghetto. But the fundamental predicament of ghetto youth remains unchanged. Recreation cannot compensate

* *Comparative Recreation Needs and Services in New York Neighborhoods,* Community Council of Greater New York, Table 18, 1963.

for the depressive realities of their lives. A score of years ago, and to some extent even today, the provision of wholesome recreational activities seemed the most urgent step toward the solution of the problem of juvenile delinquency. However, since the studies of Thraser, Shanas and Dunning, Reed, and the excellent review of research prepared by Witmer and Tufts,* the impact of recreation upon delinquency must be questioned. Given the pervasive pathology of the dark ghetto, questions must be asked whether social agencies should emphasize this restrictive role. A nice place to play is simply *not enough.* And it certainly is not evidence of the type of caring which could make the difference in the lives of the young people in a ghetto.

Many of the young people who are awaiting release from training schools or treatment centers, for example, could benefit from a concrete program to ease the transition of return to their community. To return these young people to a community or a home which has not substantially changed is to undermine the rehabilitation thought to have been begun in institutional confinement.

Young people who are brought before the courts and who are placed on probation, given suspended sentences, or released in the custody of parents or parent-surrogates are also thrown back into the very conditions which spawned their initial frustrations and rebellion. The futility and unreality of the present probation system as it relates to the reality of their predicament are beyond debate. There is ample reason to believe that for many of the young people who are given suspended sentences and are returned to the community this disposition of their cases does not necessarily reflect what is best for the child but rather the scarcity of institutional facilities. This is particularly true for the private and voluntary treatment centers. The fact that these centers can and do control their policy

* Frederick M. Thraser, "The Boys' Club and Juvenile Delinquency," *American Journal of Sociology,* 1936, pp. 66–80; Ethel Shanas and Catherine Dunning, *Recreation and Delinquency,* Chicago Recreation Commission, 1942; Ellery Reed, "How Effective Are Group Work Agencies in Preventing Delinquency?", *Social Service Review,* 1948, pp. 340–348; Helen Witmer and Edith Tufts, *The Effectiveness of Delinquency Prevention Programs,* U.S. Department of Health, Education, and Welfare, Children's Bureau, Publication No. 350, 1954.

of admission independent of the needs of a particular segment of the population means that most Negro youngsters must be referred to state training schools if they are to receive any kind of institutional help. Even in this questionable area of institutional care, these children of the ghetto are shortchanged.

These youth will have to learn eventually to function within the reality of a community if they are to lead effective lives. Even if the existing institutions were successfully rehabilitating their charges, that young person would still have to face the nonprotective community after his release. Thus, the approach to the treatment of battle neurosis in World War II, where psychiatric treatment was provided for disturbed soldiers at or near the front lines, was found to be significantly more effective than the previous approach of removing the patients far behind the battle line for treatment.

The value of involving or attempting to involve young people who are labeled as "delinquents" or "offenders" in realistic community problems and social action is twofold: first, it could give them the types of insights and understanding of their predicament which might relieve them of the need to act out their frustrations in personal and self-destructive ways; and, second, it would tap and channel the sensitivity and energy of the individual who has the ego strength to rebel by overt acts of defiance rather than succumb to apathy. It would be a valuable experiment to attempt to find out whether the defiant energies of overt delinquents could be used instead to attain socially useful goals.

For those young people who have already run afoul of the law, the Haryou program proposed Harlem Youth Junior Academies for juvenile offenders between the ages of eight and thirteen and Senior Academies for those between fourteen and seventeen. These academies would be organized to serve those young people returning to the community from a training school or treatment center and other youth placed on probation or given suspended sentences. Such academies would serve, in effect, as "halfway houses" between the institution and the community, providing work experiences and education in nonclassroom situations, using film making, tape recording, role playing, and group discussions, dance, drama, music, and the graphic arts to help these children understand themselves and their society. It would not be preposterous to think of using such academies as substitutes for the "training schools" and the misnamed "reformatories" to which these youngsters are now sent if there is room for them. The advantage of this approach would be that these young people would be kept in their own community—would be involved in discussions concerning the problems of the community and would be required, as the test of meaningful rehabilitation, to engage in constructive community action programs.

Haryou proposed, too, a Cadet Corps program, in an attempt to tap the magnetic appeal that uniforms, military organizations, martial music, and rhythms seem to have for the vast majority of Americans. The most neglected, rejected, and "all but abandoned" children are probably even more susceptible to this appeal than others would be because they have very little else in life on which to base a sense of personal worth and a feeling of pride. The failure of the Boy Scouts and the Girl Scouts to attract more than a few young people in deprived communities is due, as noted earlier, to the heavy middle-class emphasis and the relatively high cost of the uniforms and equipment of these programs.

A program for deprived young people which exploits the positive appeals of the quasimilitary, and reduces to a minimum the social class exclusion factors, might be a valuable part of a comprehensive program for Harlem's deprived youth. A Cadet Corps program could be organized and operated to use the natural appeal of uniforms, rank, insignia, and other concrete symbols of status to involve young people in more serious programs such as developing reading skills, a sense of reliability, and a sense of responsibility for the welfare and performance of others. For example, to advance up through the ranks a young cadet would have to master his manual. This might require that he enroll in a remedial reading class.

The quasimilitary aspect of the Haryou Cadet Corp program has been questioned on the grounds that this is a dangerous flirtation with the irrationality of violence on the part of an oppressed minority. There can be no question that any suggestion of violence as a way of seeking redress of the grievances of American Negroes is irrational and irresponsible. It has long been clear to some students of social change that seemingly more "rational" forms of violence such as wars and revolutions do not assure social progress. The rationale for the Cadet Corps is not to be understood in terms of its military paraphernalia but in the deeper terms of the relative ease with which uniforms, disciplined organizations, and regulations can be used to bolster the self-esteem of young people and provide them with the motivation to reinforce an awakened self-respect by developing the necessary skills in reading and communication. There are some examples of seemingly unreachable delinquents from urban ghettos who were redirected to constructive lives by their experience and training in the armed services. An experiment in attempting to provide a similar structure within the community would seem to be worth the risks. The symbols of the military imply to many a reliance upon regimentation, blind obedience, and force as a substitute for reason. Yet one of the tragedies of the ghetto is that the pervasive pathology is such, and the need so great, that the use of military symbols— with all they might mean—seems far less terrible than the evil it attempts to combat. Just as the Negro may fight racism by intensification of racism in his own self-image, so the decision for a Cadet Corps. One fights certain diseases by vaccines—the injection of an attenuated form of the disease itself—in order to build antibodies in the human system.

There now exist in the Harlem community successful cadet corps programs sponsored by the City Mission Society and by other groups. Although these programs have attracted primarily the more middle-class or upwardly mobile children of the community, their success-ful existence provides the basis for the belief that a similar program adapted for more marginal children could be successful. The cadet corps would provide a wholesome male or female image, over a sustained period of time, through intimate association of youth with older youths and adults of character and social skills. Previous at-tempts to meet the crucial need of Harlem's "abandoned" children have proved largely futile since in most cases the children and the adults have had no genuine relationship. Rather, in such traditional "big brother" approaches, without a sustained situation, the relationship necessarily remains peripheral to the child's basic human needs. It is one thing for a "big brother" from another world to take a boy to a ball game, or to his country place, once a month or so. It is quite another for a group of children and adults to take part in mutually rewarding activities for twelve or more hours a week. The first reminds the child that he has no family; the second can be a vital compensation for a shattered family life.

Narcotics Control

No young person in the ghetto is expendable, and this includes addicted as well as nonaddicted youth. The Haryou program, therefore, proposed a *Harlem Institute for Narcotics Research* to develop and maintain a community education and action program and with a special emphasis on exposure, prevention, and control of the drug traffic and detoxification and intensive aftercare treatment for young addicts. Such an institute could attempt to educate the community to support relevant bills like the Metcalf-Volker Act, which stresses a medical rather than a penal approach to drug addiction, and to explore the feasibility of legal drug use as a means of removing the profits and criminal by-products from the use of drugs. Furthermore, it should become increasingly difficult for young people of Harlem to purchase drugs in their home community if the relatively easy access which a Harlem youth has to drugs were to be dramatically dramatized. It is known that when the so-called panic is on in every other part of the city there are blocks in Harlem—117 Street between Fifth and Lenox Avenues, for example—where heroin can still be obtained. A key objective of a Harlem Institute for Narcotics Research would be to create a perennial "panic" in Harlem, making it more difficult for drug dealers to operate.

The treatment component of such an institute would have two interrelated objectives: detoxification and rehabilitation.

1. *Detoxification.* Research has revealed that a goodly number of Harlem addicts state a desire to "kick the habit." For many of them the thrill of drug use is but a distant memory; they seek the drug now for "medicinal" or physiological reasons. However, addicts who sin-

cerely wish to escape physical dependency on drugs soon learn that there is a severe shortage of available hospital beds for the short-term treatment of addicts. To get into a hospital, it often takes a degree of determination and "pull" which is beyond the resources of most Harlem addicts. More than lobbying and agitating for additional hospital beds is required, and more, too, than demanding that a "disproportionate" number of the currently available beds go to Harlem addicts.

Detoxification under proper medical supervision is a relatively short process. It should be possible to establish an inexpensive, upstate facility, perhaps a large old farmhouse, to which adolescent addicts could go for several weeks to undergo detoxification, begin the rebuilding of their physical systems, be provided with several ample meals by day and eight hours of sleep by night, and begin a program of group therapy and discussion sessions through which their psychological rehabilitation would be sought.

Given the short term of treatment, a facility with room for only twenty could, over the course of a year, serve several hundred addicts. Such a facility would require a staff: a resident physician, an on-call week-end physician, a group therapist, a housekeeper-cook, and four young counselors-in-training who are former narcotics users.

2. *Rehabilitation.* After detoxification, two distinct courses of treatment would be available in the community: counseling and referral, and group living.

a. *Counseling and referral.* For addicts who have basic skills and normal aptitudes, an outpatient aftercare program would be available. The youths would be returned to school, to a job, or enrolled in one of the Youth Occupational Training and Employment programs. They would, in addition, be enrolled in regularly scheduled group therapy and discussion sessions and encouraged to take an active part in the institute's prevention programs. Every attempt would be made to establish a "my brother's keeper" philosophy; the paid discussion leaders (all former users) would have a key role in achieving this end.

b. *Group living.* For selected addicts who have been in the drug life since the age of fourteen or fifteen, a more intensive and protracted course of treatment is indicated. Many cannot read or write; many had had no real social relations with people other than fellow addicts. These youths, to put the matter simply, have to be painstakingly trained and prepared for life in normal society. The addicts would live in houses with an around-the-clock program of basic education: reading, writing, arithmetic, basic skills training, recreation in the arts, intensive group therapy, and discusson sessions guided by members of the group. Life in this "halfway house" for addicts would be meant to provide a transition from the street drug world to normal society. The addict would remain in the society of his peers. Introduced into that society, however, would be a number of persons intended to have an influential role in his life, i.e., group discussion leaders, domestic Peace Corps volunteers, and others, prepared to give a measure of around-the-clock service as aides above and beyond the call of duty, in addition to professional group therapists who have a knowledge of the ghettto's drug culture.

The Causes of Pathology

The roots of the multiple pathology in the dark ghetto are not easy to isolate. They do not lie primarily in unemployment. In fact, if all of its residents were employed it would not materially alter the pathology of the community. More relevant is the status of the jobs held. Nor do the primary roots lie in the frustrations of bad housing. There is correlation between social pathology and housing, apparently confirming the earlier hypothesis that while better housing heightens morale, it does not affect the more fundamental variables of economic status, broken homes, and lowered aspirations; that more important than merely having *a* job, is the *kind* of job it is. And more important than housing—once human beings are removed from substandard housing—is fundamental social change. Merely to move the residents of a ghetto into low-income housing projects without altering the pattern of their lives—menial jobs, low income, inadequate education for their children—does not remove them from the tangle of community and personal pathology. But, as matters stand now, those who have achieved success move to other neighborhoods in order to better their lives. A sustained program is still to be initiated to enhance the ghetto community *as* a community. And certainly some attention should be given to a marked improvement in the physical and esthetic side of the community. Until all ghettos prove unnecessary, the nation's Harlems should be made literally so attractive and beautiful that they would affirm the highest human aspirations. As long as this is not true, the physical aspects of these communities symbolize and contribute to human degradation.

The culture of the ghetto must be reshaped so as to strike at the very roots of the ghetto's social malaise. Nothing short of a concerted and massive attack on the social, political, economic, and cultural roots of the pathology is required if anything more than daubing or a displacement of the symptoms is to be achieved. With regard to symptom displacement, it is now obvious, for example, that successful efforts to destroy the fighting gangs of Harlem merely resulted in an earlier and fuller flowering of the far more pernicious drug and "hustler" subcultures. Pyrrhic victories of this kind are the fruits of a "problem-solving" rather than an ego and "culture-building" approach to individual and social pathology. In the development of remedial stratagems, even if the major concern is the "elimination of juvenile delinquency" rather than the "building of a better life" for the people of the ghetto, stress on the latter is more likely to accomplish desired ends than too narrow a concern with the problem; be it homicide, gang fighting, burglary, drug use, or unwed motherhood.

To deal with the social pathology of adult crime in the ghetto, the pathologies of juvenile delinquency and drug addiction must be handled first, for the typical adult criminal is likely to have evolved from a juvenile delinquent, and there is evidence that such crimes as robbery, mugging, and burglary are the direct result of an expensive drug habit. And behind and beneath all of the crimes in the ghetto is the specter of unemployment, broken families, and poor education. The rise in venereal disease and illegitimacy has its source in large measure in the despair of the ghetto's young people, who seek gratification wherever they can find it as escape from the harsh realities of the many forms of racial rejection.

To explain all criminal activity, drug addiction, and other signs of personal instability solely in terms of poverty or the racial exploitation of the ghetto is, of course, a serious error, as the evidences of white-collar crimes and an increasing incidence of criminal activity among young people and adults in the more privileged communities indicate. There is a tendency toward pathology in the gilded suburban ghetto, too; an emptiness reflecting a futile struggle to find substance and worth through the concretes of things and possessions. In the struggle for affirmation and status, a homogeneous, antiseptic environment is sought, artificially isolating segments of the population in patterns of sameness: the same income level, the same-sized plot, the same neatly painted ranch houses; but even more confining, the same color of people, the same ethnic and religious background, the same age group (young couples with children), the same juvenile activities—ballet, piano, or the Little League—and the same kind of adult parties. And in this sameness, the possibility of the richness of life that can only be found in variety and individuality is negated. The residents of the gilded ghetto may escape by an acceptance of conformity, by the deadly ritual of alcoholism, by absorption in work, or in the artificial and transitory excitement of illicit affairs. The fact of the absent father in the city's ghettos is well known, but there is strong evidence that many homes are broken even more insidiously in America's gilded ghettos. The suburban pressures caused by the contrast between an apparently happy material life and a pervasive unhappiness or emptiness lead to a damning kind of personal entrapment. Such persons, unlike the lower-class ghetto members, rarely seek to relieve their frustrations in overt violence against others, but succumb rather to their fate. Why, then, would members of the city's ghettos seek to embrace a pathology of the suburb in exchange for their own? Because the middle-class culture, whatever its frustrations, still remains the norm for personal achievement of the "good life." To deny the Negro the right to exchange lower-class suffering for middle-class suffering on the grounds, in certain ways defensible, that the good life is not so good after all, is to make for a group the kind of moral decisions each individual has the right to make for himself, whether he choose well or ill. It would be psychologically naive and even cruel to ask the oppressed to transform the values of American culture. Before they can be motivated to try, they need to experience those values for themselves with all the satisfactions and all the frustrations and anxieties.

The relationship between individual pathology and permeating social pathology is much greater and clearer in the urban ghetto than it at present appears to be in more privileged communities. This suggests the hypothesis that criminal behavior among individuals from many of the more protected and privileged backgrounds might reflect a more severe form of personal instability, while the identical pattern of criminal behavior from an individual who comes out of the pathology of the ghetto may merely reflect the individual's responsiveness to and socialization within an oppressing antisocial system. The criminal from the privileged background could reflect a more severe problem of an inability to be socialized while the criminal who comes out of the ghetto reflects, however perversely, his responsiveness to social pressures and controls. One cannot push such speculation too far, however, for the lack of parental controls, the social schizophrenia and emptiness of much of suburban life may be found to be as relevant in the formation of criminal antisocial behavior as are the oppressive conditions in the slums.

The problem of controlling crime in the ghetto is primarily one of changing the conditions which tend to breed widespread violence rather than one of reforming the individual criminal. An apt analogy here may be to compare ghetto pathology to an epidemic. To prevent epidemics, necessary public health and sanitation measures are taken; one does not attempt to control the epidemic through the impossible task of trying to cure individuals. Yet the tendency has been, in terms of ghetto crimes, to concentrate on imprisonment of individuals rather than to seek to destroy the community roots of crime itself.

It is important to understand *how* a community's social pathology infects individuals. Not all persons react to pervasive pathology by resorting to antisocial criminal behavior. It is not known with enough precision why one individual reacts in overtly destructive ways and another in more passive, accepting ways. One has to accept the fact that under the best social conditions man can devise some persons will probably be criminal, some will be indigent and seek to exploit others, some will be passive, withdrawn, or lazy for reasons no one fully understands. Some possible reasons are distorted familial relations, inadequate physical constitution, defective nervous system, and a complexity of other factors that are not primarily related to community pathology. The present lack of scientific understanding cannot, however, be used to justify continuing social oppression. It is clear, moreover, that the continued existence of social pathology that could be cured increases the proportion of human casualties.

6

GHETTO SCHOOLS: SEPARATE
AND UNEQUAL

The public schools in America's urban ghettos also reflect the oppressive damage of racial exclusion. School segregation in the South had, for generations, been supported by law; in the North, segregation has been supported by community custom and indifference. It is assumed that children should go to school where they live, and if they live in segregated neighborhoods, the schools are, as a matter of course, segregated. But the educational crisis in the ghettos is not primarily, and certainly not exclusively, one of the inequitable racial balance in the schools. Equally serious is the inferior quality of the education in those schools. Segregation and inferior education reinforce each other. Some persons take the position that the first must go before the second does; others, that the reverse is true. What is clear is that the problem of education in the urban ghetto seems to be a vicious cycle: If children go to school where they live and if most neighborhoods are racially segregated, then the schools are necessarily segregated, too. If Negroes move into a previously white community and whites then move away or send their children to private or parochial schools, the public schools will continue to be segregated. If the quality of education in Negro schools is inferior to that in white schools, whites feel justified in the fear that the presence of

Negroes in their own school would lower its standards. If they move their own children away and the school becomes predominantly Negro, and therefore receives an inferior quality of education, the pattern begins all over again. The cycle of systematic neglect of Negro children must be broken, but the powerlessness of the Negro communities and the fear and indifference of the white community have combined so far to keep the cycle intact.

The central questions that lie behind the entire network of problems are these: Are Negroes such—in terms of innate incapacity *or* environmental deprivation—that their children are less capable of learning than are whites, so that any school that is permitted to become integrated necessarily declines in quality? Or has inferior education been systematically imposed on Negroes in the nation's ghettos in such a way as to compel poor performance from Negro children—a performance that could be reversed with quality education? The answer to these questions is of fundamental importance because the flight of whites from the urban public school system in many American cities is based on the belief that the first is true and the second false. If the first is false and the second true—and the centers of power in the white community can be convinced of that fact—one of the basic injustices in American life could be corrected.

The Public Schools: A Segregated System?

Unless firm and immediate steps are taken to reverse the present trend, the public school system in the Northern cities of America will become predominantly a segregated system, serving primarily Negroes. It will, in addition, become a school system of low academic standards, providing a second-class education for underclassed children and thereby a chief contributor to the perpetuation of the "social dynamite" which is the cumulative pathology of the ghetto.

In Chicago, 37 percent of the elementary schools (compared with 22 percent in New York) and 18 percent of the high schools (compared with 2 percent in New York) are now segregated; 48.3 percent of the pupils in Chicago are now Negro. In Cleveland, 60 percent of the elementary schools and 58 percent of the high schools are segregated, white or Negro. In Detroit, more than 40 percent of public school children are Negro. In Philadelphia, more than half of the public school children are now Negro. By 1963 the Washington, D.C., public schools, which ten years ago had been one-third Negro, had become more than three-quarters Negro; by 1970, more than nine out of ten children in the public schools in the nation's capital may be Negro.

In the public schools of Manhattan as a whole, 73 percent of the children are already nonwhites. Ninety percent of school age children in Harlem are in public schools; only two-thirds of the children in the rest of Manhattan are—the others have moved into private or parochial schools. Despite the fact that segregation has been illegal in the public school system of New York State since 1902, virtually all the 31,469 children in Harlem's schools (twenty elementary schools, four junior high schools, and no high schools) are Negro. Only two of the elementary schools have less than 89.9 percent Negro enrollment; and all the junior high schools are at least 91.4 percent Negro. This means that the bulk of the community's children in elementary and junior high schools are educated in *de facto* segregated schools although the city's Board of Education has an official policy of full integration.*

The trend toward school segregation, in fact, is accelerating. Seventy-eight New York schools below high school became segregated between 1958 and 1963. Open enrollment and the free choice transfer policy, allowing parents to seek the transfer of their children to nonsegregated schools, have done little to improve the situation— less than 3 percent of the nonwhite students moved to other schools. Many whites point to this apathy on the part of Negroes as evidence that Negro families in general prefer segregated neighborhood schools to unsegregated distant schools. *Any* parent prefers a neighborhood school, all things being equal and often when not all is equal, and no public school desegregation plan that demands voluntary individual decisions is ever accepted by the majority of Negro or white parents. Yet even if more students did transfer out of the ghetto few, if any, whites would move into the ghetto, and while the schools of

* *Toward Greater Opportunity*, New York City Board of Education, June 1960, p. 1.

the ghetto themselves would probably decline in population, they would remain segregated.

The pairing system, often called the Princeton Plan, which merges the populations of two nearby elementary schools, one predominantly Negro and the other predominantly white, also offers little chance of success in complex urban residential patterns and school systems. The New York City Board of Education proposed in 1964 that twenty-one such pairings be made. If all were introduced at once —though the board responded to further reflection and to community pressures by reducing the proposed twenty-one to four—segregation in the city would be reduced by only 1 percent. If twenty schools a year were so paired, an unlikely move, the school system would still be one-quarter segregated in 1970. Sprawling, densely populated cities are not manageable, peaceful suburban communities like Princeton, and because the plan works in one area is no guarantee it will work in another.

In 1963, 45 percent of New York's nonwhite children attended segregated junior highs. The Board of Education proposals to change the system of feeding students from elementary schools into junior highs would reduce this percentage only slightly. At this rate, and providing that the city's population did not itself change, the junior high schools of New York would be desegregated by about 2010. On the other hand, efforts to desegregate the twenty-five schools dominated now by nonwhites would make a difference in a single decade. If important efforts to achieve school integration are not adopted, segregation in the public schools will increase from the 22 percent of the elementary schools in 1963 to 38 percent in 1975; from 19 to 29 percent of the junior high schools; from 2 to 6 percent of the high schools. The schools by 1980 would be three-quarters Negro and Puerto Rican in the city as a whole and in Manhattan would probably exceed 90 percent, though the proportion may be expected to stabilize at that point.*

One of the remedies suggested has been long-distance transporta-

* These projections were made in 1964 by the staff engaged by the Advisory Committee on Human Relations and Community Tensions to James E. Allen, New York State Commissioner of Education.

tion of elementary school pupils, or "busing." This plan seems to offer immediate desegregation, but in many cases it would lead to bad education and, in the end, therefore, to even more segregation. Whites would pull out of the public school system even more rapidly than they are presently doing. In Brooklyn, for example, if real integration were the goal, about 70,000 Negro and Puerto Rican children, under eleven, would have to be transported twice a day, some of them ten miles away. In Manhattan, where schools have an even higher proportion of Negro and Puerto Rican children, even longer travel time would fail to bring about meaningful integration. As the Allen Commission Report said:

It should be obvious, but does not always appear to be, that integration is impossible without white pupils. No plan can be acceptable, therefore, which increases the movement of white pupils out of the public schools. Neither is it acceptable, however, unless it contributes to desegregation.

Therefore, any effective plan must (1) reduce school segregation; (2) bring better educational services; and (3) hold white pupils, even bring more back into the public school system.

One cannot help noting, however, that the interest in neighborhood schools, however valid, seems to have some relation to human hypocrisy. The white Parents and Taxpayers (PAT) groups in New York threatened boycotts over the school system's plan to transfer 383 children no more than a mile and a half for a ten-minute ride. Assistant Superintendent of Schools Jacob Landers noted that 77,000 children, including 25,000 in parochial schools, have been transferred regularly, and not for purposes of integration. The largest number were children in kindergarten and first and second grades, the same age group whose welfare is invoked fervently in behalf of the neighborhood school.

Many who have been themselves deeply damaged by past patterns of racial segregation will continue to resist the demands of the present. The demands of Negroes for desegregated schools will be met by many and continued forms of subtle and flagrant resistance. The school boycotts organized by civil rights groups in New York to force desegregation in the schools were rooted in the belief that such desegregation was immediately possible. But given the timidity and moral irresolution of whites, any such assumption is unrealistic, and the strategy doomed to fail. All white families need to do in event of forced desegregation is to form a countermovement, as PAT did, and threaten to leave the community, as thousands have already done, or shift their children to private or parochial schools.

Whenever minority group membership in a community increases in the neighborhood of a public school, white families who can afford it tend to take their children out of public school and either move to a new community or send the children to the comparative safety of the private and parochial schools. The white protest groups that arrange community boycotts against integrated schools represent the marginal families who can neither move nor pay private school tuition. These groups react out of that despair which Negroes themselves often reflect when they see no alternatives in a threatening situation.

Less than 10 percent of the private and parochial school population in New York is Negro—about 32,000 pupils; the 90 percent who are white students represent 30 percent of the city's white student population. So, while nine out of ten Negro children are in public schools, only seven out of ten white children are. An ironic possibility is that the present middle-class flight from the public schools which is explained in terms of the desire for quality education will not result in quality education at all. It is conceivable that with the proliferation of private and parochial schools in the urban areas, these schools will not be able to obtain the necessary finances and faculty for a truly quality education. They might then have to base their appeal only on status needs.

Most of New York City's private schools are parochial or church-sponsored, Roman Catholic and Episcopalian predominantly, with a few sponsored by Quakers, Jews, Ethical Culture societies, and others. Roman Catholic and certain Jewish schools give primary emphasis to the parents' desire to reinforce their children's religious loyalty. The Protestant and Ethical Culture groups, in particular, give quality of education as the chief reason for the existence of these private schools. But whatever the intent of the sponsors, many parents —some Negroes as well as whites—send their children to these schools not only for religious training or the sake of quality education but also to escape the growing influx of low-income minority group members into the public school system. There is a real question, of course, whether religion is best served by a displacement of a city's leadership into a private school system. There is a real question, also, whether socially insulated education *is* really education for leadership. The middle- and upper-class parents who defend their decision for private schools with the plea: "I won't sacrifice my child," give perhaps less weight to their children's resilience than the evidence would support, and certainly less weight to the importance of democratically based education than the times demand. But such arguments have little weight when parents fear for their child's future. In American life, where education is considered the first prerequisite for adult success, the issue is especially sensitive. When the question of education, therefore, is combined with the even more sensitive question of race, the emotions of persons are aroused as they seldom are by a public question.

Educational Inequality

One thing is clear and that is that meaningful desegregation of urban ghetto public schools can occur only if all of the schools in the system are raised to the highest standards, so that the quality of education does not vary according to income or the social status of the neighborhood. The goals of integration and quality education must be sought together; they are interdependent. One is not possible without the other.

A number of individuals prominent in the civil rights movement claim, however, that a demand for excellence in ghetto schools is really camouflage for acquiescence in segregation. On the contrary it is, given the intransigence of the white community and the impossibility of immediate integration, a decision to save as many Negro children as possible now. The struggle of the civil rights groups for a better life for these children is made more difficult, if not impossible, if the methods of the struggle become dominated by inflexible emotional postures. Heroics and dramatic words and gestures, over-

simplified either-or thinking, and devil-hunting might dominate
headlines; but they cannot solve the fundamental problems of obtaining high-quality education in the public schools and the related problem of realistic and serious desegregation of these schools. These
children, Negro or white, must not be sacrificed on the altars of
ideological and semantic rigidities.

Negroes in the ghetto have long been concerned with the quality
of their children's education. There have been committees for better
schools in Harlem going back to the 1930s. After the 1935 Harlem
riots, Mayor Fiorello La Guardia asked E. Franklin Frazier, the distinguished sociologist, to study the state of things in Harlem. Among
the inflammatory conditions he reported were the flagrant deficiencies
of the ghetto schools. As the proportion of Negroes in the schools
increased over the years it became clear to everyone that the quality
of education decreased.

In 1955, the Public Education Association, in cooperation with the
New York University Research Center for Human Relations, conducted a "full, impartial, and objective inquiry" into the status of the
public school education of Negroes and Puerto Ricans in New York
City.* The picture they discovered at that time was one of sub-

* *The Status of Public School Education of Negro and Puerto Rican Children in New York City,* Public Education Association, October 1955. Ironically, New York did not look seriously at the problems of its ghetto schools
until the school segregation cases in the South forced its attention upon them.
Justin Moore, a Southern lawyer defending Virginia's school segregation, asked
the NAACP consultant how he could give testimony about the detrimental
effects of segregation on children in Virginia when New York, his home state,
had schools as segregated. Moore was substantially correct: *de facto* segregation in the North and *de jure* segregation in the South had the same psychological consequences. In 1952, as a result, after returning to New York, the
consultant told the New York Urban League of Justin Moore's question. It
was imperative to find out just what were the consequences of the ghetto
schools. Mayor Wagner, responding to a similar presentation, later, called a
meeting with the superintendent of schools, who labeled the NAACP consultant's charges impertinent and irresponsible and even demagogic. *De facto*
segregation, he said, was a geographic accident, and the children in Negro
schools were receiving quality education and performing according to the
level of their I.Q. This the consultant denied, demonstrating that the I.Q.
scores often reflect quality of teaching, reading level, etc., and suggested that
low performance indicated rather educational rejection of the children. Certain basic principles of psychology in regard to modifiability—the capacity
to change—and learning capacity could be applied to the New York City
schools.

standard staff, facilities, and pupil performance. The situation has deteriorated since then. To do nothing does not maintain the *status quo;* social inertia leads to social regression. The warnings of the past thirty years had gone virtually unheeded. Harlem felt increasing anxiety, alienation, and concern and an inability to do anything about it. The hopelessness of the ghetto led to inaction.

It was not true, however, as some said, that the situation in Harlem reflected general deterioration of public education in New York City. In neighborhoods composed predominantly of middle-class whites, the schools were generally good. New York City had several high schools as severely rigorous in quality of education as any—public or private—in the nation. These high schools are predominantly white.

The 1964 Allen Report declared:

Total desegregation of all schools, for example, is simply not attainable in the foreseeable future and neither planning nor pressure can change the fact. Yet if nothing more is done, or too little is attempted, the outcome will inevitably be more extensive and more extreme segregation and a larger number of poor schools. More can be done, however, and should be. With thoughtful planning, bold policies and vigorous action, there are sound reasons to believe that the spread of segregation can be slowed, its severity reduced and the effectiveness of school programs substantially improved.*

The job of obtaining excellent education for the children in deprived urban areas is now a national problem. A serious and responsible program to attain this goal transcends local, sectional, or racial considerations. John Kenneth Galbraith of Harvard University has suggested an emergency education program as probably the most effective single step in the attack on poverty in America.

The basic story of academic achievement in Harlem is one of inefficiency, inferiority, and massive deterioration. The further these students progress in school, the larger the proportion who are retarded and the greater is the discrepancy between their achievement and the achievement of other children in the city. This is also true for their

* "Desegregating the Public Schools of New York City," the State Education Commissioner's Advisory Committee on Human Relations and Community Tensions, May 12, 1964. p. 13.

intelligence test scores. This deterioration can be traced in sequence, beginning with the elementary schools and following through the junior high schools to the high schools.*

In reading comprehension, the ability to understand what one is reading, 30 percent of the Harlem third grade pupils are reading below grade level, compared to 21.6 percent who are reading above. For sixth grade pupils, the story is even more dismal; there 80.9 percent of the pupils score below grade level in reading, while 11.7 percent score above, indicating a rather rapid relative deterioration in reading comprehension within three school years.

Between grades three and six, word knowledge falters also; in third grade, 38.9 percent score below grade level, 18.7 percent score above; in sixth grade, 77.5 percent are below, 10.6 percent above. Arithmetic shows a similar pattern of underachievement, though figures are only available for the sixth grade (57.6 percent are below grade level in "computation," 66.6 below in "problems and concepts"). By eighth grade, three-quarters of the Harlem junior high school students score below grade level in reading comprehension and word knowledge; in arithmetic, their performance is even more discouraging—83.8 percent are now below.†

The academic performance of Harlem pupils in reading and arithmetic is still more depressing when compared to the performance of other children in New York City and in the nation as a whole (see

* The data, summarized in the following pages and discussed in considerable detail in *Youth In the Ghetto,* are drawn from standard tests applied in the third, sixth, and eighth grades throughout the New York City school system and from I.Q. tests given at the same time. These data were made available to the Haryou research staff by the New York City Board of Education. The standard tests given during the third, sixth, and eighth grades, include: *Third grade:* intelligence—Otis Quick Scoring Alpha Test; reading—Metropolitan Achievement Reading Test. *Sixth grade:* intelligence—Otis Beta; reading—Metropolitan Achievement Intermediate A; arithmetic—Metropolitan Intermediate A. *Eighth grade:* intelligence—Pintner General Ability and Intermediate Test, Form A; reading—Metropolitan Achievement Advanced; arithmetic—New York City Computation.

† These figures probably present a more positive figure than the realities of academic performance of these children in the Junior High School would warrant since it is the custom for some school officials to withhold the scores of those students who score too low on these standardized tests in Elementary and Junior High Schools because these very low scores would "distort" the averages.

Charts 1, 2, 3*). In the third grade, New York City pupils, on the average, are about equal to those elsewhere. By the eighth grade they have slipped almost a half grade behind. During those same grades, the pupils in Harlem slip further and further behind the achievement levels of both the city and the nation. In the third grade, Harlem pupils are one year behind the achievement levels of New York City pupils. By the sixth grade they have fallen nearly two years behind; and by the eighth grade they are about two and one-half years behind New York City levels and three years behind students in the nation as a whole.

In I.Q. the picture is just as alarming; a sharp drop for ghetto children between third and sixth grades, with a slight improvement by the eighth grade, but still behind where they were in the third grade. Although the ghetto's pupils show a decrease in mean I.Q. scores from the third to the sixth grade and a slight recovery by the eighth, New York City pupils as a whole show a slight, but steady, increase in I.Q., until by eighth grade they match national norms (see Chart 4*). These findings strongly suggest that for Harlem pupils I.Q. tests reflect the quality of teaching and the resulting educational achievement more than intellectual potential, since I.Q. as an index of intellectual potential was at one time thought to be constant, and still is considered generally to be more constant than achievement fluctuations. Only 2.8 percent of Central Harlem junior high school pupils are in "special progress" (SP) or "special progress enrichment" (SPE) classes for the academically alert youngster, while 13.4 percent of all New York City junior high school pupils are in these classes. At present, students who excel are skimmed off into pitiably few classes for the "Intellectually Gifted Child," special progress classes, and special progress enrichment classes, where great things are expected of them. Those who fail are shunted into classes for "children with mentally retarded development" and "opportunity" classes. Most stay in their regular classes that "meet their ability." Little is expected of them; they are rewarded for mediocre performance, and

* These charts were prepared for *Youth in the Ghetto.*

Chart 1. Median Equivalent Grades In Reading Comprehension For Central Harlem And New York City Pupils Compared To National Norms

	3rd Grade	6th Grade	8th Grade
Central Harlem	2.5	4.1	6.0
New York City	3.6	6.1	8.1
National	3.7	6.2	8.5

Chart 2. Median Equivalent Grades In Word Knowledge For Central Harlem And New York City Pupils Compared To National Norms

	3rd Grade	6th Grade	8th Grade
Central Harlem	2.7	4.1	6.0
New York City	3.6	6.1	8.1
National	3.7	6.2	8.3

Chart 3. Median Equivalent Grades in Arithmetic For Central Harlem And New York City Pupils Compared To National Norms

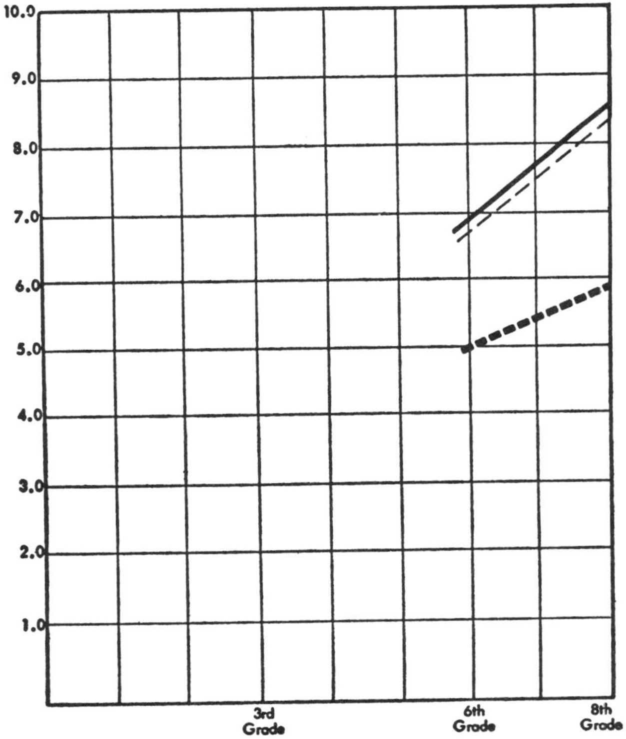

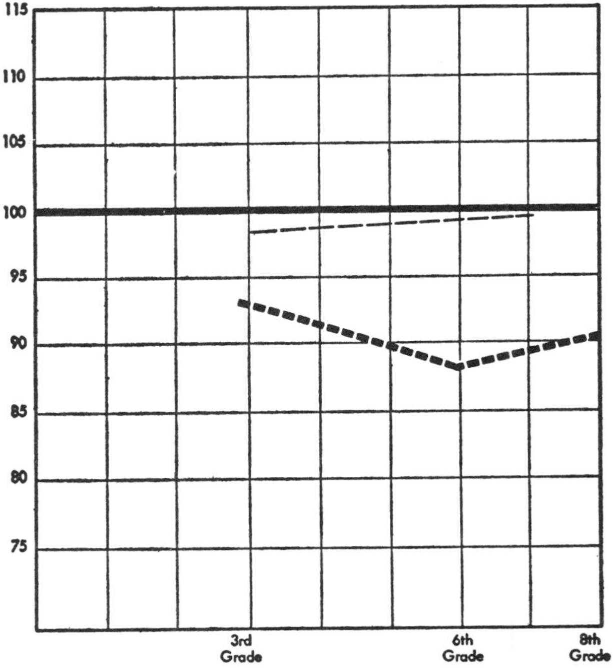

Chart 4. Median I.Q. Scores For Central Harlem And New York City Pupils Compared To National Norms

consequently accomplish increasingly less than pupils at their grade level should accomplish.

It is an ironic and tragic inversion of the purpose of education that Negro children in ghetto schools tend to lose ground in I.Q. as they proceed through the schools and to fall further and further behind the standard for their grade level in academic performance. The schools are presently damaging the children they exist to help.

Scarcely surprising then are the high figures for school dropouts— one out of ten from Harlem schools. Four out of five of the pupils from Harlem's junior high schools who do go on to high school, go to academic high schools; but this reflects not a plan to enter college or to seek a white-collar job, but the fact that the city's vocational schools now have higher entrance requirements; the "academic" high schools, in a reversal of the earlier situation, have become the "dumping ground" for inferior students.

Of the 1,276 students from four Harlem junior high schools who started high school in 1959–1960, less than half were graduated in 1962 (records were located for 1,012; 117 others transferred to other schools. Of the 1,012, 44.6 percent were graduated). The Board of Education of the City of New York awards "general" diplomas to any student who stayed in school for the required period of time but who is not prepared for any further education; an "academic" diploma indicates that a student satisfactorily completed a college preparatory curriculum. Of the academic high school graduates from Harlem, only one-seventh received "academic" diplomas—compared to about half of the academic school pupils for the city as a whole. More than three-fourths of the academic high school diplomas that went to Harlem students were "general" diplomas. But even this picture of the relatively small proportion of Harlem's young people who graduate from high school with "diplomas" does not reflect the full negative picture of the educational wastage which afflicts this community.

Thousands of students drop out of school before graduation, thereby increasing the chances that they will end up unemployed or with a menial job. Harlem has far more than its share of such alienated teen-agers. A survey by the New York State Division of Youth showed that in 1960–1961, about 10 percent of Harlem's pupils attending high school in Manhattan left that year. Of the students from Harlem who entered academic high schools in 1959, 53 percent became dropouts; 61 percent who entered vocational schools that year left before graduating. Even though attendance at school is compulsory until sixteen, more than a fifth of the boys and more than half of the girls leaving junior high (during 1960–1961, 3.8 percent of these pupils left school) were under sixteen. A number of these boys were sent to correctional institutions, a number of the girls were pregnant—but the schools do not mention reform schools in their own records and far underestimate the number of pregnancies; they generally refer instead to "overage."* Nor do the schools mention discouragement over academic failure as a cause, though the dropouts themselves do, and their records show the evidence: 88.1 percent of the boys and 68.5 percent of the girls leaving high school were inferior in reading; in mathematics, 89.5 percent of the boys and 84.6 percent of the girls were inferior. One cannot avoid the question whether it was the inability of these young people to learn or the failure of the schools to teach that led to this pattern of deterioration in learning skills, decline in I.Q., and eventual dropout. Fewer than half of the ghetto youth seem likely, as matters now stand, to graduate from high school. And few of them are prepared for any job; fewer still will go on to college.

The Debate on the Causes of Inferiority

The fact of the academic inferiority of Negro students in ghetto schools is no longer in dispute. Some Negroes resent this and consider it a key problem of the civil rights struggle; some whites argue that this justifies the continued segregation of these children—or at best, the acceptance of only the few superior Negro children in predominantly white schools. What remains in dispute is: How does one explain the continued inferiority of Negro students? How much validity is there to the hypotheses used as a basis for explaining and

* According to a study of ninety-six school dropouts serviced by the Urban League of Greater New York, *Youth in the Ghetto, op. cit.,* p. 185.

dealing with this persistent problem? Among the most tempting of these assumptions now in vogue are:

1. That each child should be educated in terms of his own needs and his capacities. On the surface this seems like a perfectly logical position and has been offered by individuals whose humanitarian and democratic instincts should certainly not be questioned. But it has led to a great deal of confusion, misunderstanding, and injustice in the educational process.

2. That children from workingclass cultures (and this second assumption necessarily follows from the first) need not only a different approach in the educational process, but a different type of education from that provided for children from middle-class families.

3. That one cannot expect from culturally deprived children adequate educational performance in the classroom because they come from homes in which there is no stimulation for educational achievement. This generalization is usually supported by such specifics as the absence of books from the home and of discussions that would stimulate intellectual curiosity. (It is assumed that in homes in which there are books, these books are read or that the presence of books in some other manner influences the child in a way relevant to his ability to learn to read in the primary grades.) Every child has to be taught how to read, however, and, as present evidence indicates, a child whose parents have no books can learn to read in school as quickly as a child whose home is well equipped.

4. That children from deprived communities bring into the classroom certain psychological problems that are peculiar to their low socio-economic status and that interfere with the educational process in the classroom.

5. That one can predict the future academic success of the child by knowing his I.Q. score, which is obtained early in the elementary grades. Some educational systems begin to give children I.Q. tests by the first or second grade, and classify them and relegate them to various types of educational procedures on this basis. The test scores will follow them for the rest of their lives. This is considered efficient and economic: Time is not wasted trying to teach children who cannot learn. This is related to the first assumption,

that a child should be educated according to his needs, his status in life, and his capacities.

A second group of assumptions can be categorically recognized as subtle forms of social class and racial snobbery and ignorance, arguing, for example, that it is not really worth it to put time and effort into teaching Negroes because, after all "they" will only become frustrated. There is no point in "their" having high academic aspirations since "their" lives will be restricted to menial jobs. In the late 1950s a number of teachers in the New York public school system told white student interviewers assigned by the author that Negro children are inherently inferior in intelligence and therefore cannot be expected to learn as much or as readily as white children; and that all one would do, if one tried to teach them as if they could learn, would be to develop in them serious emotional disturbances, frustrations and anxieties. The humanitarian thing to do for these children, the proponents of such theories maintain, is to provide schools that are essentially custodial, rather than educational institutions.

Each of the above assumptions is primarily an alibi for educational neglect, and in no way is a reflection of the nature of the educational process. Each of these assumptions—the well-intentioned as well as those that reflect clear prejudice and ignorance—contributes to the perpetuation of inferior education for lower-status children, whether their lower status is socio-economic or racial. Each intensifies racial and class cleavages in schools and therefore perpetuates and extends such cleavages in society. Each, when implemented in an educational procedure, makes the public schools and public education not instruments in facilitating social mobility, but very effective instruments in widening socio-economic and racial cleavages in our society and in imposing class and caste rigidities.

Educational Atrophy: The Self-fulfilling Prophecy

The most insidious consequence of these assumptions is that they are self-fulfilling prophecies. The fallacy in the assumptions does not mean that a system based upon them will be demonstrated to be ineffective; for once one organizes an educational system where children are placed in tracks or where certain judgments about their ability determine what is done for them or how much they are taught or not taught, the horror is that the results seem to justify the assumptions. The use of intelligence test scores to brand children for life, to determine education based upon tracks and homogeneous groupings of children, impose on our public school system an intolerable and undemocratic social hierarchy, and defeat the initial purposes of public education. They induce and perpetuate the very pathology which they claim to remedy. Children who are treated as if they are uneducable almost invariably become uneducable. This is educational atrophy. It is generally known that if an arm or a leg is bound so that it cannot be used, eventually it becomes unusable. The same is true of intelligence.

Children themselves are not fooled by the various euphemisms educators use to disguise educational snobbery. From the earliest grades a child knows when he has been assigned to a level that is considered less than adequate. Whether letters, numbers, or dog or animal names are used to describe these groups, within days after these procedures are imposed the children know exactly what they mean. Those children who are relegated to the inferior groups suffer a sense of self-doubt and deep feelings of inferiority which stamp their entire attitude toward school and the learning process. Many children are now systematically categorized, classified in groups labeled slow learners, trainables, untrainables, Track A, Track B, the "Pussycats," the "Bunnies," etc. But it all adds up to the fact that they are not being taught; and not being taught, they fail. They have a sense of personal humiliation and unworthiness. They react negatively and hostilely and aggressively to the educational process. They hate teachers, they hate schools, they hate anything that seems to impose upon them this denigration, because they are not being respected as human beings, because they are sacrificed in a machinery of efficiency and expendability, because their dignity and potential as human beings are being obscured and ignored in terms of educationally irrelevant factors—their manners, their speech, their dress, or their apparent disinterest.

The contempt of these children for school is clearly related to the high dropout statistics, the hostility, aggression, and the seeming unmanageability of children in such schools. They are in a sense revolting against a deep and pervasive attack upon their dignity and integrity as human beings.

Educators, parents, and others really concerned with the human aspects of American public education should dare to look the I.Q. straight in the eye, and reject it or relegate it to the place where it belongs. The I.Q. cannot be considered sacred or even relevant in decisions about the future of the child. It should not be used to shackle children. An I.Q. so misused contributes to the wastage of human potential. The I.Q. can be a valuable educational tool within the limits of its utility, namely, as an index of what needs to be done for a particular child. The I.Q. used as the Russians use it, namely, to determine where one must start, to determine what a particular child needs to bring him up to maximum effectiveness, is a valuable educational aid. But the I.Q. as an end product or an end decision for children is criminally neglectful. The I.Q. should not be used as a basis for segregating children and for predicting—and, therefore, determining—the child's educational future.*

"The clash of cultures in the classroom" is essentially a class war, a socio-economic and racial warfare being waged on the battleground of our schools, with middle-class and middle-class-aspiring teachers provided with a powerful arsenal of half-truths, prejudices, and rationalizations, arrayed against hopelessly outclassed workingclass youngsters. This is an uneven balance, particularly since, like most battles, it comes under the guise of righteousness.

The Cult of "Cultural Deprivation"

Among the earliest explanations of the educational inferiority of Negro children was that the poor average performance was to be accounted for in terms of inherent racial inferiority. After the re-

---

* In 1963, on the initiative of top staff of the New York City Board of Education, a policy was adopted to de-emphasize the use of I.Q. scores in placing of pupils in the elementary grades.

search findings of Otto Klineberg and others in the 1930s came a serious re-examination among social scientists of the racial inferiority explanation.

More recently, it has become fashionable to attempt to explain the persistent fact of the academic retardation of Negro children in terms of general environmental disabilities. Taking their lead from the Klineberg type of research, these explanations tend to emphasize the pattern of environmental conditions as the cause which depresses the ability of these children to learn—economic and job discrimination, substandard housing, poor nutrition, parental apathy. The most recent version of the environmentalistic approach comes under the general heading of "cultural deprivation." The literature on this topic has used a variety of synonyms for this concept. Among them are: culturally disadvantaged, the disadvantaged, minority groups, socially neglected, socially rejected, socially deprived, school retarded, educationally disadvantaged, lower socio-economic groups, socio-economically deprived, culturally impoverished, culturally different, rural disadvantaged, the deprived slum children.

The cultural deprivation approach is seductive. It is both reasonable and consistent with contemporary environmentalistic thought, which seems to dominate social science thinking. Indeed, it is presented as a rejection of the inherent racial inferiority theories of the nineteenth and early twentieth centuries. The recent rash of cultural deprivation theories, however, should be subjected to intensive scrutiny to see whether they do, in fact, account for the pervasive academic retardation of Negro children. Specifically, in what way does a low economic status or absence of books in the home or "cognitive deficit," referred to constantly by proponents of this point of view, actually interfere with the ability of a child to learn to read or to do arithmetic in the elementary grades?

What is meant by "cognitive deficit"? How remediable or unremediable is it? If it is remediable, how? Is it merely a jargon tautology which says only what everyone knows: that these children are not learning? In what way does it explain difficulties in learning to read? What are the implications of these cultural deprivation theories for educational prognosis and methods? What is the relationship between the methodology for educating these children suggested by proponents of these theories and the theories themselves? A rigorously objective study of these problems and attempts to answer these questions might provide answers which will not only increase our understanding of problems of education of lower status groups but might contribute to our understanding of problems of education in general —the teaching and learning phenomena. Cultural deprivation theories might also be crucial to the important problem of determining the reasonable expectations and limits of education.

To what extent are the contemporary social deprivation theories merely substituting notions of environmental immutability and fatalism for earlier notions of biologically determined educational unmodifiability? To what extent do these theories obscure more basic reasons for the educational retardation of lower-status children? To what extent do they offer acceptable and desired alibis for the educational default: the fact that these children, by and large, do not learn because they are not being taught effectively and they are not being taught because those who are charged with the responsibility of teaching them do not believe that they can learn, do not expect that they can learn, and do not act toward them in ways which help them to learn.

The answers to these and related questions cannot be found in rhetoric or continued speculative discourse. Speculation appears to reflect primarily the status of those who speculate. Just as those who proposed the earlier racial inferiority theories were invariably members of the dominant racial groups who presumed themselves and their groups to be superior, those who at present propose the cultural deprivation theory, are, in fact, members of the privileged group who inevitably associate their privileged status with their own innate intellect and its related educational success. Such association neither proves nor disproves the theory in itself, but the implicit caste and class factors in this controversy cannot and should not be ignored. Many of today's scholars and teachers came from "culturally deprived" backgrounds. Many of these same individuals, however, when confronted with students whose present economic and social predicament is not unlike their own was, tend to react negatively to them, possibly to escape the painful memory of their own prior lower status. It is easy for one's own image of self to be reinforced and made total by the convenient device of a protective forgetting—a refusal to remember the specific educational factor, such as a sympathetic and understanding teacher or the tutorial supports which made academic success and upward mobility possible in spite of cultural deprivation. The role of empathy, the understanding and identification of a teacher with his students in eliciting maximum academic performance from them, is an important educational question which should be studied systematically. The problems of empathy and identification between Negro students and their teachers are complex in an essentially racist society. It is significant that this relationship, as a systematic examination of the cultural deprivation literature reveals, has been so far totally ignored.

Looked at one way, it seems the epitome of common sense—and certainly compassion—to be convinced that a child who never has had toys to play with, or books to read, who has never visited a museum or a zoo or attended a concert, who has no room of his own, or even a pencil he can call his own, ought not to be expected to achieve in school on a level to match a more fortunate child. His image of himself is certain to be poor, his motivation weak, his vision of the world outside the ghetto distorted. But common sense and compassion may not tell the whole story. The evidence of the pilot projects in "deprived" schools—odd though it may appear to many—seems to indicate that a child who is expected by the school to learn does so; the child of whom little is expected produces little. Stimulation and teaching based upon positive expectation seem to play an even more important role in a child's performance in school than does the community environment from which he comes.

A key component of the deprivation which afflicts ghetto children is that generally their teachers do not expect them to learn. This is certainly one possible interpretation of the fact that ghetto children in Harlem *decline* in relative performance and in I.Q. the longer they are in school. Furthermore, other evidence supports this conclusion: Statistical studies of the relationship between social factors such as broken homes, crowded housing, low income with performance in

Harlem schools show a very tenuous link between environment and performance.* Depth interviews and questionnaires with Harlem teachers and school supervisors sustain the same observation. There are some school personnel who feel that the learning potential of the children is adequate. Though the majority believed one-fourth or less had potential for college, they did believe the majority could finish high school. One suspects that the children's level of motivation is, to some extent, set by their teachers. One guidance counselor said: "The children have a poor self-image and unrealistic aspirations. If you ask them what they want to be, they will say 'a doctor,' or something like that." When asked, "What would you say to a child who wanted to be a doctor?" she replied, "I would present the situation to him as it really is; show him how little possibility he has for that. I would tell him about the related fields, technicians, etc." One suspects, from this type of guidance reinforced by poor teaching and academic retardation, that the poor motivation and absence of a dignified self-image stem from the negative influence of such teachers more than from the influence of home and community.

The majority of teachers and administrators interviewed, nevertheless, talked of lowering standards to meet what they considered the intellectual level of their students. Assistant principals, who expressed this view with particular frequency, are in a position to influence curriculum. If they view the ghetto students as unteachable, one could scarcely blame the teachers they supervise for adopting a similar skepticism. When schools do not have confidence in their job, they gradually shift their concept of their function from teaching to custodial care and discipline.

Defeatism in Ghetto Schools

As Haryou gathered data on the schools, it became increasingly clear that the attitude of the teachers toward their students was emerging as a most important factor in attempting to understand the massive retardation of these children. It was necessary to find out what they really felt, and so the schools were asked to recommend teachers

---

* *Youth in the Ghetto, op. cit.,* pp. 212–213.

to discuss the problems of teachers in slum schools. Interviews were held; group discussions were conducted; questionnaires were distributed. They tended to make clear what a crucial role the teachers really played in the success or failure of their students. The problems of identifying with children of different backgrounds—especially for persons from the white middle class—the problems of rejection of children deemed unappealing or alien, and the problems of achieving empathy are multiple. Courses in educational philosophy and psychology as presently taught do not prepare these teachers for the challenge of their job.

The pattern of teaching in Harlem is one of short tenure and inexperience. Many white teachers are afraid to work in Harlem; some Negroes consider a post outside of Harlem to be a sign of status. Discipline problems pervade a number of the schools, as students show contempt for teachers and principals they do not respect; and, in turn, the emphasis on "good discipline" displaces an emphasis on learning, both in evaluating a teacher's record and in a teacher's estimate of his own effectiveness. Apathy seems pervasive.

A pattern of violence expected from students and counterforce from the teachers creates a brutalizing atmosphere in which any learning would be hard. One teacher reported: "The children are not taught anything; they are just slapped around and nobody bothers to do anything about it."

Some teachers say or imply that Harlem children expect to be beaten:

When I came to school "X," I had never seen anything like that school. I cried, they behaved so badly. I soon learned that the boys like to be beaten; like to be spoken to in the way in which they are accustomed, and when I learned to say things to them that, to me, would be absolutely insulting and to hit them when they needed it, I got along all right and they began to like me. Somehow that made them feel that I liked them. I talked to them in the terms and in the way to which they are accustomed, and they like it.

Another white teacher said:

Here, both the Negro and white teachers feel completely free to beat up the children, and the principal knows it. They know he knows it and that nothing will be done about it. The principal is prejudiced. Because he knows he is prejudiced, he covers it by giving the Negro teachers the best classes. The Negro teachers are the best teachers because they are more stable. Some colored and white teachers ask for the worst classes because they don't want to work. In the worst classes they don't have to work because whatever happens, they can just say, "It is the children." The white teachers are largely inexperienced—the principal does not expect very much from the teachers. He often says, openly, "Why did they put me here?" The Board of Education should have put an experienced principal there. There is a lot of brutality—brutal beatings, and nobody cares—nothing is done about it. The parents, the principal and the teachers don't care.

One teacher told of a teacher who exploited his students:

The teacher should set a good example; not a teacher who comes to class to shave, clean his teeth, and sleep—as does one of the teachers in my school. Then, so that he will be free of responsibility, he tells one of the bullies of the class to strong-arm the class and keep order.

One teacher of some sensitivity commented on the reaction of Negro children to the often severe, even brutal punishment inflicted upon them:

A child won't respond to minor discipline and will more often only respond to a more brutal form of discipline. There is inconsistent discipline and a lot of brutality in the Harlem schools. Many children are immature and, therefore, are extremely hurt by being disciplined. I have had the experience of children running out of the room after they had been yelled at—there seems to be a very low frustration point at which they can take discipline.

It is only in a context of utter apathy that such behavior could be tolerated. If only one teacher could talk of children expecting to be beaten, this would be evidence of inhumanity. The fact is that in the ghetto schools many teachers believe that such discipline is necessary for children who come from ghetto homes. In such an atmosphere where the priority is not on superior teaching, it is not surprising to discover that nearly half of the school personnel report that they find their work in the ghetto "more demanding and less satisfying" than work in other parts of the city.

Negro teachers tended to feel that the Negroes in Harlem are better teachers than the whites, in part because they stayed longer and could keep better discipline. One Negro woman teacher said that a white male teacher constantly asked her to restore order in his classroom. Whites, in turn, often feel a Harlem post is a step down. A Negro teacher said Harlem schools are "a dumping ground for condemned white teachers." Some white teachers report that they feel uneasy with Negroes. One white teacher interviewed said, "When I walk through the streets here I feel conspicuous; I would like to be able to blend into the scenery." Yet there are a number of dedicated men and women for whom the job of teaching the many neglected children of Harlem brings satisfaction and reward.

White teachers who feel they are in hostile territory and Negro teachers who resent their presence can hardly be expected to work together without friction. Much of the feeling is repressed, however, and only emerges in depth interviews conducted in confidence. Negroes express the feeling that whites feel and act superior and "cold" even when they are less well educated. Many of the white teachers are Jewish; for some of them this fact brings a sense of identification with another oppressed minority; for others, an impatience with an ethnic group, unlike their own, where the tradition of eager learning has not yet been firmly established. One Negro teacher expressed her view on the subject in these words:

I find that the Jewish people, in particular, will protect their own and are protected by their own. In our school, this young teacher says that the children "just can't be taught" and even when the method used to teach is not a good one, she blames the children for not having the mentality to learn.

Unless she is a lackey, the Negro teacher has a hard road to travel. Mostly, they are doing a good job, but I don't think that there are enough Negroes in the teaching field with the guts to fight against the things that should not be. Negro teachers are too often trying to placate and please the white teachers. Most of the white teachers are Jewish. They respect the Negro who will fight, but if they find that they will not fight, they will walk all over them.

Negro teachers generally prefer not to associate with white teachers. As one said:

I, by choice, try not to socialize with them because I get sick and tired of hearing how our children will never amount to anything, our children are ignorant, the homes they come from are so deprived, these children are nothing, and so forth, and so on. I get tired of hearing this conversation even though I realize there is a problem.

Another Negro implied that friendliness to white teachers was taboo, and would be frowned upon or punished by her Negro colleagues:

I am a person who has been around and I get tired of "Oh, you feel white today, you're eating with the white teachers." "Oh, ha, she's joining their gang, she's turning on us." I won't eat with any of them. You know what, I'd rather go down to the Harlem Embers and eat by myself.

The dominant and disturbing fact about the ghetto schools is that the teachers and the students regard each other as adversaries. Under these conditions the teachers are reluctant to teach and the students retaliate and resist learning.

Negroes seldom move up the ladder of promotion in urban school systems. There are only six Negroes out of more than 1,200 top-level administrators in New York City, and only three Negroes out of 800 are full principals. Practically all of the Negroes are to be found quite far down in the organizational hierarchy—a fact discouraging in the extreme to Negro teachers and indirectly damaging to the self-image of Negro children who rarely see Negroes in posts of authority.

In past attempts to obtain experienced and qualified teachers for the schools in deprived communities, the Board of Education of the City of New York has not used its statutory power to assign teachers to these schools. The implicit and explicit reasons for not doing so were based upon the assumption that, given the "teacher shortage," teachers would refuse to accept such assignments and would leave the New York City school system if the board insisted upon exercising its power to make such assignments. The board, therefore, sought "volunteers" for these schools and flirted with proposals for providing extra bonuses for teachers who sought assignments in them. These methods have not been successful. The Allen Report declared that:

A spurious "reward structure" exists within the staffing pattern of the New York schools. Through it, less experienced and less competent teachers are assigned to the least "desirable" yet professionally most demanding depressed area schools. As the teacher gains experience and demonstrated competence, his mobility upward usually means mobility away from the pupils with the greatest need for skilled help. The classrooms that most urgently need the best teachers are thus often deprived of them.

Schools in deprived communities have a disproportionately high number of substitute and unlicensed teachers. Some of the classes in these schools have as many as ten or more different teachers in a single school year. Although precise figures are unavailable, nearly half of the teachers answering a Haryou questionnaire said they had held their posts for three years or less—far more than the citywide average (20 percent in present post three years or less).

The persistent failure on the part of the New York Board of Education to solve the problem of the adequate staffing of these schools points to the need for a new approach to this problem. It is suggested that teachers be selected for assignment in these schools in terms of their special qualifications, training, and human understanding. Rather than seek to entice, cajole, or bribe teachers into serving in such "hardship or ghetto outposts," the board should set up rather rigorous standards and qualifications for the teachers who would be invited or accepted for this type of service. These teachers should be motivated and recognized as *master teachers* or individuals working toward such professional recognition. Realistic professional and financial incentives must be provided if this professional status is to be other than perfunctory or nominal. Extra pay should be specifically tied to superior skill and more challenging responsibilities. A high-level professional atmosphere of competent and understanding supervision, a system of accountability—objective appraisal of professional performance—and a general atmosphere conducive to high-quality teaching and clear standards for differentiation of inferior, mediocre, and superior teaching with appropriate corrections and rewards must be maintained.

Excellent teaching can be obtained and sustained only under conditions of excellent supervision. The roles of field assistant superintendents, principals, and assistant principals must be re-examined. Those individuals who are assigned to schools in deprived communities must be selected in terms of special competence and in terms of the highest professional and personal standards. It should be understood that they would be judged primarily, if not exclusively, in terms of objective evidence.

Evidence of Effective Learning

The schools in the ghetto have lost faith in the ability of their students to learn and the ghetto has lost faith in the ability of the schools to lead. There are two conflicting points of view—one, that the pupils do not learn because they cannot; the other, that they do not learn because they are not taught. The fact is they are not learning. The problem is to see that they do, and only when the attempt is made with enthusiasm and competence will the answer be clear. As the Haryou report said:

Children do enter school with individual differences in experience, skills, and attitudes which make teaching more or less difficult. It is not unreasonable to expect that some of these differences will stem from differences in cultural or economic background. What has not been demonstrated, however, is that these differences constitute a permanent barrier to learning.

How long does it take to learn the colors of the spectrum, or develop the manipulative skills needed in order to do first grade work?

The studies cited by school administrators are silent on this point. Further, the data here presented show that the major deterioration in learning takes place between the third and sixth grades, not in the first and second grades. This leads to the inference that underachievement is the result of an accumulation of deficiencies while in school, rather than the result of deficiencies prior to school.*

Given no evidence to the contrary, the assumption can be made that cultural and economic backgrounds of pupils do not constitute a barrier to the type of learning which can reasonably be expected of normal children in the elementary grades—however much of a barrier such backgrounds are in respect to social problems such as

* *Youth in the Ghetto, op cit.,* pp. 239–240.

delinquency, emotional stability, and the like. Only when it is permitted to be a barrier does it become a cumulative deteriorating force.

What are the facts that are presently available that would substantiate this point of view? A few examples follow:

1. A "crash program" of remedial reading for one summer month starting in 1955 and continuing until the summer of 1964 (the data available, however, cover only 1955–1959) at Northside Center for Child Development in New York discovered that a child who has one month of extra daily instruction can gain on the average of almost one school year in reading. The children with the least retardation gained the most—those with I.Q.'s of above 110 gained more than two years in reading achievement, but the most retarded gained at least five months. The 104 children helped came eagerly and voluntarily to the program. Attendance never was less than 85 percent. Those who came more learned more.

This study of large numbers of woefully retarded, economically inferior Negro and Puerto Rican students reveals that such children can learn if taught. Nothing was done to change their "cultural deprivation." The only thing that was done was that they were being taught to read by individuals who believed that they could learn to read and who related to them with warmth and acceptance. Under these conditions they learned. And what is more, they sustained what they had learned during the school year. It is ironic, however, that when they returned to school they sustained their summer gains but they did not advance further.

All studies of the problem of education in deprived communities agree in concluding that the central problem in ghetto schools is the fact that the children are woefully deficient in reading. It has been suggested by the remedial reading staff of Northside Center that as a necessary first step in the development of a program to attain educational excellence in the Harlem schools, the Board of Education drop its normal curriculum in these schools for a period of half a school year, or perhaps a full school year, and immediately mobilize all of its resources toward the goal of raising the reading level of all children in the Harlem schools, especially those from the third to the eighth grades. During this *Reading Mobilization Year* the total school program in these schools would be geared toward the improvement of reading. All other school work would be temporarily postponed for those children who are retarded until they are brought up to grade level.

There is general agreement also, supported by Haryou's research findings and by the Board of Education itself, that there is a desperate need for afterschool remedial centers. Space is available in churches, renovated store fronts and lofts, social agencies, and community centers. What is not agreed upon, however, is the most effective type of remedial program. There is serious question whether submitting the child who has already experienced defeat in school to the same teachers, techniques, classroom settings, and general atmosphere is likely to result in any great educational achievement. An effective remedial program would require a revised curriculum, advanced teaching techniques and materials, a stimulating atmosphere, and generally increased motivation.

2. "Culturally deprived" children have learned in those public schools in which they are expected to learn and in which they are taught. Children attending Harlem schools in the 1920s and 1930s had average academic achievement close to, if not equal to, the white norms. Klineberg's study of the performance of Negro children migrating from the South to the North and those already in Northern schools during the thirties can be used as evidence that at that time the discrepancy between norms of white students and those of Negro students was minimal compared with the present gap.* It would be difficult to argue and to prove the contention that Negroes at that time were less culturally deprived than they were in the 1950s or than they are now.

3. Junior High School 43 on the periphery of Harlem, like most Harlem schools, was holding largely a custodial program for the "culturally deprived." In 1956, before the pilot project began, the teachers felt helpless to teach. Their students seemed then to be hopeless, and considered themselves failures, their teachers as

---

* Otto Klineberg, *Negro Intelligence and Selective Migration,* New York, Columbia University Press, 1935.

enemies. Then the school became a pilot demonstration guidance program and what looked like a miracle occurred. Six times as many students went to college (25 percent) than had earlier (4 percent). The dropout rate fell one-half, from 50 percent to 25 percent. Eighty-one percent were judged to have greater intellectual capacity than their earlier I.Q. and achievement scores would have predicted— their I.Q.'s in the eleventh grade went up an average of eight to nine points. In the more than two years during which the tests were made, the average student gained 4.3 years in reading scores compared with 1.7 years during a similar earlier period. When one studies this pilot project, one does not find any revolutionary educational methods. Most of the New York City schools had both curriculum and individual counseling, trips and programs for parents, as did JHS 43, prior to the project.

The "miracle" seemed due primarily to an implementation of the belief that such children can learn.

School personnel were told to adopt an affirmative view of their students and give up their earlier negative views. Therefore, certain educational methods previously considered questionable for lower-class children were now used. Those who had openly blocked changes before became less influential in the wake of the prestige of the new project. Most of the emphasis on discipline was toned down. Teacher responsibility for maintaining order was relaxed. Students felt that they were "special," and that they were expected to achieve and learn. Teachers were evaluated more on their teaching skill than on their discipline. Because the school administration was eager for the success of the experiment, it opened many previously clogged channels of communication between itself and teachers, parents, and pupils. Originally this was meant to win their support, but also, the administration was unconsciously stimulated to solve some of the problems and attend to some of the grievances not necessarily related at all to the question of race. Teachers began to consider themselves competent and their students capable. Pupils were told that they were trustworthy and that their teachers were committed to helping them succeed. Parents were advised that they could help in their children's education and progress. There was no attempt, because the task was too formidable, to reverse the environment of cultural deprivation of the community's children.

The cyclic relationship between educational effectiveness and heightened morale is indicated by the fact that a serious program designed to increase educational effectiveness invariably heightens the morale of pupils, teachers, and supervisors; the heightened morale increases the chances of success of the educational program. Conversely, inferior education in a school decreases morale of teachers, pupils, and supervisors, and the decreased morale tends to reinforce the educational inefficiency.

4. The Banneker Project in St. Louis, Missouri, showed similar striking results.

In 1957, St. Louis high schools inaugurated a three-track system of ability grouping based upon standardized I.Q. and achievement scores. Students scoring high on both tests were placed in Track I and given college preparatory courses. Those scoring below average were placed in Track III and given vocational and technical courses. Average students fell into Track II.

The Banneker School District is one of five elementary school groups in St. Louis and is one of two having the largest proportion of Negroes. The neighborhood is characterized by old housing, slums, high crime rate, high unemployment, etc. Of the 16,000 pupils in the Banneker schools, 9,590 are Negro.

The initial test scores for students in the Banneker District showed that only 7 percent had Track I scores, whereas 47 percent went into Track III. The median scores for reading, arithmetic, and language achievement were consistently below grade level. Otis Intelligence Test scores for 1958–1959 showed Banneker children with an I.Q. median of 90.5, with 12.1 percent below I.Q. 79.

The district director, Dr. Samuel Shepard, immediately moved to improve performance, suggesting that the children had not been properly prepared for the testing experience and for that reason did not measure up as well as they might have if well motivated. Shepard initiated a program designed to stimulate teachers to teach students to learn, and parents to facilitate learning. The initial scores were graphically and comparatively represented to teachers, principals, students, and parents. It was made quite clear, however, that the low standing of Banneker children relative to children in other parts of the city was not to be ignored or explained away as the inevitable consequence of underprivilege. Rather, it was to be used to bring about improvement.

Principals were asked to help teachers have a more positive attitude toward the children and their chances for success. Teachers were to visit the homes of their pupils to familiarize themselves with the social and familial situation. In addition, teachers were asked to ignore I.Q. scores and to treat all children as if they had superior ability. As a result of this intensive, yet inexpensive and relatively uncomplicated approach, eighth graders went from 7.7 years in reading to 8.8 in two and one-half years; from 7.6 in language to 9.1; and 7.9 to 8.7 in arithmetic. Children assigned to Track I increased from 7 percent to 22 percent, while Track III assignments fell from 47.1 percent to 10.9 percent. Attendance in one school reached an unprecedented 97.1 percent. The median I.Q. was raised almost ten points.

In spite of the fact that there had been no drastic change in curriculum, instructional technique, or the basic "underprivileged" social situation, improvements were definitely evident. What had changed was the attitude and perspective of teachers which influenced the way in which the students were taught and learned.

5. Baltimore, Maryland, has tried another interesting program— this one a preschool year for sixty children of four years of age in two of the city's most depressed neighborhoods, both Negro, where crime and delinquency rates have been so high that teachers hesitated to make home visits alone or at night. Francis Keppel, U.S. Commissioner of Education, reports that the school administrator in charge, Mrs. Catherine Brunner, has found that: Every child who entered in 1963 began kindergarten the following year, a record their older brothers and sisters had not matched. In kindergarten they did as well as children from middle- or upper-class families. In first grade, they showed better use of language, superior understanding of ideas and problem solving than other children from the same depressed neighborhoods. In the first grade, two-thirds of the original

sixty were in the top half of their class; ten in the top quarter. Keppel quotes one kindergarten teacher's "candid and heartwarming judgment" of the project:

I've always been in the habit of dividing my kindergarten classes into two sections—those who come from poor neighborhoods and lack much background for learning, and those who come from better homes and are accustomed to books and cultural experiences in their families. In a sense, this has also seemed a logical division between the dull children, the ones who need help, and the bright ones, who go along very quickly.

But what seemed so logical before the project started now doesn't seem logical to me today. The youngsters who have this new preschool experience, I'm finding, belong among the highest achieving children in my classes and this is where I place them. It makes me wonder now whether many of us in teaching haven't a great deal to learn ourselves.

Despite the evidence of the effectiveness of early childhood education for the growth and development of children, public schools have not made adequate provision for extensive preprimary education. For children who live in disadvantaged circumstances, well-organized centers for early childhood education can partially compensate for lack of opportunities for wholesome development in these formative years.

There are more than 12,000 children between three and six years of age in Harlem. All of the twenty elementary schools in the area have kindergartens which children may enter at the age of five, but there are at least 4,000 children under five who should have preschool education if community pathology is to be resisted. Haryou proposed that in each school zone, two preschool academies be established, each serving 100 children three through five years old. At first, preference would be given to the four- and five-year olds. But preschool experience, however desirable for its own sake, will not lead children to learn basic skills in the primary grades if, when they reach these grades, the schools react to them as though they cannot learn.

One variable held constant in each of these programs is the nature and extent of the cultural deprivation found in the particular group before the program began. The programs' success then would have to be due either to the unlikely fact that the culturally deprived are particularly responsive to a program of education or that their deprivation is less important in their success than other factors— such as the faith of the teachers, the quality of the education. The common denominator in all these successful programs was more efficient teaching—these children can be taught if they are accepted and respected. But how does one transform an apathetic teacher into an empathic, accepting, and enthusiastic one?

If it were assumed on the other hand that teachers could only teach children who came from homes where learning is respected and encouraged, it would be analogous to physicians asserting that they could only help patients who are not too ill, or who are not ill at all.

If the cultural deprivation theories are valid and relevant explanations of the widespread problem, then it would follow that the extent and degree of academic retardation would be constant, that is, the same, under different conditions and at varying periods of time as long as the social, economic, and cultural conditions of the Negro group remained the same. A related hypothesis would be that the degree of retardation would increase or decrease in proportion to similar changes in the status of the Negro. Any evidence showing constancy in the degree of retardation in spite of changes in the economic and social status of the Negro would seem to raise serious questions about the cultural deprivation theories, and it would then be necessary to seek explanations of the academic retardation of Negro children in terms of variables directly related to the educational processes: What is happening in the classroom? Are these children being taught or are they being ignored? What is the attitude of their teachers toward them? Are they seen as primitive, unmanageable discipline problems and burdens, rather than as modifiable human beings who will respond positively if they are reacted to positively? In short, are these children seen as essentially uneducable because they are racially or culturally inferior? In the 1930s, Otto Klineberg, as noted earlier, succeeded in demonstrating that the academic performance of Negro youngsters in the New York City public schools was nearly equal to that of whites. The economic conditions of Negroes at that time were significantly lower than today. To assume that Negro children are inherently inferior or that environmental inferiority is responsible for poor school performance is educationally irrelevant—and even false. The assumption of inferiority might be the controlling fact which restricts the educational responsiveness of children to the alleged educational experience. In this regard, racial inferiority and cultural inferiority have identical practical educational consequences. This might, therefore, be the chief obstacle—the subtle, insidious human obstacle—which must be overcome if lower-status children are to be educated up to a level of efficiency necessary to bring them within a useful and creative role in society.

There is considerable evidence that this can be done. It has been done. The resistance to accepting this evidence and implementing it, the insistence upon labeling these children with euphemistically derogatory terms, might be the key human and educational problems to be studied if our society is to obtain the benefits of the trained intelligence of these children.

This is not to say that a teacher's affirmative attitude toward children is the only relevant factor influencing the performance of children in ghetto schools and that overcrowded classrooms, inadequate plants and facilities, unimaginative curricula, and the like, are irrelevant. All of these influence a child's educational growth. The point is rather that these factors cannot be given equal importance; in the light of available evidence the controlling factor which determines the academic performance of pupils and which establishes the level of educational efficiency and the over-all quality of the schools is the competence of the teachers and their attitude of acceptance or rejection of their students. Competent teachers who have confidence in children strive to achieve the other dimensions of good education also. But without such competence and confidence, children do not learn even if the textbooks are new and the classes small. There are ghetto schools which are brand new. There are some ghetto schools with comparatively small classes and with adequate facilities. But there are few ghetto schools where the morale of teachers and pupils is high and where the teachers truly believe in the humanity and capacity of the children to learn. In those few schools the children learn.

The pilot experiments in St. Louis, New York, and elsewhere are encouraging evidence that children can learn when they are expected to learn. The Negro child, like the Negro teacher, must be held to the same high standards of academic performance as their white counterparts in white schools. Obviously some Negroes, like some whites, will not have the innate capacity to respond. But many will, and each deserves the chance. Negro students cannot be excused for shoddy performance *because* they are Negro. To do so makes more rigid and intolerable the pathology, injustices, and distinctions of racism. There can be no double standards in education, no easy alibi. Schools are institutions designed to compensate for "cultural deprivation." If this were not true there would be no need for schools.

The schools are crucial to any positive resolution of the problems of the ghetto. As long as these ghetto schools continue to turn out thousands and thousands of functional illiterates yearly, Negro youth will not be prepared for anything other than menial jobs or unemployment and dependency; they will continue the cycle of broken homes, unstable family life, and neglected and uneducated children. The tragic waste of human resources will go on unabated.

The Role of Leadership

Some powerful voices are now being raised in major colleges and universities in behalf of quality education for children of the ghetto. For the first time, leaders outside of the civil rights movement itself are joining in such demands. James Bryant Conant, Francis Keppel, John Kenneth Galbraith, John Monro, and others have endorsed the Negro's urgent quest for equality in public education. Galbraith has called for an emergency education program as part of the war on poverty, a program that would select one hundred of the lowest-income counties or slum areas as special educational districts to be equipped with superior school plants and an elite corps of teachers—after the manner of the Peace Corps—"tough and well-trained enough to take on the worst slums, proud to go to Harlan County or to Harlem." John Monro, dean of Harvard College, proposed to Haryou a total reorganization of the Harlem schools, with revision of curriculums, teaching methods, testing, guidance, remedial work, in a deliberately "avant garde, experimental, inventive" program. Such schools would need to be "expensive schools, just as any really good school is expensive"; and if the project in Harlem were successful, he said, it could serve as a model for projects elsewhere. Universities like Harvard, Yale, Columbia, the City University of New York, Princeton, and Howard would, Monro believes, be willing, even eager, to be potential sponsors of such a program, more cognizant than they used to be of their social responsibilities, less proud of the detachment of the ivory tower.

But the trouble with most such imaginative proposals is that they often end with the expression of them. To translate them into action takes more than the imagination of individuals; it takes the power of society. If some have initiative, others are gripped with inertia, not the least among them educators themselves, some of whom have come to believe that ghetto children are really inferior and cannot learn, others of whom know better but sense the helplessness of the ghetto parents and of the ghetto's political, economic, social, and religious leaders.

The first voices raised to demand quality education for ghetto children, embarrassingly enough, came not from educators but from civil rights leaders. Unfortunately, major social change within institutions usually comes only in response to outside force, seldom in response to self-criticism. But any sustained ghetto force so far has been muted and ineffective.

In the North much of the energy of civil rights groups has been directed toward the goal of quality integrated education. But their sporadic demonstrations, dramatic and fervent though they have been, cannot succeed in achieving sustained fundamental change in the schools. Such change can only come when the majority sources of power recognize the danger to themselves and to their communities and proceed to act. Otherwise, reports and recommendations will come and go, and the energy of protest will be dissolved in cathartic, sputtering explosions.

In 1964, at the request of James E. Allen, Jr., commissioner of education of the state of New York, the commissioner's Advisory Committee on Human Relations and Community Tensions posed its series of recommendations to the city, pointing out that integration and quality education are dependent on each other.* If there were no white children in the public schools, the schools could not be integrated. The Allen Committee, thereupon, interested itself in the reasons for the flight of middle-class whites from the New York City public schools—a flight that has its counterpart in every Northern city. They found that whites were leaving the public schools at an alarming rate to escape what they believed to be the inferior— and deteriorating—public schools, those in which the proportion of Negroes was increasing. In the minds of such middle-class whites, inferior schools and Negroes went together. They can only be disabused of that belief if such schools are, in fact, superior. At present, the reasons given for middle-class flight into the suburbs or into the private and parochial schools become self-fulfilling prophecies, for as whites leave the schools, the quality of the schools does indeed decline—*not* because Negroes are inferior, but because the school system behaves as though they are. The Allen Committee proposed a comprehensive plan which would change the pattern of segregation in the schools and move toward quality education in a variety of ways: by shifting grades now heavily segregated (like the ninth) into more integrated schools (in this case, into high schools); by building any new schools neither in the ghettos nor in segregated white neighborhoods but in neighborhoods that, though predominantly white, are moving toward integration; by using shuttle buses for middle-school children in the fifth through eighth grades for ten- to fifteen-minute rides to integrated schools; by extending the definition of "neighborhood" for primary schools; by moving toward a system of educational complexes, clusters of schools for children of different

* The members of the committee were John H. Fischer, Judah Cahn, and Kenneth B. Clark.

age levels and ethnic background with shared activities, and to be replaced eventually by educational parks of groups of schools on new sites. The plan called also for preprimary programs to help young children from deprived backgrounds prepare for the demands of the elementary grades, and for special methods to recruit superior teachers and administrators for ghetto schools. This part of the program is similar to the Haryou recommendations.

A preprimary program, limited in scope, has begun. But in other ways, business as usual is underway despite the public support which the Allen proposals received. Plans to build new schools in segregated white neighborhoods continue. So, too, successful pilot programs—like Harlem's Junior High School 43 project—have not only failed to stimulate educational reform in other schools, but the pilot projects themselves have been dropped. It is almost as though a pilot demonstration was meant to serve as a diversionary method and was never intended as a test whose results would lead to action. But, though the failure was doubtless due more to inertia than anything else, it is especially cruel to the neglected child to offer him hope by showing that he can succeed if someone believes in him and then to withdraw that hope. One of the few exceptions to this dismal rule seems to be the work of Dr. Samuel Shepard in the Banneker School project of St. Louis. When this project was found successful, it was continued.

In general, the more responsible and skillful educational officials seem to have perfected the ability to ride out the periodic ghetto storms of demands for integrated quality education by gracious discussions and negotiations with representatives of local civil rights groups. The officials make what seem to be promises and agreements, only to ignore or modify them after the storm has died down. Once again, the energies of the ghetto that might lead to constructive change are dissipated and distorted. The more advantaged children, whose parents own practical power—parents with whom the educators themselves identify—continue to get preferential treatment in the public schools and to respond by superior educational achievement. The public schools, as a result, are beginning to betray the purpose for which they were founded: to give each child an equal chance to education and to serve as an impetus for progress of the poor and neglected into the circle of democratic opportunity. Instead, the public schools are becoming an instrument for the perpetuation— and strengthening—of class and caste, while the elite cluster in their safe suburban schools or in the exclusive private schools.

Such a default in leadership by professional educators can only reduce their total influence in the community at large. A default in leadership from school boards can only make such boards futile exercises in democratic control. Yet in matters of health, the medical profession seldom submits to the fears and anxieties of the uninformed or to the pressures of vested interests. Can educational leadership consider the educational health of a community to be less important? If leaders do not lead when the need is urgent, what is the nature of their leadership? If educators respond merely to pressure, whether it is *against* integration, like the Parents and Taxpayers groups, or *for* it, as in the case of the civil rights boycotts, they have abdicated their right to decision on the basis of their knowledge and insight as educators, and submitted to force for the sake of peace at almost any price. This is a passive rather than a dynamic, socially responsible role. They must respond rather to need, for the poor and neglected are generally too intimidated by authority, too fearful of rejection and humiliation, to press their own cause. It is the responsibility of strong leadership to represent the common good—not only because it is right, but because the despair of the weak in the end threatens the stability of the whole.

Crucial to the issue, too, is the fact that educators themselves, and the boards of education, do not see themselves as having power. Indeed, the failure to assert and use what they had may have atrophied the power that remained. And it may be true that genuine power does lie elsewhere, that educational power is secondary to political power, and political power secondary to economic power. The real decisions can only be made by those who have the most to lose from social decay. The time has come when the economic princes of power can no longer take their cues from those marginal middle class whites whose immediate anxieties do not necessarily coincide with their own long-term interests or with the good of society as a whole. If the middle class white leaves the heart of America's cities, the cities will wither. The response of economic power to the blight of the city must be as creative and daring as the need is great. Ways must be found to mobilize the power of industry and business to sustain the economic, social, and intellectual life of urban America.

In New York, a conference of top business leaders like David Rockefeller, John Whitney, Robert Dowling could assume responsibility for deciding what must be done with the city's public educational system if the stability and viability of the metropolis are to be assured. A consensus and commitment for action from such a group— and its counterparts in other cities—would impel political leadership to action. Political power would, in turn, demand of the educational bureaucracy that it take appropriate measures to effect change. This is not contrary to the democratic process but the justification of it. The people—both white and Negro—have already called attention to their need for quality education and agitated for action. They have, in a sense, "voted" a mandate for their leaders to act. The future vitality of democracy may depend on the response of power to this demand and therefore upon the capacity of a free society to achieve its own transformation with intelligence, thereby minimizing the possibility of chaos.

7

THE POWER STRUCTURE
OF THE GHETTO

Power must be understood to be used properly, if it is to avoid dilution into the appearance of power. Power, misunderstood or miscalculated, increases the dangers of its explosive dissipation or stagnation. It is essential to analyze the sources of power—the strengths and weaknesses—within America's dark ghettos if any realistic diagnosis and predictions about their future are to be possible.

The ghetto is, in a manner, self-perpetuating, and while it encourages some for attempting change, it rewards others for loyalty to things as they are. Inside the ghetto lie sources of energy that are ordinarily mobilized, overtly or covertly, to prevent change and to perpetuate and exploit the *status quo*. Outside the ghetto, too, are sources of energy that depend on the ghetto for their own security—all exploitation rests upon real or imagined advantages to the exploiters. Therefore, any social action to transform the ghetto must expect to face apathy and hostility from both Negroes and whites—for a ghetto can be a cocoon as well as a cage.

Social institutions—the church, the courts, the legislature, the executive regulatory agencies, the police and, in ultimate cases, the military—are intended generally to protect society-as-it-is, though

154

at times, they themselves may—as the Supreme Court did in the 1954 school desegregation cases—be a powerful stimulus to change. Democratic government tends to be limited in its capacity to respond to the demands of minority or lower-status groups because it is necessarily dependent either upon majority support or upon those groups that already have economic, political, and social status and power. The successful politician seeks to find a balance between the demands of those who wish to change and the resistance of those who are determined to prevent it. American political history is the record of adjustment to the needs of those minorities most restless at any one time—and a postponement or dilution of the requests of those groups that are, at the time, relatively satisfied or quiescent. The strategy of such compromise responds to tension among competing forces and is inevitable in a democratic society. Ironically, the earlier minorities whose needs have been satisfied may themselves join to form a coalition against the rising demands of a newly articulate minority, as many labor unions have done in the past, in response to the claims of Negroes.

If Negroes are to use their new-found energy most effectively, it will be necessary for them to learn the ways of power and to avoid the delusion of pseudopower.

Political Power

The most obvious of the social sources of power is political, yet Negroes have failed so far to translate their vote into effective action in their own behalf. In the South, persecution has combined with apathy to keep Negroes from the polls, but registration drives and some federal protection have reversed the trend in recent years. In the North, Negroes vote, though usually in smaller proportion than whites. There is a circular pattern in political behavior, for ineffective use of the vote limits a group's political influence while its political powerlessness may in turn seem convincing evidence that voting is useless, leading to apathy. But votes alone do not necessarily imply actual political power, in the sense of control of the direction of social changes, for seldom are the issues of an election clear-cut enough for victory to imply a mandate for a particular program.

The effective exercise of power in the urban ghetto is crippled severely by the inexperience of the ghetto's own political leaders. Their inexperience and political unsophistication have a fundamental root—the psychology of the ghetto with its pervasive and total sense of helplessness. It is difficult, if not impossible, to behave as one with power when all one's experience has indicated that one has none. Because their house of political power is built on sand without a solid base of economic or social influence, ghetto politicians are likely to accept a limited jurisdiction and to seek immediate and concrete rewards. They often subject themselves to the control of others they believe to hold the primary power, and some are prepared to make petty deals and to toy with political corruption. But even in corruption the Negro is accorded second-class citizenship. Negro urban leaders, to illustrate, seldom have access to decisions on bids for multimillion-dollar construction projects. Those who are susceptible to temptation are restricted to marginal graft like the numbers racket. Negroes felt it an ironic confirmation of their low status that when the first Negro to be borough president of Manhattan lost his position it involved not a million-dollar conspiracy but a less than $5,000 apartment renovation. In political patronage, too, Negro politicians are restricted to the lower levels of reward. The hard facts generally tend to limit the outreach and the effectiveness of the ghetto politicians. Unable to compete successfully for power or patronage, they tend to compete among themselves for the available crumbs; and this struggle, in turn, makes them more vulnerable to manipulation by real political leadership—i.e., white leadership. When no one has much patronage or much power, rivalry for a minimal share keeps everyone divided and everyone impotent.

Politics, like other aspects of American culture has been afflicted with Jim Crow. Before 1935, the Democratic organization in Harlem was strictly segregated. Negroes had their "own" clubs (generally in the basement of the regular club) and elected their own leaders. No Negro was on the Democratic County Committee.

The first official Negro member of the Democratic County Committee from Harlem was Harlem businessman Herbert L. Bruce. He succeeded in winning a leadership post through a merger of two competing Negro clubs which managed to get more votes together than the white candidate, although the white candidate had more votes than either one of the Negro clubs separately. Bruce took his place on the County Committee in 1935 and resigned undefeated in 1953. During his tenure, he proved to be a dynamic and respected leader. He took no money from Tammany to run his district and, therefore, when he went "downtown," he could demand, and did not need to beg.

With the exceptions of Congressmen William Dawson of Chicago and Adam Clayton Powell of New York, and J. Raymond Jones, no Negro political leader in America has ever moved from his constricted ghetto position into any really top post. Top posts have gone to others. For example, William Hastie, who was the first Negro judge of a federal circuit court, was appointed from his vantage post of experience as dean of Howard University Law School and as governor of the Virgin Islands. Thurgood Marshall, the second Negro to reach the United States Court of Appeals, moved there from his job as director of the NAACP Legal Defense and Educational Fund. Ralph Bunche accepted a position as undersecretary in the United Nations after a distinguished career with Howard University as professor of political science, with the Office of Strategic Services, and with the State Department. Carl Rowan became director of the United States Information Agency after a strong newspaper career in the "white press," followed by a brief but distinguished service in the State Department. Robert C. Weaver arrived at his post as director of the Federal Housing and Home Finance Agency after a career as economist and as an authority on state and local housing problems. Edward Brooke, the first Negro attorney general of a state, achieved this position by way of a successful legal career in Massachusetts and through his recognized effectiveness as a member of the Boston Finance Commission. He was appointed to this post in 1960 by a Republican governor. He was elected in 1962 and reelected in 1964 despite an overwhelming national Democratic landslide. Franklin H. Williams, United

States Ambassador serving on the Economic and Social Council of the United Nations, moved to this post from an apprenticeship on the staff of the NAACP, and was West Coast representative of that organization until he joined the Peace Corps under Sargent Shriver. Negroes who have made a name for themselves through competition in the white community in the professions and through the civil rights movement have therefore been far more likely to reach a place of power than have the Negro politicians themselves. Most Negro politicians have never been given a chance to operate outside of the ghetto sphere, in part because they have not focused their energies on civil rights or matters of general public concern but on representing Negro constituents within their districts—in the manner of politicians generally. Whereas this does not handicap a white politician unduly from advancement, it is part of the nature of the ghetto that the white power structure comes to see Negro political figures as reflections of the limitations of the ghetto itself, as men without potential for other larger jobs. Some top civil rights leaders, who have operated within the nonghetto power structure, e.g., in the courts, which are essentially white-dominated, have been compelled to meet the competitive standards of the community at large, which is white, and they have been able to wrest concessions from it and thereby to gain respect and further power.

Traditional Negro politicians would have preferred that Negroes appointed to federal judgeships, for example, be those who had moved gradually up the political ladder. But white officials have tended rather to appoint Negroes who have achieved stature by another route. Where the Negroes chosen were of stature, as with Hastie and Marshall, the politicians had to accept the appointments in good grace. Where the prospective appointees have not been of commanding stature, the Negro politicians have succeeded in blocking the promotions even at the cost of losing the post for a Negro altogether. Negro politicians have justified such pressure as a simple political expedient; if rewards go to those who have not served a political apprenticeship, Negroes will not have the patience to persist in the political effort necessary to build sound party structure.

It should be pointed out, moreover, that some Negroes express concern about the increasing tendency of government—federal, state, and local—to tap the limited pool of Negro talent available to the civil rights movement. There is some justification for the contention that if this continues it will weaken the civil rights movement itself. Some Negroes have even been cynical enough to ask whether this result is intended; and others, in turn, question the motivation of the civil rights leaders who do take such jobs, suggesting that this "proves" that they were only using the movement as a stepping stone to personal success. Such cynicism is consistent with one of the main character-istics of ghetto psychology—suspiciousness and doubt concerning the possibility that anyone, either white or Negro, can be motivated by other than self-serving interests. According to the laws of the ghetto, everyone has an angle.

J. Raymond Jones, Harlem political leader, is unusual because, though he began as a leader within the Harlem ghetto and was sub-ject to these same debilitating conditions of leadership, he refused to submit to its conditions. He approached white political leaders with a style and manner—and demands—that did not fit the stereo-type of Negro leadership. He was not willing "to settle for the Negro's share." He moved out of the Harlem ghetto into the larger and more demanding political arena of the larger city, into the borough of Man-hattan. In 1958 he dared to challenge the authority of the Tammany head, Carmine De Sapio, and sought to organize the rest of the Negro leaders to back Adam Clayton Powell in defiance of constituted white political leadership when De Sapio sought Powell's ouster from his congressional seat. He knew that De Sapio was seriously mistaken in thinking that Tammany Hall could defeat Powell in Harlem. It took courage even to know this obvious fact—many other Negro politicians had gone along in the style of the ghetto. But in the end the others reverted to the old competition; and after the Powell vic-tory, the coalition of Negro leaders fell apart, though Jones tried to hold it together. An important reason might be that some of these leaders suspected Jones of trying to build his own political empire at their expense. The irony is that their suspicions of him left them in the same kind of predicament of dependence on white leadership.

Jones had failed to calculate the tremendous power of the past patterns of ghetto deprivation that expressed themselves in suspicion and rivalry.

In the 1961 mayoralty election, in a stand of Tammany against reform leadership forces, De Sapio refused to back Mayor Robert Wagner. Here Jones, once again taking the initiative, convinced Wagner that competing political machines could be formed into a coalition to oppose and defeat the regular organization. Jones moved outside the ghetto and, armed with little more than the power of his own personality, organized the machinery for obtaining the petitions necessary to assure that Wagner's name would be placed on the ballot. The De Sapio–backed candidate lost and Wagner kept his control. The reform movement rode the crest of triumph. The question immediately arose: Who will succeed De Sapio as head of the New York County Democratic Committee—Tammany Hall? On criteria of political astuteness, independence, power of personality, consistency of position, and successful defiance of the regular bosses, Jones seemed likely to be De Sapio's successor. But never in the history of American politics had a Negro held such a powerful party leadership post. The reform Democrats opposed Jones on ground that he was not a member of a reform group, a charge that was technically correct. Still, if the reform goal was to lead a successful revolt against De Sapio and the common enemy, Jones had acted like a reformer. When a group of Negro leaders went to discuss the problem with former Governor Herbert H. Lehman, whom they considered a liberal, they learned that Lehman would not back Jones. A reform leader could not himself get the post, Lehman agreed, but Jones was not a suitable alternative. It was a prevalent rumor in Harlem that Wagner finally called Jones to his office and said that a number of his liberal supporters had told him that they did not believe the time was right for a Negro to serve as head of Tammany. He could not defy their wishes, he said. Instead, he offered Jones the innocuous position of his confidential political secretary. In the end, the reformers agreed on Edward Costikyan; and New York Negroes, rightly or wrongly, continued to believe he got the job primarily because he was white.

The incident indicated that even the most highly prepared and experienced Negro could not then be permitted to enter the primary councils of political power in New York City. This seemed particularly true of the Negroes known to be militant and independent. The problem posed for the white power structure has been the difficult one of how to use the talents and assets of such a Negro without letting him share the basic power and rewards of the system. As for the forces within the ghetto itself, the question was whether genuine social change could be expected to come from the primary sources of power in the "larger city" and, if not, how the ghetto's own latent and derivative power could be mobilized and transformed into actual primary power that does not depend on the *noblesse oblige* of others for its effectiveness.

Two years after Jones was bypassed for chairmanship of the County Committee, upon the resignation of Costikyan the issue was raised again since many persons, Negro and white, still believed that the most qualified person for the job was J. Raymond Jones. Jones had indicated earlier his intention of retiring, but it was clear that he would postpone any such plans if Mayor Wagner indicated a desire to have him serve as chairman. A complexity of forces, doubtless including the fact of the overwhelming election of President Johnson with its massive demonstration of Negro support for the Democratic party, led to the Mayor's decision to back Jones. With this support, Jones was, in the fall of 1964, elected to the post, the first Negro chosen as county leader of a major political party anywhere in the United States.

But the nature of the ghetto is such that one must face certain questions about the extent of Jones's future power:

1. Will he be permitted to have and exercise the political power traditionally associated with the post or will his power be diluted?

2. What kind of accommodation will be reached between Jones and the Reform wing of the Democratic party, which opposed his election?

3. What accommodation, if any, will he be able to work out with Adam Clayton Powell and other regular Democratic leaders, white and Negro?

Prior to his election as chairman, Jones was engaged in major conflict with Powell. The source of the dispute was both political and economic and the depth of the conflict seemed to have blocked the development of a powerful united political front in the Harlem community. In this regard, it is significant that one of Jones's first acts after his election was to seek a meeting with Powell, a meeting described by each as "amicable."

The New York daily newspapers generally questioned the advisability or the motives behind this haste on Jones's part to establish an alliance with Powell. This is consistent with the tendency of the metropolitan press to view him as "The Fox," a cunning and old-style machine politician. Their picture of Jones tends to rest largely upon the fact that he had remained loyal to the regular party apparatus even when in conflict with De Sapio. Such party loyalty has often been considered a virtue in other political leaders and was certainly viewed tolerantly by the public in two of the nation's most respected Presidents, Franklin Roosevelt and Harry Truman. Jones is unquestionably a political realist in the tradition of Roosevelt and Truman and a man of more stature than generally recognized. He is usually not given credit for his real social sensitivity, for his depth of concern for racial justice, and, perhaps, even most important in terms of his uses of power, a sense of his own personal human dignity. These characteristics, together with his acknowledged political craftsmanship would seem to demand a new evaluation of Jones as more than an ordinary machine politician. He is a proud man.

The election of Jones may well mean that Adam Clayton Powell is no longer the dominant figure among Negro political leaders. If the power of Jones's position is not diluted, then he will be the most important Negro in American politics. This is a major breakthrough, suggesting some hope for the dark ghetto. The test of his political acumen and a clue to the future of the ghetto may be found in the degree of his success in forging a strong unified political structure within the ghetto—and outside the ghetto—without compromising with or being drawn into the maelstrom of the ghetto's pathology.

Just as Jones's role as political leader has been, in the past at least, controlled in scope by the white power structure so, in a quite different way, is Adam Clayton Powell's. Powell's effectiveness in the ghetto is a consequence, in part, of his suave charm. Here is a man who is always in complete control of the gesture and posture, as sensitive to his role as an actor on a stage. He is narcissistic, but even his narcissism is under his control. He holds sway over his predominantly female congregation at the Abyssinian Baptist Church by dramatizing himself as the prototype of the desirable male aware of his power. He uses his appeal without apology. But Powell must be understood also in terms of the massive pathology of the ghetto, where a powerless people seek a concrete hero who will fight the battles they cannot fight for themselves. All the better if the hero defies and taunts the white enemy. Here is the gratifying joy of vicarious revenge without the attendant penalties of a real encounter.

In his flamboyant personal behavior, Powell has been to the Negroes a symbol of all that life has denied them. The Negro can in fantasy journey with Adam to the Riviera, enjoy a home in Puerto Rico, have beautiful girls at his beck and call, change wives "like rich white folks." Powell plays the role the Hollywood star may for whites but even more powerfully, for added to the magic and glamour of personal fame is the excitement and virtues of defiant racial protest.

The Negro masses do not see Powell as amoral but as defiantly honest in his protest against the myths and hypocrisies of racism. What whites regard as Powell's violation of elemental ethics, Negroes view as effective and amusing defiance. Whatever is the personal ethical moral standard of the individual Negro, it tends to be suspended in judgment of Powell. He is important precisely because he *is* a caricature, a burlesque, of the personal exploitation of power. His behavior merely focuses on the fact that certain respectable white congressmen, too, may use public funds for personal junkets or put their wives on the public payroll. The white power structure never successfully calls him to account and the Negro sees this and applauds. The *Amsterdam News* reacted to one of the more flagrant examples of Powell's defiant personal behavior with a front-page headline: "Ho Hum! They're 'After Adam' Again."* Whenever a *New York Times* editorial criticizes Powell, he is strengthened in the Negro com-

* February 9, 1963.

munity. When Powell is condemned by respectable whites, this is taken merely as evidence of his effectiveness, for clearly whites would not be concerned with an impotent Negro! Powell understands all this and uses the knowledge deliberately in an intelligent and effective way.

In the 1930s Powell became the symbol of the struggle for minimal Negro rights, his name a household word. He led picket lines to help Negro girls get jobs as clerks at Woolworth's on Harlem's 125th Street. In the early 1940s he demanded to know why no Negroes were teaching on the faculties of the city colleges. In 1945, he went to Congress, representing the Eighteenth Congressional District, and in the 1950s, before civil rights was popular, his name was appended to every antisegregation amendment proposed for federal appropriation bills. He was fearless in the face of the use of power against him, and convinced powerless Negroes that their cause was his only concern. His credentials for leadership depended totally on his challenge to whites. He was to Negroes an image of certainty and of emancipation. Yet at all times he was the prototype of the American urban politician, white and black, for whom practical political rewards were more important than sentiment. Probably more than any other Negro politician, Powell understood the hard, tough realities of politics.

The question arises whether Powell is not actually contemptuous of his constituents. He has nothing in common with the workingclass Negro who provides the bulk of his support. He does not live in the community; he has never shared its problems but, since infancy, has lived a life of privilege and indulgence. Yet he has an almost instinctive ability to exploit the deep and elemental emotional needs of the average Negro. Like every successful charismatic political leader who attracts a mass following, he is sensitive and responsive to the needs of the masses. He can use their words, their idiom, their fashionable jargon, to communicate to their emotions just as, on Adam Clayton Powell Day, in extolling his own virtues as a congressman, he cried: "Big Daddy will take care of you!" The *New York Times* quoted him as saying to his constituents: "When you come to Washington and walk into my new offices, you'll see 19 rooms . . . two kitchenettes

. . . four sanitary facilities." One may ponder whether this is the response of affectionate concern or of patronizing disdain.

Does anything really matter to Powell? He behaves with that freedom and flexibility usually available only to a person who is unencumbered by illusion, delusion, principle, or loyalty. For Powell, any idea and any person seems to be an instrument for use. This leaves the further question—use for what? To what is Powell committed? Not to party loyalty: He could and did support Eisenhower and temporarily desert the Democratic party without apology. Not to democratic ideology: He accepted at one period in his career the support of the Communists, the only politician able to survive involvement with the Communists without injury, the only one able to use the Communists and then discard them when they no longer proved useful. Powell appears rather to employ all resources available to him for the gratification of his own ego. He seems a simple hedonist above all else. He appears free of any sense of guilt. Guilt is the consequence of a sense that one has violated what one believes in, a consequence of behavior in conflict with one's conscience. To be rid of such conflict is to be free of much anguish.

But more important than an attempt to probe Powell's motivations—a risky and inconclusive venture for any human being—is the question of the extent of his present power. If he is important in the civil rights movement it is because the civil rights movement itself is important. Yet he is no longer a primary power source in the civil rights movement, but rather a successful fellow traveler with the ability to act as if he is directing a movement he is merely following. He attempts always to align himself with the more dramatic sources of power. When the Muslims seemed to be the cutting edge of the Negro movement, he rejected the NAACP forces in their behalf. When the Milton Galamison–sponsored school boycott in New York City was considered a potent effort, he associated himself with it. He attempted to join with Martin Luther King in the early stages of the Montgomery bus boycott, but King and his admirers were shrewd enough to recognize the tactic, and the liaison failed to materialize. In the genuine thrust of the civil rights movement, Powell is a has-been, still seeking to give the impression of leadership. The fascinating thing is that this façade becomes something more because whites in positions of power still respond to Powell as though he were able to deliver or withhold Negro votes. When U.S. Attorney General Robert Kennedy was faced with the possibility that Powell might attempt to exploit the Haryou-Act program in development of Harlem for personal political gain, he was quoted in the daily press as saying, "I have no fault to find with Adam Clayton Powell." The Democratic party nationally seems afraid of Powell, despite the fact that Powell's own party loyalty is flexible. The fear among whites compensates for Powell's actual loss of power in the civil rights movement. If people believe one has power it is almost as good as having it—particularly if one's needs require not the substance but only the illusion of power.

In his role as chairman of the House Committee on Education and Labor, on the other hand, Powell does in fact have the substance of power. This position is not directly related to leadership in the civil rights movement, but Powell gives many Negroes the impression that it is. He attempts to consolidate his slipping influence by arguing also that if he is ever defeated for his congressional seat—it is unlikely that he will be; he is now in his middle fifties—many years will elapse before another Negro achieves a post of chairman of a congressional committee. Negroes are urged, therefore, to discourage him from any thought of retirement. The white public and press attacks on Powell are said to be understood in terms of the desire of whites to oust a Negro from a powerful congressional post. Even the 1964 poll by *Pageant* magazine in which members of Congress and the Washington press corps named Powell the "least effective" Congressman (and, ironically, named the segregationist, Goldwater-supporter, Senator J. Strom Thurmond of South Carolina, the "least effective" senator) would have little impact in Harlem and has been seriously questioned by others outside of Harlem.

Even more effective than the contribution to Powell's influence of the white power structure is the sustaining help of certain Negro leaders of the civil rights organizations. Small imitation Powells compliment him by attempting to copy his style and militancy. But more serious is the silent support of responsible leaders, who justify their refusal to criticize Powell publicly—though most of them do so scathingly in private—by arguing that the civil rights movement itself would suffer from public expression of conflict among well-known Negroes. Powell is not part of this gentlemen's agreement, for he has repeatedly and harshly criticized as subservient to white power responsible civil rights leaders like those of the NAACP and Urban League. But they consider it a sign of self-discipline and statesmanship to refrain from responding to his charges even when the integrity of their own staff is challenged.

The power of Powell to elicit solid support was perhaps most clearly illustrated by his success in inducing one of the most respected civil rights leaders to act as chairman of a self-promoted Adam Clayton Powell Day in Harlem in the summer of 1964. Whitney M. Young, Jr., who had been dean of the Atlanta School of Social Work before his appointment as executive director of the National Urban League, has been recognized by Negroes and whites as one of the most thoughtful, balanced, and forthright of Negro leaders. Under his leadership the Urban League has learned to talk without equivocation with the princes of economic power in the white society. The fact that a man of his personal and professional stature felt he could advance the cause of civil rights by assuming an active role in a mass adulation of Powell reveals a most important aspect of the phenomenon of effective illusion of power. It may well be that this jeopardy of a deservedly high reputation was assumed on the ground that goals important to the Urban League could be attained only by respecting the very real power which the chairman of the House Committee on Education and Labor holds. It must be pointed out, however, that such justification would hold equally to justify a similar participation by civil rights leadership in a public ceremony lauding any other powerful public figure, even Senator James Eastland, chairman of the far more powerful Senate Judiciary Committee. For if one decides to concede primarily to power, the logical decision to concede where the source is Negro would be no different from the logic of decision to concede to power where the source is white. Most severe of all the burdens upon civil rights leaders may be the requirement that they refrain from compromise of fundamental principle, of morality and justice. The only weapon the Negro has, as a minority in American society, is his moral strength, the justice of his cause. Even if, in the short run, Powell as a phenomenon seems justified by the illusion of the Negro that vicarious revenge on the white will compensate for his anguish and despair, in the long run Powell is, to the Negro, a major liability.

As long as the predicament of Negroes in American cities endures, just so long will Powell. The amorality of the larger society makes the amorality of the ghetto possible. Those who oppose Powell must oppose the ghetto first, for Powell is a creature of the ghetto; and for Powell to survive, the ghetto itself must survive. To transform the ghetto would lead to Powell's political destruction.

The Power of the Press

If political power of consequence is withheld from the ghetto, does power lie elsewhere—in its social agencies, in its press, in its churches, in its personalities of strength and talent?

In American society, though the extent of its influence is hard to assess, the press is considered to be an instrument of power, an influence for social change or for preservation of the *status quo*. The Negro press is, in character, very different from the white-owned press, but it also has power. If a Negro newspaper is to be successful it must reflect the atmosphere of the ghetto it serves and at the same time express both aspiration and protest. These goals have often been at odds with each other; and as a result the Negro newspaper, like Harlem's *Amsterdam News,* may contain bizarre inconsistencies. The *Amsterdam News* has to make money like any other paper to survive, and therefore addresses itself, through flamboyant headlines, makeup, and front-page articles on crime and scandal, to those it considers its audience, thereby ironically reinforcing the white stereotype of the Negro, against which it argues vehemently on its editorial page. Many of its local advertisements are devoted to fortune telling, the sale of dream books and skin bleaches, exploiting the misery and fantasy of ghetto life. The editor defends the paper by pointing to its editorial support of racial militancy, arguing that in its news stories and advertising the paper must serve the people. He does not wrestle with the implications of contradiction implicit in his stand. And by exaggerating the importance of Negro successes—the first Negro to do this or that—the paper contributes to the fantasy of denial that tends to refute the need for militancy at all.

Though the Negro press has articulated the Negro's demands for social change, by its stand for uncompromising militancy, it may contribute to fantasy as surely as it does in its hawking of dream books; for militancy that allows for no rational assessment of strategies may deceive the Negro into believing that the potential effectiveness of a plan is to be judged by one standard—absolutism. It tends to ally itself with or support the more sensational leaders and to give excessive coverage in its news columns to the Powell-type of extremist leadership. It tends to use as its barometer the prevailing white view on any issue and to support whatever irritates whites. Its reaction to militant proposals is generally uncritical; it saves its most caustic barbs for the more judicious, hardheaded strategies, thereby oversimplifying the issues of civil rights for masses of Negroes. Most attempts to think reasonably about Negro problems are greeted as "Uncle Tomism." Some ironic inconsistencies in policy result: The editor argues with equal vehemence *for* developing a superior quality of medical services at Harlem Hospital and *against* improving the quality of education in the Harlem schools. He sees the first as beneficial to the Negro, the latter as a strengthening of segregation. Yet Harlem Hospital is also segregated. In another contradictory position, he argued in support of the earlier militancy of Malcolm X and the Black Muslims, who represent the ultimate in the philosophy of segregation; yet he demands immediate integration. He was against attempting to persuade the New York City Public Housing Authority to regulate the percentage of whites and Negroes assigned to lower- and middle-income housing projects to insure greater integration. Left to the natural process of social change in New York City, public housing would rapidly become Negro-dominated, for there is a tendency among whites to escape public housing when Negroes enter. He maintained that integration by regulation would deny Negroes free access to such housing and hence would be a support for a philosophy of exclusion. Yet when exclusion has previously been the rule or practice in any institution, the imposition of quotas could be the *beginning* of free access. Otherwise, the excluded minority may become the majority as the natural majority of whites moves away in search of a "haven." The hard realities may require the acceptance of some form of quota as a necessary strategy of regulated social change. The complexity of this issue can be avoided by a rigid, simple reaction against the symbol of "quota," but this absolutism does not contribute to the solution; the alternative to quotas may be a perpetuation and extension of segregation. One could only accept a quota as a transition to a society where the fears and behavior of the majority do not require artificial attempts to circumvent a "natural" tendency toward racism.

The *Amsterdam News* is in its own way consistent, not in terms of ideas but in its emotion—one argument may negate another, yet whatever is emotional is exploited.

Students of the press, white as well as Negro, may point out that inconsistencies of view are characteristic of newspapers generally— news columns and syndicated columnists may present what editorials reject. They may also point out that there is little evidence that editorials sway the nation—the overwhelming majority of the nation's papers have been, with the widely noted exception of the Johnson-Goldwater campaign, solidly Republican, but the nation often elects Democrats. The *New York Daily News,* with the largest circulation of any American daily, seemed unable to influence its millions of New York readers who voted for Franklin Roosevelt again and again despite the paper's virulent anti–New Deal editorials. Yet in the Negro ghettos, where few voices of reason are raised and where few institutions have influence, and the balance of mood is volatile, it would seem that the influence of the press would be far greater and its responsibility correspondingly greater. But the owners and publishers of the Negro press tend to be successful, balanced, even conservative persons who appear to draw a careful line between the role of the publisher and the role of the editor. They seem to believe that the editor's job is to meet the needs of the community and sustain the paper's economic strength. Though they as owners will decide the paper's position at elections, the editor himself may use wide latitude at other times.

The Negro press itself tends to dissipate any sustained or long-range power it might have not only because the white power structure tends to become immune to Negro sensationalism, but also because repeated flamboyance dulls the emotions to any real need for response. It concentrates on skirmishes, on specific immediate problems, and its power, if it can be called that, is the colorful but spent power of the skyrocket whose flash is forgotten a moment after it bursts. The Negro newspaper is a symbol of pseudocathartic power; it neither satisfies the deeper psychological needs of its readers nor does it assume responsibility for sustained fundamental social change.

Much of the criticism of the Negro press comes from better-educated, upper-middle-class Negroes who have little patience with the paper's need to maintain mass appeal. They tend to judge the Negro press as they judge the best of the white press; and, seeing its inadequacies, they tend to reject it. The press's anti-intellectualism reflects and encourages a deep suspicion of the intellectual on the part of large numbers, perhaps the majority, of Negroes, and the upwardly mobile Negro must constantly turn from anything that reminds him of what he seeks to escape. Many Negroes in New York take pride in announcing that they never read the *Amsterdam News*. They rely on the "metropolitan" or "white" press, which is basically unsatisfactory, too, since it has underscored his own feelings of self-doubt by its own past tendency to ignore the Negro community though the *New York Times* has recently initiated what must be a high policy decision to present Negro models in fashion pages and an occasional Negro bride in the society columns. With the rise of the civil rights movement, the metropolitan press—in its ignorance of the Negro community—often made the embarrassing mistake of overplaying the more sensational and self-seeking Negro leaders and thereby inadvertently assisting in building up their influence and undercutting the more responsible, less flamboyant leaders. Every major New York daily now has at least one Negro on its reporting staff. There appears to be a dilemma, however, as to how best to use these reporters; whether to use them as reporters of Negro news or as reporters. Some make a point of using them to cover general stories; others tend to assign them to cover the "Negro" angle. The major papers are tending now to accept Negroes simply as reporters.

Some of the more obvious deficiencies of the Negro press seem to be absent in the national magazines which are devoted to Negro news, aspirations, and achievements. The most successful of these magazines are published by John H. Johnson of Chicago. Johnson is a shrewd man, deceptively calm in manner, one of the few Negroes who has succeeded in breaking out of the constricted standards of the ghetto. His magazines are significant not only because of their nationwide circulation, which for the first time demonstrates that Negroes can sustain a national press, but because they show that publications controlled by Negroes can meet the competitive, aesthetic standards of the "larger," i.e., the white, society.

The Johnson publications provide for Negroes concrete images of middle-class success in their stories and pictures of Negro doctors, teachers, businessmen, and others. While there is some exaggeration in the implication that Negro achievement is more prevalent than it is, thereby reinforcing the Negro's fantasies about himself, these are fantasies of affirmation, and if they encourage in the Negro the motivation to seek achievements of his own, they may eventually be translated into reality. When the magazines describe A. G. Gaston of Birmingham and his successful insurance company and savings and loan associations, Negro young people see that there are certain opportunities and rewards for them, too. The middle-class image is further projected in the magazines' pages in even more discreet ways, with emphasis on quiet, tasteful language, dress and grooming, design, and interior decoration. The ostentatious is muted; the attractive but restrained is approved. The names of the magazines themselves are a subtle endorsement of a positive Negro image: The names *"Ebony,"* and *"Jet,"* and *"Tan"* are fashionable synonyms for the colors "black" and "brown" in the white world.

Because the Johnson publications, unlike the Negro newspapers on the whole, are directed toward the middle-class and upward-striving Negro on whom the Negro community must depend for leadership, they may well prove to have a more powerful impact on the civil rights movement in the long run than all of the Negro newspapers combined.

The Power of Social Services

There is increasing debate—though chiefly confined to the professions of social work and philanthropy—as to the actual effectiveness of social work and philanthropy in transforming society, and indeed as to the desirability of their seeking to do so. In Harlem such debate has special and poignant significance because the need is so great.

The major social agencies which operate in Harlem depend on sources outside the community for support, and must compete for limited philanthropic funds. Foundations and philanthropists tend to view the ghetto as a single problem of "civil rights" or "minority status," and to distinguish less clearly than they do elsewhere the merits of a particular project. The competition for dollars is thereby enhanced. Nor have Harlem social agencies generally been adjudged good risks for grants, or capable of using large funds effectively. Agencies whose boards are chiefly composed of Harlem Negroes have greater difficulty in the race for funds, for those who need help most are often inexperienced in the ritual of how to get it.

To arrange for an agency board to be dominated by whites instead is often assumed to solve the problem. But for these whites Harlem is necessarily only one of their own many interests. They agree to serve out of a commitment to racial justice, or because of a personal confidence in an agency's professional leadership, but they seldom bring power that is transferable to Negro leadership. At the same time they unconsciously reinforce the patterns of colonialism and dependency that reflect the essential powerlessness of Negroes themselves. When financial help from outside the ghetto leads to influence over policy, the direction of social change in the ghetto itself may be indirectly controlled; though, of course, the fact of guidance of agency programs by financial power is not restricted to social agencies in Negro ghettos.

Some community agencies are outposts of a larger, more affluent nonghetto social agency. When the real authority lies beyond the boundaries of the ghetto, it may fail to respond to the ghetto's actual needs, and if the services offered are considered primarily as a benevolence, they may be modified and cut back at the discretion of those who do hold the power. When this happens the community has no recourse but protest.

Harlem is a philanthropic, economic, business, and industrial colony of New York City. Few persons of wealth live in Harlem; and, as we have seen, upper-class Negroes tend to get out of Harlem, to send their children to private schools, or, if they stay in Harlem, to withdraw from community problems. Without a tradition of Negro support for community services, Negroes must either accept white help or do without. There are too few wealthy Negroes in Harlem, or anywhere else, to sustain strong community programs backed by private funds. Negroes continue to believe that the white power structure is responsible for the ghetto and therefore believe that it must pay for all of the problems that emanate from the ghetto. One must say that social work and philanthropy as instruments of constructive social change have so far had little impact in any of the nation's urban ghettos.

The Power of the Church

Have the churches of Harlem themselves any power—real or latent—to stimulate and direct constructive social change? Or are they, too, victims of the ghetto?

The need of the average Negro to compensate for the daily subservience and emotional restraints imposed upon him by his inferior status can be satisfied either in the bars, on the street corners, or in the churches.

Established Negro churches, the many storefront churches, and the sporadic Negro quasireligious cult groups, like Father Divine's and the late Daddy Grace's followers, play chiefly a cathartic role for the Negro. These churches and cults and their leaders provide an opportunity for their followers to "let off steam," to seek release for emotions which cannot be expressed in overcrowded homes or on the job. The Negro church is a social and recreational club and a haven of comfort for the masses of Negroes. Within the church, a Negro porter or maid can assume responsibilities and authority not available to him elsewhere. Only there can he engage in political intrigue and participate in financial decisions open to whites in many other aspects of their lives. Here the Negro domestic exchanges her uniform for a "high-fashion" dress and enjoys the admiration and envy of other friends. The value of the church in providing personal affirmation and self-esteem for Negroes is great enough to permit them to tolerate almost any degree of personal, theological, or educational inadequacy upon the part of their minister, so long as he holds the church together as a successful social and financial institution. Prominent Negro ministers of Negro churches are indulged by their congregations. They are permitted considerable personal freedom, and they are often given presents of clothing and cars. They are symbols of the social and civic success of the church and give the members of their congregation the vicarious satisfaction of relationship to an important church and identification with an influential minister.

This is the source of both the power and the weakness of the Negro church in the ghetto. The potential power of the Negro church lies in the fact that it does attract large numbers of the masses of Negroes. The weaknesses of the Negro church, however, cannot be ignored: They are inherent in the general pathology of the ghetto of which the Negro church is a part. Among its more flagrant weaknesses is the fact that its potential strengths can all too easily be dissipated by preoccupation with trivia, with competitiveness, suspiciousness, and a desperate struggle for the empty status, bombast, and show of the ghetto world.

Many Negro ministers have, nevertheless, managed to mobilize the positive power potential of their churches and have harnessed it to the democratic and idealistic ideologies of religion for effective racial protest and action. It was inevitable that, in addition to their escape function, Negro churches would have a direct protest role. The dream of heaven that sustained Negroes for so long has been transformed into hope for life on earth. The roles of such Negro ministers as Adam Clayton Powell, Martin Luther King, Jr., Ralph Abernathy, and Fred Shuttlesworth in the Negro protest movement reflect the historical and unavoidable relationship between Negro religion and Negro protest. The role of the Negro church in the early stages of the Negro movement may have owed its strength to the fact that the Negro church was the only institution in which the Negro was allowed that degree of autonomy and freedom from white domination which permitted even a minimal degree of organization for a sustained protest movement. The Negro was required to finance and build his own churches. He hired and paid his ministers without any major help from the white community. In all other aspects of life—in all economic, educational, and other institutional contacts—even under a pervasive and rigid biracial and segregated system, the Negro was still dependent upon white financial control. His schools were controlled by white authorities or white philanthropy. His job, his business, and his home were controlled by white industries and banks. His rights as a citizen were determined by white politicians and government officials. Only in the most segregated of social institutions, the church, was he able to exercise that degree of personal and racial freedom necessary for the initial stages of an effective campaign against racial injustices. The Negro church, therefore, cannot be understood primarily in traditional theological terms, but rather in terms of the religion of race. For the Negro, his church is his instrument of escape, his weapon of protest, his protective fortress behind which he seeks to withstand the assaults of a hostile world and within which he plans his strategies of defiance, harassment, and, at times, his frontal attacks against racial barriers. The ministers and laymen of the white Christian churches are responsible for making the Negro churches effective as vehicles of racial protest by their historic unwillingness to incorporate Negroes into their houses of Christ and by their inability to share with the Negro his passion and action for justice and equality. One of the earliest civil rights controversies, dating back to the beginning of human slavery in the New World, was the argument whether the African slaves should be taught to read and converted to Christianity. A paradox of Protestantism, the dominant religion of the early North American colonists, was the need to reconcile the practical fact of human slavery with the ideals of Christian brotherhood. The advantages of slavery demanded that the religious and moral conflicts of the early American Christians be handled by the comparatively simple device of denying to the African slave the status of a fully developed human being. The contemporary Negro churches, whether in an all-Negro denomination or as part of a white denomination, are concrete symbols and citadels of this exclusion and rejection.

Given the special origin of the Negro church and Negro personal need, one must be prepared for the possibility that in spite of very compelling religious and idealistic reasons for desegregation of American churches, the church is likely to be the last of the social institutions to be effectively integrated. Paradoxically, bedrock resistance to desegregation may be found more among Negroes than among whites, for only in the church have many Negroes found a basis for personal worth. If one demands that the Negro give up the Negro church before total integration is achieved, on the grounds of consistency with the goals of the civil rights movement, the demand will be rejected, for the Negro has managed to salvage some personal self-esteem from his church, and until he achieves such self-esteem elsewhere he will not give up this, his last and only sanctuary.

This point is no less true merely because there exist, in the larger community, churches with interracial congregations. Such churches tend to offer themselves as examples of the type of religious democracy toward which all other churches should strive. An analysis of the social class structure of the membership of such churches would probably reveal that the members are well above the American mean in social, economic, and educational status. The chances are that Negro members of interracial churches are of the upper middle classes or upwardly mobile groups, probably superior even to the average white member of the church in educational background. The interracial church outside the ghetto is a social instrument for the upwardly mobile and upper-middle-class Negro who uses the fact of his membership as additional evidence of his success. He therefore tends to demand of the church that it protect this image of himself above any other ideal. Any issue which would tend to remind the Negro of his racial identity would necessarily come in conflict with the basic needs which he sought to satisfy by joining. Even to discuss race may shat-ter the delusions of denial and the fantasies of acceptance which are part of his identification with the interracial church. Such Negroes are nonetheless able to derive satisfaction through their jobs and personal success and are less dependent upon the church for a more basic psychological support than are the masses of Negroes. Segregated Negro churches in the ghetto not only serve the needs of whites but of Negroes, too; and therefore there are no genuinely interracial churches in the heart of any Negro ghetto, and there cannot be. If the ghetto churches were genuinely interracial the needs of Negroes for self-esteem and for escape would remain unfulfilled.

The Negro intellectual, on the other hand, tends to reject the church altogether as a multiple symbol of fantasy. He tends to regard the church as basically irrelevant to the hard and difficult realities of race. He tends to emphasize the fact that the church has, histori-cally, compromised on moral social issues, obscuring them by abstruse theological debate. In his view, the churches have, in a sense, sought to have the cake of moral leadership and eat it, too, refusing to come in conflict with those power groups that support racial in-justice, determined to hold on to their major contributors, who are usually conservative, fearing to offend them by commitment to social change. It has seldom dared to question the validity of the uses of power by the princes of power. This looks like hypocrisy to the Negro intellectual, and as a result he often rejects not only the church as an institution, but religion itself.

The church as an institution has not yet found the formula for effecting change without alienating its strongest supporters. If any reconciliation or resolution of this conflict is possible it would seem to depend on the ability of the church leadership to state clearly and unequivocally the terms for such resolution which are consistent with the basic moral and theological positions of the church and thereby to assume the risk that the practical controllers of power within the church will accept, comply with, and use their power to reinforce this position, rather than rejecting it as in many Southern and Northern churches. But even if, in response to this challenge, the lay leaders of the church oppose its stand for justice, the moral strength of the church would have been affirmed and the issue between the demands and the direction of practical economic and political power on the one hand and moral and spiritual power on the other hand would be clarified. The façade of power which the church now presents would be removed, and the church would be forced to develop a genuine prophetic role. The fact that the churches are the most pervasive social institutions in the Negro ghetto, and the fact that churches do not hold primary power in American society, are cruelly related. If religion were a powerful social force, either the white society would have to restrict church strength in Northern Negro communities—witness the bombings of Negro churches in the South—or the ghettos themselves would be transformed.

Religion in Harlem, as among Negroes generally, is primarily Protestant, though the number of Negro Catholics has been gradually increasing in recent years. For many Negroes, in a reversal of the pattern some immigrant groups have followed, to become a Roman Catholic is part of a move to a higher status because of the association between poverty and inferiority and their Protestant past.

The number of Negro Roman Catholics, from 1953 to 1963 rose from roughly 450,000 to 700,000, an increase of 55 percent. Yet nationally, among 237 Roman Catholic bishops, none is Negro; and in New York City, there is no Negro priest among the 433 priests in charge of parishes serving approximately 80,000 Negro Catholics.

There are some large and prosperous Negro churches in Harlem and some distinguished churchmen. The majority of Negro church members belong to segregated Negro denominations (Negro Baptist and Negro Methodist, including African Methodist Episcopal, A.M.E. Zion, Christian Methodist Episcopal,* and Wesleyan Methodist) and most of the rest either to evangelical sects or to churches belonging to white-controlled denominations (Presbyterian, Protestant Episcopal, Lutheran, and Congregational). The former are segregated by decision of the white denominations to live apart, though the Metho-

* In response to the Supreme Court's 1954 decision, the C.M.E. denomination changed its name from Colored Methodist Episcopal.

dists are now moving slowly toward abolishing their Negro Central Jurisdiction; the latter by the same kind of *de facto* segregation, justified by geography, that affects the city's school system.

In the past, Negro church leaders have tended to concentrate their energies on building and maintaining the institution itself, but as the civil rights movement gained in impact and Southern Negro ministers took leadership in the struggle for justice, Northern Negro ministers, affected by a newly stirring social conscience, began to assume a firmer role in attempting to influence social change. The segregated denominations, which raise their own funds and control their own affairs, have, doubtless in part for this reason, been able to provide most of this leadership. One does not find a similar leadership within the evangelical sects like the Pentecostal and Holiness, perhaps because these are oriented more to the next world than to this. Negro ministers whose churches belong to white-dominated denominations have a tougher decision to make. They must pay attention to the opinions of their national hierarchy. They are less free. Seeking to avoid the charge of "Uncle Tom" churches, with its attendant loss of status in both Negro and white communities, they often try to support themselves without help, though this pressure inevitably means that the time and energy and funds spent on providing an educated ministry, a dignified setting, a well-run institution, are not available for social action. "Negro work" does not receive priority in Protestantism; and Protestantism, less unified than either Roman Catholicism or Judaism and less identified than Catholicism and Judaism with the needs of recent immigrant and refugee groups, has been far less effectively organized to help Protestants of low income and persistent need, and particularly Negro Protestants. Yet the vast majority of Negroes in the urban ghettos, as well as elsewhere, hold on to the Protestant faith that has served their spirit while it has neglected their other needs as human beings.

In the wider uses of power, the Negro churches have played a peripheral role. Only rarely has a Negro churchman been accepted in a position of influence by the wider community. One such occasion was the election in 1964 of the Reverend Edler Hawkins to be moderator of the United Presbyterian Church in the U.S.A., the first and only Negro chosen to head a white-dominated denomination. Hawkins is not well known to whites, but in Harlem he has been regarded as forward-looking and sound and not at all as one of the flamboyant Negro religious leaders.

In the Protestant Episcopal church, despite the fact that large numbers of Negroes belong—especially members of the so-called middle and upper classes—and despite the presence of a number of highly trained and educated Negro Episcopal priests, there are only two Negro bishops nationally: one is Bishop John Burgess of Greater Boston; the other has been relegated to missionary work in Liberia. The Episcopal church has spoken forcefully on race, but acted timidly and inconsistently in the march toward racial justice, reflecting conflict within the church itself on its role in society. A number of hospitals, agencies, and schools identified with that denomination continue to exclude or segregate Negroes. The 1960 denominational budgets for race relations and alcoholism were the same—$7,500—both of obviously low priority. When an advisory committee on intergroup relations was appointed in 1960 to report to the Department of Social Relations of the National Council, its critical findings were never presented and debated openly. The House of Bishops, to whom the committee appealed in 1961, felt at the time that it had a more urgent matter than race to discuss, a matter later revealed to have been concerned with the personal behavior of Episcopal priests.

Within the Methodist body, two separate denominations have existed; one, the segregated Negro Central Jurisdiction is now a matter of considerable embarrassment to liberal white Methodists who led a "kneel-in" at the 1964 General Conference to try to stir the denomination's conscience to prompter action. The vote was to abolish the Central Jurisdiction over a three-year transition period. Some Negro Methodists have and will continue to resist its abolition just because the parallel Negro hierarchy makes possible Negroes' achievement of power. But in 1964, two Negroes were chosen as bishops, among the forty-four in the Methodist Church, to serve integrated jurisdictions, one, Bishop Prince A. Taylor, Jr., of New Jersey; the other, Bishop James Thomas of Iowa.

Open competition in religion, as in other areas of life, is always hard for Negroes themselves to face. Yet the very satisfactions of segregation reinforce it. The transition from a closed society to an open, nonsegregated one requires that Negroes and whites both surrender the advantages of the closed society for the dangerous but hopefully more rewarding open competitive society.

Religious Leaders and Social Action

The outstanding example of religious leaders who address themselves not just to religious institutional problems of fund raising and the general duties of the parish ministry, but to community problems also, without moving from the ghetto altogether is, of course, Adam Clayton Powell, who uses the platform of his church and his concept of a social ministry as a basis for projecting himself directly into the sphere of politics. Others, like the Reverend Milton Galamison, one of the instigators of the New York City school boycotts, have not moved directly into the politics of elective office but have concerned themselves with the periphery of politics. Reverend Gardner Taylor of Brooklyn served as a member of the New York City Board of Education; Reverend Obadiah Dempsey was aggressive in the fight against narcotic addiction and drug traffic in New York City; Reverend Eugene Callender, who succeeded Dr. James Robinson as pastor of the Church of the Master, was active in Harlem Neighborhoods Association and a member of the board of Haryou. In other cities, Negro ministers have taken similar leadership, as did Reverend Leon Sullivan of Philadelphia, leader of the effective boycott against businesses that had hired few if any Negroes.

The weakness of such leadership lies in the possibility that even the relative independence of the Negro church does not provide a genuine source of power. It does not in itself provide the financial or the organizational stability for a long-range conflict. If the Negro minister is to be successful, he must collect followers outside of his church, as Powell and King have done, attracting them by strength of personality and articulateness or by sound and sincere leadership. In Sullivan's case, the church provided a springboard to help him win over a wider community support. He was also successful in gaining the cooperation of his colleagues, a significant fact in itself, for the Negro minister who seeks to project himself beyond his own congregation, like the Negro politician, almost invariably arouses the competitive spirit of his fellows. Just as Negro political leaders tend to squabble among themselves for the scraps of power, so the ministers tend to distrust each other's leadership—each is a rival for a congregational following and for recognition and status.

Martin Luther King is the prime illustration of the Negro minister's success in moving to the rostrum of the community at large, partly because of the charisma of his own personality, partly because in the South the Negro church has been the only available rallying place for Negroes and a more potent force in the life of the community than is true in the North. In King, the thrust of religious and of political power come together. The inherently dramatic quality of the Montgomery bus boycott led by King caught the imagination not only of Negroes but of the country as a whole and catapulted him into the status of leader beyond the reach of competitive resentment from his fellow ministers. But he has had no permanent immunity and has not altogether escaped resentment in the succeeding years. His methods, actions, and words are subjected to constant scrutiny. This scrutiny, while reflecting the general pattern of intra-ghetto rivalry, controls the extent to which any single individual is permitted to become a spokesman for Negroes. Again the one exception is Powell, who, in spite of mounting criticism, has been able to consolidate his power within the community, reinforced by the real power of his role in Congress. King is more immune from criticism among whites than among Negroes, for to whites his leadership, reinforced strongly by the award of the Nobel Prize for Peace, personifies quiet intelligence, gentlemanly conduct, the Christian philosophy of love and disciplined nonviolent protest, which on its face is less threatening and more acceptable than are other civil rights strategies. Although King does not so intend it, his approach is, to whites, not inconsistent with the familiar view of Negroes as long-suffering and amenable. King, for his part, believes that this philosophy and method "has a way of disarming the opponent. It exposes his moral defenses. It weakens his morale and at the same time it works on his conscience. He just doesn't know how to handle it."* Among Negro civil rights leaders, King's ideology, as distinct from his methods, is either accepted as a strategy for disarming whites or is personally rejected. Some of his followers will personally admit to another Negro that they neither love whites nor understand what King really means by love of the oppressor, but that they will go along with this so long as the philosophy is associated with effective protest.

The best illustration of this accommodation is SNCC, clearly one of the most effectively militant groups in the Deep South. SNCC (Student Nonviolent Coordinating Committee) uses the nonviolent confrontation method and adheres to the use of King's method. Nonetheless, it divorced the nonviolent method from any need to express love of the oppressor.

But in the North, especially in the urban ghettos, King's method and the methods, too, of SNCC and CORE are not as relevant or appropriate to the problems of Negroes. The more dramatic techniques such as boycotts have been concentrated on schools, as in Boston, New York, and Cleveland. They have not been sustained, as have the campaigns in the South, over a prolonged period of time, but have been used primarily to call dramatic attention to a problem. In the North, racial exclusion is more subtle and rarely defended by law. In the South it has been direct and flagrant and sustained by local and state law. To the concrete problem of the segregated bus or water fountain, the concrete answer—physical presence of the Negro himself—has been effective. Against the more subtle problem of *de facto* segregated schools in segregated Northern neighborhoods, such methods have been futile. Against whom was the protest directed? Effective methods must be immediately related to the object of protest. In the North, the object is the entrenched bastions of political and economic power, and therefore the most effective instrument of change is direct contact with leadership, not sit-ins and other forms of mass protest. In the Philadelphia boycott, Negroes did not

* *The Negro Protest,* James Baldwin, Malcolm X, Martin Luther King talk with Kenneth B. Clark, Boston, Beacon Press, 1963.

sit in in business buildings to force employers to hire them. Rather they applied the method to the center of power—economic loss threatened by selective buying—and business yielded. The NAACP has begun a campaign to apply this same principle widely in an attempt to break down employment barriers in business and industry.

King does have strong appeal among Northern Negroes, but this is related to respect for his courage and a sense of identity with Southern Negroes, rather than to the conviction that his methods are relevant to their own problems. When Northern Negroes try to use his approach they almost always fail. King comes to the North primarily to elicit support for work in the South, but generally he himself has not taken the initiative in trying to project his philosophy in Northern cities. When Mayor Wagner invited King to New York City to advise him about the problems of Harlem after the 1964 summer riots, the invitation resulted in considerable resentment from Northern Negro leaders. The fact is that King did attempt some form of communication with community spokesmen in Harlem before he accepted the invitation, but in general these spokesmen tended to deny that they had advised him to speak to the Mayor. Some advised him to stay out of Harlem, on the grounds that the Mayor was merely seeking to use him as a cover for his own inaction, trying to hoodwink the Harlem community. Some, particularly the more militant nationalistic leaders, said that the invitation was a sign of King's "softness" and willingness to compromise. Whatever their reasons and almost without regard to differing ideology, the consensus was that Mayor Wagner, and King in accepting, had committed a major blunder. It reinforced what Negro leaders believed to be the Mayor's disrespect for them and eroded thereafter whatever power they had or might have in the future. King said, on the contrary, that he had acted to strengthen local Negro leadership. An additional factor in the discontent of Negro leaders was the fact that a number of national civil rights leaders have their headquarters in New York. Both Roy Wilkins of the NAACP and Whitney Young, Jr., of the Urban League were available for open or quiet consultations. Was King chosen instead because of his reputation as a charismatic social leader or as a temperate religious leader? Either Wagner was inadequately briefed, Negro leaders concluded, or he did not understand the complex psychology of the ghetto. The Negro leaders may be justified in their indignation. On the other hand, the fact that they themselves have no real basis for power means they cannot expect to be taken seriously in time of genuine crisis when there is much at stake. Often, in fact, they are competitive, petty, and unrealistic and do not justify respect. But justified or not, few are respected by white power. The contamination of the ghetto is pervasive. In times of crisis, the reputation of the ghetto is such that those responsible for decision look almost everywhere else for help except within the ghetto. And so the pattern of community pathology and powerlessness reinforce each other. Those who are treated as if they have no power can have none, just as those who are treated as if they have power tend to have it.

Experiments in Power

Negroes are sensitive to the pervasive pattern of powerlessness in the ghetto. They recognize that the real influence of Negroes in the nation's cities is woefully below what their numbers would suggest. They see that other groups, the Irish, the Italians, the Jews, have power—religious, economic, social—far beyond their own.

A few years ago, in an attempt to bring coherence and effectiveness to leadership in the New York ghetto community, a group of about fifteen Negroes formed themselves into an organization which they referred to simply as the Group. Some were at high-level positions in the municipal government; others were former judges, lawyers, directors of civil rights agencies; one was a college professor. The incident which united them was an attack they considered unjust upon one of them. His forced resignation from a government post had come on the heels of a similar onslaught on a Negro magistrate and on the Negro borough president of Manhattan. It seemed to these fifteen Negroes that here was a common pattern of exaggerated civic scrutiny of the behavior of Negroes in public positions. More seemed to be demanded of them in their public and private lives than was demanded of whites. These stringent requirements seemed to reflect a desire on the part of white political power to avoid any sharing of real influence with Negroes.

The Group's goal was to combine individual power, such as it was, to protect Negroes exposed to public examination because of their conspicuousness in top positions. Its strategy was for each to share information with the others, for each to do what he could to influence public understanding, and to form direct personal contacts with the primary sources of government. Each incident was to be dealt with separately. For example, members of the Group visited former Governor Lehman to try to persuade him that J. Raymond Jones deserved the post of head of the New York County Democratic Committee, Tammany Hall. As noted earlier their mission was in vain.

Members of the Group communicate with one another orally, never by written invitation. Its existence has been known to few Negroes and fewer whites. For the past four or five years it has met fairly regularly and, over brandy and cigars, discussed the persistent problems of the Harlem community. While the Group cannot claim credit for effective social change, it did have some success in terms of the Harlem press, bringing pressure for some retractions of statements it considered irresponsible. Those whom the Group tried to protect often did not know they were protected. When the issue at stake was clear-cut and concrete, success was more likely. One of its major achievements was a change in administration of an important city commission.

The Group's failure to influence the city administration's decision on J. Raymond Jones was due in large part to the fact that it could not promise that any threats made could be fulfilled. They knew Negroes would go on voting Democratic without regard to what happened to Jones, and both Lehman and Wagner knew it, too. The Group had no resources with which to cajole or threaten. The only power they had was what they believed to be the rightness of their cause. They believed, undoubtedly naively, that the combination of a just cause and a well-planned and appropriate strategy could influence public opinion and win for the Negro his rightful place in city affairs. There was an element of fantasy in this confidence.

The Group talked frankly about the psychological problems of ghetto leadership, including the personal ambition which allowed itself to be satisfied with mere fragments of power. The discussions were thoughtful, balanced, and dignified, and came to have value more for their own sake as the members shared their troubled feelings and concerns, cathartic in the sense of communion.

Yet, when a genuine crisis arose in which the integrity of the Harlem community seemed to be at stake, the Group found itself immobile and silent. The dimensions of the crisis were too formidable. Ironically, and perhaps appropriately, the Group did not even meet to discuss what could be done. It sought to explain its silence by pointing out that the individual whom they genuinely wished to protect had not asked for their help. Later, with real self-reproach, they chastised themselves for failing in the task they had been organized to fulfill. But the fact was that the Group did not possess the power it thought it had, and its guilt was unnecessary; responsibility can be demanded only for duties which one has the capacity to achieve. In law, no one can be convicted of a crime he has not the ability to commit or prevent.

Whatever the causes—naiveté, personal vested interest, lack of real power—the Group was never able to face directly the fact of its own impotence. The evidence of helplessness intruded itself after the repeated experience that the Group could not obtain even limited goals. The Group sought, then, to expand its membership indirectly as chief agent in the formation of a larger group known as the Hundred Men, not as intimate or as confidential as the Group, but intended as a forum to talk over the basic problems of the ghetto, and hopefully to resolve some of them. As the Hundred Men grew, the inherent weakness of the quiet sponsorship by the Group became even more apparent, for in the end it lost any control over the affairs of its offspring.

Why was not the Group more effective? The most obvious reason was that the majority of its members were themselves office holders. Each had something to protect and something to lose. Only two were totally independent, in the sense of freedom from reliance on elective or appointive office. No one in the Group had achieved the level of

economic independence that would permit him to be publicly identified with the conflict at issue. Indeed, few persons with such freedom
exist in the entire Harlem community. The psychology of the Negro
of wealth, like that of the Negro poor, is in its own way a psychology
of insecurity. The wealthy Negro is not sure that his wealth will
bring power, though he sees that money often brings power in white
society. He uses most of his psychic energy to protect his wealth;
he is conservative and careful of his wealth and does not easily share
it with the ghetto community at large.

The present generation of Negroes is the first to break through
to that economic level on which philanthropy is possible; for a
tradition of philanthropy seems to require at least two generations
of fairly secure, nonspeculative wealth before civic responsibility
can be assured. In the entire country there are probably no more
than three or four Negro families who can support the claim of inherited wealth. Negroes have not had enough time or enough opportunity to accumulate family fortunes. Even Negroes who are
"comfortably off" are not yet meaningfully involved in Wall Street,
nor is any Negro well known for philanthropic leadership. The civil
rights agencies, local and national, are not generally supported by
large grants from individual Negroes but by large grants from
whites and many smaller gifts from Negroes.

Basically, too, the ghetto pathology includes an unwillingness
to make any personal sacrifice beyond those already required by the
ghetto itself. *The ghetto fails to prepare one for voluntary sacrifices
precisely because it demands so many involuntary ones.* Negroes
who are successful financially usually escape from the ghetto, though
a number continue to depend upon the ghetto economy for their own
source of wealth—Negro physicians, undertakers, publishers. Most
Negro wealth comes from businesses that white society did not wish
to control or from services peculiarly personal—newspaper publish-
ing of the segregated press; real estate and insurance, which grew out
of Negro burial societies; and undertaking, which owes its Negro
monopoly in the ghetto to the fact that white undertakers did not
wish to handle Negro bodies. Whatever the source of wealth, those
who attain it tend to divorce themselves from the community itself and

refuse to assume generally any major responsibility for the community.

Wealth that comes from illicit or marginal activities such as the numbers racket, however, does tend to maintain its residential roots within the ghetto. The source of wealth determines the level of social acceptance; Negroes whom the Negro suburban "upper class" would refuse to accept stay in the ghetto.

The Negro community views as "marginal" many occupations and sources of wealth which the white community would accept as respectable. Marginal occupations—the not quite respectable—in the Negro community tend to be those which represent the Negro stereotype as it is construed by the white community. The Negro who owns a bar or a liquor business, or a Negro entertainer or athlete is, therefore, viewed with some opprobrium by other Negroes of money or position. This is not true for Negro writers such as James Baldwin and Ralph Ellison and Negro dramatic stars such as Ruby Dee, Ossie Davis, and Sidney Poitier. Negro actors and actresses are admired and respected if they refuse to play stereotyped "Negro" roles.

The social class distinctions among Negroes, which are intended to reflect positions of influence in the wider community, are defined most clearly by a Negro fraternal organization, a group of about 1,000 throughout the country. Sigma Pi Phi, founded in Philadelphia in 1904, and known informally as the Boulé, is a conscious attempt to bring together Negroes who have demonstrated outstanding ability to compete successfully with whites. It is the most concrete form of a truly upper middle class Negro group. E. Franklin Frazier in *Black Bourgeoisie* said: "Although the original aim of the society was to bring together the 'aristocracy of talent,' it has become one of the main expressions of social snobbishness on the part of the black bourgeoisie."* One of the Boulé's cardinal rules is to shun publicity. It refuses to cooperate with the Negro press. It systematically rejects the mores which govern the ghetto. It applies rigorous standards for its members; men of similar interests and values. The personal conduct of all members must be beyond re-

* E. Franklin Frazier, *Black Bourgeoisie,* The Rise of a New Middle Class in the United States, Glencoe, Ill., The Free Press, 1957.

proach. The stable family is the ideal—a counterresponse to the pattern of family instability in the ghetto community. Achievement in the "larger world," as the white society is often called, is essential for recognition in Boulé. Negroes must have been weighed in fair competition with whites on the whites' own terms and been found not wanting. The source of achievement is also important. Originally, most members of Boulé were physicians and lawyers; others have since joined them—college professors, clergymen, businessmen. Robert Weaver, Whitney Young, Jr., John H. Johnson are members. Adam Clayton Powell is not. Nor have most Negroes prominent in political life received invitations. Outstanding Negro performers like Sidney Poitier and Harry Belafonte are not members since the rules demand that all members be college graduates. And no matter how wealthy or well known an individual is, if the source of wealth is illicit or marginal, the person fails to be recommended for admission. Negroes from such businesses as the liquor industry, undertaking, and the stage are generally excluded. So, too, are all persons who are symbols of stark nonconformity of whatever nature—scandalous personal behavior, too keen a sense of self-promotion, or even the dramatic brilliance of the artist: James Baldwin and Ralph Ellison are not members of Boulé nor was Richard Wright. They are outstanding American writers, but they are not college graduates.

There is some pretense and artificiality in Boulé. In an attempt to build a tradition of inherited status, sons and grandsons of members may be admitted who do not quite match the high standards required of their fathers and grandfathers. It is a kind of family, a community of mutual acceptance, of congeniality and compatibility. On the surface it may seem to be snobbish, superficial, and stuffy. Yet though it provides no program of action, it does provide a sense of belonging.

As late as 1964, Boulé members engaged in a revealing debate on whether it would be legitimate for the group to contribute $5,000 to the NAACP. The main argument against such a step was that the group did not exist to provide leadership in the civil rights movement. An important aspect of Boulé's value was said to be that Negroes could enjoy friendship with persons of similar status without needing to be reminded continually of the everyday problems of being a Negro. Essential to the Negro's psychological health was his creation of a safe oasis. Precisely because the realities of life for the Negro in America do demand continuous involvement in racial problems, he must fight against insidious attempts to allow these problems to invade every crevice of his life. They argued for the right of Negroes to enjoy frivolity, even irrelevance, and to be preoccupied even with inconsequential matters.

Those who took the contrary position—including a Negro millionaire—maintained that the Negro cannot find even temporary isolation from the conflict and tensions of race. They declared that no thinking, sensitive Negro could avoid involvement with the racial struggle, and that an attempt to do so would be a flight into unreality, a symptom of personal and group irrelevance, if not of sickness.

The issue was finally resolved by a majority decision to contribute $5,000 each to the NAACP and to the NAACP's Legal Defense and Education Fund, with an additional $5,000 to the Association for the Study of Negro Life and History. The understanding was that these contributions were evidence of the group's desire to be relevant to the civil rights struggle, yet that such relevance was not necessarily inconsistent with the needs of Negroes to find some shelter from racial bombardment. The Negro cannot demonstrate strength and virtue all the time. No human being can. Not even soldiers are under constant attack, but are rotated at the front with men fresh and rested for battle.

But there are signs that some of the leadership of Boulé is urging more direct involvement. Percy L. Julian, a distinguished businessman and scientist, in his memorial address to the group published in the October 1964 *Boulé Journal,* said:

So goes the great dialogue and rebuke of "do-nothingers" especially Scholars in this day of human travail. I cannot comprehend the remotest possibility that the noble men of Sigma Pi Phi, whose tradition is that of Scholars, will continue to defame the sacred memory of our beloved forbears, by sitting on our inherited stools of intellectual eminence and merely watching the streams of life go by. Make no mistake about it. This is largely what we are doing.

Creative Power Transcending the Ghetto

A few Negroes—among them, Ralph Bunche of the United Nations; Howard Thurman, chaplain of Boston University; John Hope Franklin, the distinguished historian; James Robinson of Crossroads Africa—have succeeded in gaining acceptance outside the ghetto not through civil rights leadership or business ventures but through their own personal efforts and accomplishments.

Robinson, though a Harlem minister, sought to exert influence beyond the confines of his church. Unlike King and Powell, however, he sought to support effective religious leadership not by moving into the realm of politics or civil rights power primarily, but by developing contacts with universities and philanthropic organizations and by broad international interests. His development of Crossroads Africa, as one of the pioneer efforts in the use of American students overseas, became one of the precedents for the successful Peace Corps. This was a testament to a stature and a vision capable of breaking through the demands and dimensions of the ghetto. It did not, however, impressively increase Robinson's power or status within the ghetto. In fact, it is possible that as he demonstrated the capacity for outreach and the ability to deal with larger problems, his influence within the ghetto, which demands a focus on the ghetto's own specific problems, tended to decrease. The decision to give up his church and to move completely out of the ghetto, basing his activities outside, was consistent with this inevitable fact.

To take another example, James Dumpson, New York City's Commissioner of Welfare, gained his position not because he is a Negro but because of his exceptional professional competence. He is widely respected in professional circles and is considered one of Mayor Wagner's top commissioners. He has brought a tough, practical, realistic approach and a professisonal skill to his job. But because the ghetto does not control his skill or his performance, he holds no power in the ghetto itself and is criticized in the ghetto for failing to consider his role to be primarily one of responsibility for Negroes. If the skills and talents of Negroes like Dumpson are to be available to the total community, the ghetto cannot possess them;

nor can the ghetto demand that their contributions be restricted to the problems of the ghetto.

This would suggest the general principle that as a Negro succeeds in mobilizing and directing his energies on larger problems and is accepted and regarded as successful in competition in the larger arena, his usefulness and his ability to function within the dynamics of the ghetto decline. The ghetto appears to weed out individuals of certain levels of interest and competence, excluding them from effectiveness in the ghetto and thereby contributing to the self-perpetuating pathology of the ghetto itself. Such persons may be regarded as deserters, and the ghetto has no role for them to play. They are psychologically unprepared to meet the ghetto's demands, which are essentially demands of a restriction of vision. The inner turmoil, stress, and confinement of the ghetto demand that all of one's energies be devoted either to exploiting or rebelling against the ghetto. This choice is inconsistent with artistic standards or with any deep or serious concern with problems of national or international scope; an effective leader in the ghetto may be absolutely ignorant of the most elemental issues of public affairs. Ralph Bunche, as one of the world's outstanding statesmen, has no function in the ghetto. During the Lumumba affair at the United Nations, after Bunche raised a critical voice against the Negro nationalists who demonstrated in the UN, the Negro press and, interestingly enough, some Negro intellectuals rebuked Bunche. He had no right, they said, to criticize Negroes. They had sought to impose upon him the rules of the ghetto:

1. *One basic rule* is to present to the hostile white world a single voice of protest and rebellion. No Negro who is concerned with his acceptance in the ghetto dares to violate this rule.

2. *Another basic rule* is that no issue can take precedence over the basic issue of race and, specifically, of racial oppression.

The Negro who dares to move outside of the ghetto, either physically or psychologically, runs the risk of retaliatory hostility, at worst, or of misunderstanding, at best. To do so requires strength and individualism. It may reflect, in addition, a desire to escape a negative racial identification and an urgent, anguished, realistic desire to affirm himself as an individual without regard to the white or the Negro world, without regard to the tendency of whites to shackle or imprison his spirit, or the tendency of Negroes, in a different but just as effective way, to do the same. Yet escape, whatever the motive, can never be complete as long as racial oppression exists. The Negro, no matter how successful his flight may appear, still remains in conflict, a conflict stemming from his awareness of the ambivalence of other Negroes toward him and from his awareness that the larger white society never accepts him fully. He is in conflict within himself, with whites, and with Negroes, confronted by a sense of guilt, alienation, resentment, and random bitterness directed as much against Negroes as against whites.

Some do step outside altogether and violate the ghetto's taboos, but not without penalty. It is interesting that almost every well-known Negro writer, artist, and performer has left the ghetto: James Baldwin, Richard Wright, Lorraine Hansberry, Harry Belafonte, Sidney Poitier, Lena Horne, Louis Lomax, Sammy Davis. But even though they leave the ghetto physically, they do not do so psychologically. They are still bound to it. Baldwin is the clearest illustration of this; his writings are ghetto-bound. The artist may flirt with trying to find a meaningful and acceptable place by himself in the fight against the oppressiveness of the ghetto. At the same time, he feels reluctant to go back and is probably literally incapable of returning.

The problem for the Negro scholar is even more acute in view of the fact that he is not permitted to escape into the subjectivity and emotion that are an expected part of the life of the artist. He must deal with facts and ideas, and must articulate and interpret complex social processes. If he is faithful to his craft, he must confront directly not only the dilemmas of his society, but the dilemmas within himself. The dilemma becomes even more focused when the Negro scholar is required to use his skill and insights and training in a critical and evaluative role, forced to look dispassionately at all aspects of his society and to describe as faithfully as he can the difficulties of both the white and the Negro worlds. To rise above the accepted defenses, the fantasies, the rules and regulations governing accommodation within the ghetto and within the larger society, demands of the Negro scholar, writer, and artist not only intellectual and artistic skills but a pattern of intangible and complex personal and psychological strengths, the value and source of which are not clearly known. One thing is clear; the artist and scholar cannot have power inside the ghetto. The fantasies and delusions of the ghetto are not permitted the artist or scholar; for them a pitiless vision is required.

The constricted opportunities and the racially determined limits of the rewards available to the ghetto tend to intensify petty status competitiveness and suspiciousness in the ghetto, particularly against those who break through the barriers of the invisible wall. It stimulates, too, a capricious flirtation between a superficial hostility and an equally superficial and exaggerated admiration for even minor achievement of a fellow ghetto dweller.

Those who have been deeply damaged by the ghetto seem unable to trust even their own feelings. They cannot afford the psychic luxury of depth of emotion. Even their hostility must be kept manageable. Their praise or castigation of Negro leaders or of the Negro masses seems verbal, and related only to the moment. The same person might move from indifference to adoration to condemnation of a fellow Negro within a single conversation without his or his audience's seeming to be conscious of any inconsistency. A member of the Negro middle class may both idealize and reject the masses of workingclass Negroes. A workingclass Negro may at the same time be proud of the skill and poise of Negro leaders and resent and suspect them because of their education and achievement. Negro leaders may work effectively with each other at the same time that they confide to their "white friends" their doubts and reservations about each other. Beneath the surface of apparent Negro unity remains the psychological turbulence arising out of past and present racial injustice.

Given the chronic debasement and assaults on his ego, probably the most difficult feeling for any American Negro to maintain toward himself or any other Negro is that of stable and unqualified respect. His core of doubt about the qualifications and the price in integrity or honesty which the successful Negro must have paid, or even concerning his right to prominence in the face of the pervasive failure of his group, protrudes and contaminates the ability of one Negro to respect and to accept another Negro without ambivalence and skepticism. This seems particularly true when the Negro seeks—and wins—recognition in fields not usually open to Negroes, and where competition and promotion are rigorously controlled by the most powerful whites of our society, e.g., diplomacy and the upper echelons of the academic, business, and industrial world. It is less true in such fields as the arts, the theater, and athletics, where the talent and personal accomplishments of an individual Negro are not subject to ambiguous interpretations: Marian Anderson met the clear test of a great singing voice; it is evident to all that Sidney Poitier and Sammy Davis, Jr., are great talents; that Jackie Robinson was a great ball player; and that Joe Louis knocked out nearly all of his opponents. But even in these cases of outstanding talent and skill among Negroes, it is possible for the masses of Negroes to obtain vicarious satisfaction and release of their frustrations by identifying with them, admiring the talent without, ironically, respecting the person who possesses it.

The effective use of the potential power of the Negro masses and the ability of Negro leaders to discipline and mobilize that power for constructive social change may well be determined by the ability of a critical mass of Negroes to control their ambivalence toward themselves and to develop the capacity for genuine and sustained respect for those Negroes who are worthy of confidence and respect. The present unrealities and distortions of ghetto life make it difficult to differentiate between empty flamboyance and valid achievement; between hysterical, cynical, verbal manipulations and sound judgment. It is difficult for the uneducated, exploited, and despised Negro to know whom he can trust and whom he must continue to suspect. He knows for sure only his own deep despair and resentment, and he sees that as long as the conditions which give rise to these feelings persist he will continue to be their victim. The compounded tragedy is that he will remain the chief victim also of himself. The real tragedy for the Negro is that he has not taken himself seriously because no one else has. The hope for the Negro is that now he is asserting that he really is a human being, and is demanding the rights due to a human being. If he succeeds in winning these rights he will respect and trust himself, but he cannot win the right to human dignity without the ability to respect and cherish his own humanity in spite of pervasive white rejection.

8

STRATEGY FOR CHANGE

Stagnant ghettos are a monument to the dominance of forces which tend to perpetuate the *status quo* and to resist constructive social change. If the ghettos are to be transformed, then forces superior to those which resist change must be mobilized to counteract them. The problem of change in the ghetto is esssentially, therefore, a problem of power—a confrontation and conflict between the power required for change and the power resistant to change. The problem of power is crucial and nuclear to any nonsentimental approach to understanding, planning, and predicting.

Power is defined, in physics, as any form of energy or force available for work or applied to produce motion or pressure. Used in terms of social dynamics, the term power has essentially the same meaning, namely, the force required to bring about—or to prevent—social, political, or economic changes. It is relevant to an understanding of the problems of disadvantaged minority groups and their confinement within ghettos that one of the meanings of the term power emphasizes the possession of control or command or authority over others and directly relates to the problem of status. The form of power that is most significant in the understanding of social change is that combination of energies required to determine and to translate goals into a desired social reality.

Power and Social Change

The effective, constructive use of power is indicated not merely by expressing a desire for change, but by the demonstration of the ability to achieve it. There is an important and often overlooked distinction between *pseudopower,* which is restricted to a verbal or posturing level of reality—by word or by acting "as if"—and *actual power,* demonstrated in *social action* and *social change.* But it may be useful to carry the distinction one step further, that is, to differentiate between social action and social change, the significant social power. Social action may be used as a form of diversion of power under the conditions where the significant political and economic forces permit certain action as a mere escape valve and as a displacement of energy. It is possible for the forces aligned for the perpetuation of the *status quo* to permit the power of those who desire social change to be dissipated into mere appearances of social action—catharsis—without observable and meaningful progress. This can be a most effective technique of control, exploiting as it does the democratic ritual of freedom of protest. In the final analysis, however, the key criterion—the significant basis of actual power—must be a demonstrated change in a desired direction.

It would be reasonable to assume a necessary relationship among the forms of social power—words, action, and change; that is, that the verbal manifestation of power would tend to precede social action, which in turn would precede the ultimate actual power in social change. Many would accept such a progressive continuum uncritically as a correlate of democratic social processes, assuming that one who begins at the stage of protest moves on to demonstration of this protest—an acting out, as in a picket line, of the fervor and resolution of intent—and finally triumphs in the effective mobilization of power. It is conceivable, however, that effective control of a verbalization of power might instead preclude the possibility of progression either to the intermediate stage of social action or the climax of social change itself.

It is also conceivable that skillful manipulation of the social action level of protest, too, could interfere with the ability of a disadvantaged group to move meaningfully to the level of social change. The ultimate of skill in blocking this transition would be for the resistant forces not to resist social action overtly but so to identify with the goals, techniques, and demonstrations as to obscure for the protesters the real goals of the protest. Under these conditions energy is diverted away from the hard demands of complex strategy into the securing of friendship, the enlisting of allies, the achievement of affability and accommodation. Those genuinely concerned not just with the satisfactions of social action but the achievement of actual power must resist flagrant and particularly subtle attempts to obscure the goal if they would not find themselves regressing to the relatively easier stand of mere verbal protest.

Probably the most dramatic example of the effective use of the power of social action can be found in the March on Washington, organized by civil rights groups in August 1963. More than a quarter of a million Americans, white and black, converged on Washington to demonstrate their concern for racial democracy in America and "For Jobs and Freedom." The speeches were inspiring, and some were considered classic. The spirit was akin to that of religious fervor and conversion. The mass media contributed to the belief that it was a most effective demonstration. The marchers were well organized, orderly, peaceful, and united. In the planning the largest effort seemed directed toward insuring that fears of violence and disorder would be frustrated. The value to America was illustrated by the fact that the Voice of America carried this demonstration throughout the world as an example of the ability of Americans to petition their government for redress of grievances. The fact that a significant proportion of those participating in the march were white, the fact that the National Council of Churches, Catholic Interracial Council, and Jewish groups joined predominantly Negro civil rights groups in making the March on Washington a success, gave further testament to the strength of American democracy. Although President Kennedy did not address the assembled crowd, he made it clear that the demonstration had his blessing. There was a general air of festive acceptance of the rightness of the cause, unquestioned faith that justice would eventually prevail, and that the ceremonies of democracy are themselves evidence of the inevitability of progress. It has often been said that the Civil Rights Bill of 1964 was a direct consequence of this mobilization of power.

Whatever the forces responsible for the Civil Rights Act of 1964, they cannot be reduced to the single fact of a demonstration in August 1963, on the evidence alone that the March on Washington occurred earlier than did the passage of the act. The march was followed, also, by a prolonged filibuster on the part of Southern senators. Within two months after the march four Negro children were murdered in a church bombing in Birmingham. Within a year, scores of Negro churches were bombed or destroyed by other means, and three civil rights workers were killed in Mississippi. Of utmost significance is the fact that the term "white backlash," a popular phrase for intensified white resistance to integration, became a part of the colloquial language within the year immediately following the march.

The demonstration did not affect the day-to-day lives of the masses of oppressed Negroes in the Southern states or in the Northern ghettos. The poor housing, the poor schools, job discrimination, and the stigmatized and rejected status which were the lot of the Negro in America in July 1963 remained precisely his predicament in July 1964.

Yet the march had a dramatic impact on the morale of middle-class Negroes. For many Negroes in the North, participation in the march was their first decision to assume the risks of action. For many alienated Negroes in the South, it revealed for the first time the extent of support for their cause in the rest of the country. In addition, it may be that the march was not so much an effective instrument of social change—for it probably was not—as an evidence of a consensus of support from respectable middle-class groups, white and Negro, hitherto inarticulate, disorganized, and irresolute. It may have helped to convince some persons in the seats of power that some degree of social change was desirable, if only to contain the energies of protests. But it could also, and very likely did, release the energies of others, opposed to civil rights, in reciprocal protest. One could speculate on the possibility that as the intensity of the Negro's verbal and action demonstrations of power and desire for change increased, the expressson of the verbal and social action resistance on the parts of whites increased correspondingly. This pattern seems to be true both in the North as well as in the South. Action produces counteraction—a school boycott by civil rights groups stimulates a boycott by those who wish to preserve the *status quo*—and then the question becomes: To which group do the forces of actual power choose to respond? Will the actual power follow the direction of the verbal demands of Negroes for change or the verbal resistance of the majority of whites to change? The power to bring about a legislative consensus for change may not necessarily be the same power required to implement or enforce the consensus.

The problem posed for Negroes and those whites who are committed to actual social change as a reality and not a mere social posture is that of identifying, mobilizing, and using that power necessary to translate laws into meaningful changes in the day-to-day lives of those whom the laws are intended to protect. This problem of power is one of the more difficult ones to resolve positively because masses of whites believe that they stand to gain by maintaining the Negro in his present predicament, because some whites and a few Negroes actually do gain economically and politically by maintaining the racial *status quo,* and because energy must always be mobilized to counteract social inertia.

The conflict of power then becomes a struggle between conscience and economic loss or between conscience and political pragmatism. If economic loss—or anticipated loss—is great, as in the fear of a worker with low seniority that a Negro will take his job, moral power does not count heavily in the scales. And if conscience counts only when the threat of loss is minimal, then the avenue of effective social change in civil rights must lie in identifying those groups who will not be directly threatened by change and encouraging the release of their latent moral energy in effective action. Social progress seems to depend on a combination of such forces, for where advance which is not triggered by military force would be to the detriment of the essential sources of power, advance does not take place.

Social change that appears on the surface to benefit a minority—as in the case of civil rights—rarely engages the commitment of the majority.

Continuing evidence of the pervasive moral apathy and political cynicism in the American mass culture is a significant negative in weighing the possibilities for social democracy. If the practical imperatives for constructive change were to be controlled by the chance of profound moral conversion, there might be cause for pessimism. Negroes must convince the majority, who are white, that continued oppression of the Negro minority hurts the white majority too. Nor is it sophistry to argue that this is indeed the case. If it were not the case, the Negro cause would be hopeless. Certainly the Negro cannot hope to argue his case primarily in terms of ethical concerns, for these historically have had only sentimental and verbal significance in themselves. They have never been the chief source of power for that social change which involves significant alteration of status between privileged versus unprivileged groups. Child labor legislation was not the direct result of a moral indignation against the exploitation of children in factories, mines, mills, but rather reflected a growing manpower shortage and the new rise of the labor unions. The value of ethical appeals is to be found only when they can be harnessed to more concrete appeals such as economic, political, or other power advantages to be derived from those with the power to facilitate or inhibit change. Ethical and moral appeal can be used to give theoretical support for a program of action, or in some cases to obscure and make the pragmatic aspects of that program more palatable to conscience. If moral force opposes economic or political ends, the goal of moral force may be postponed. The reverse may also be true. But where moral force and practical advantage are united, their momentum is hard to deny.

Conflicting Forces

A summary of the positives and the negatives in the present civil rights crisis would seem to highlight the following as clear gains within the past two years:

Religious groups have become more seriously involved in action geared toward the elimination of racism in our society. The activities of the National Council of Churches of Christ in America, and the intensified activities of the Roman Catholic church, together with the clear commitment of the organized Jewish groups, have contributed significantly to the awakening of the dormant conscience of the American people.

There is also evidence that the leaders of business and industry are now beginning to understand more clearly that it is not to the interest of the capitalistic system to have one-tenth of our nation underemployed and blocked from the consumer market. The artificial reduction of the gross national product, which inevitably results from racial discrimination, may turn out to be the pivot of change. The vitality and growth potential of the American economy may well depend upon the capacity to change old patterns of attitudes and behavior and make it possible to exploit constructively the nation's underdeveloped group. One is reminded of Gunnar Myrdal's recent observation, in his *Challenge of Affluence,* that at this period in history practical economic imperatives and American idealism have converged.

On the negative side one still is confronted with the fact that American labor unions reflect for the most part a racial rigidity which is inimical to the national interest and, of course, is detrimental to the interests of organized labor. This paradox, this blindness, can only be self-destructive. In that lies the hope for change.

Countering the forces resistant to the effective social change are other forces not related directly to civil rights but with an impact upon the problem. Among these are the shift in population from a predominantly rural and agrarian to an urban industrial society; the tremendous technological revolution in transportation and communication; the major political and economic developments throughout the world; rapid changes in status and relationship among previously subject people; and the accelerated momentum of political and economic democracy which triggered and propelled the end of European colonial domination. The psychological impact of these seemingly impersonal changes on the morale and the drive of the American Negro is obvious. His aspirations are compatible with the world-wide democratic momentum; the resistance of those who would deny these aspirations is incompatible with this momentum, and therefore it is the Negro who has the most potential for actual power. In one sense this factor appears abstract and nebulous. But it may determine whether the power of the American Negro will remain largely either a verbal pseudopower, cathartic but inconsequential, or will culminate in actual social change.

The success of the Negro revolution is inevitable, given the long-term view. But the pace of that revolution within the lifetime of those now living depends upon the soundness of the strategy and the methods that derive from it which are adopted by civil rights leadership. Negroes have a variety of alternatives of strategy to consider. Direct action and nonviolent demonstrations have been effective, but they must inevitably decrease in impact. Intense and dramatic experiences are subject to the psychological law of diminishing returns—a decrease in sensitivity both on the part of the participant and the audience. This principle of adaptation holds even on such levels as specific sensory experiences, e.g., the adaptive automatic fatigue of the nerves of sight and sound and smell. To a sight or noise or smell that is often repeated and that persists, a person becomes oblivious. Furthermore, these demonstrations appear to be more difficult to sustain psychologically than military operations, for example, because those who take part in civil rights demonstrations, unlike the military, must tend to the day-to-day routine of living independent of the campaign. They must work and take care of their families. Demonstrations are psychologically exhausting, and the more they are used the more they tend to become routine, and the less their impact and effect.

These demonstrations will only retain some value if they do not become diffuse and unrelated to specific targets and goals. It would be unfortunate if these demonstrations became a form of *bread and circuses* which provided an outlet for emotional catharsis for Negroes but did not deal with the pressing social, economic, or political problems. This would be a dissipation of precious human energy and a cruel hoax. In this regard, one could look with suspicion on the tendency of some white political officials to join some of the more respectable demonstrations, and the equally disturbing tendency of some Negro leaders to embrace this type of superficial but skillful neutralization of a protest movement.

Another danger which threatens the future effectiveness of these demonstrations is the tendency to use them as vehicles for the projection of the egos and personal ambitions of local and would-be leaders of Negroes. These persons, who often do not have responsibility for the burdens of a complex organization, can assume postures of militance and make flamboyant statements which appeal to the crowd without regard to whether the statements lead to change. They need not concern themselves with such mundane things as planning, strategy, and follow-through. It is enough that they have an arsenal of words and are adept at name-calling and are ruthless in their ability to ascribe nefarious motives to anyone who disagrees with them. The most successful of these wildcat civil rights leaders use the technique of demagogic intimidation of the more responsible civil rights leaders. To the extent that they are allowed to be successful, they are serious threats to the movement. The potential anarchy is in some ways similar to that of a military organization in which a corporal is permitted to intimidate, or countermand the orders of, a general.

It is not enough, however, to criticize and attempt to dismiss as ineffective various responses by Negroes to their cumulative frustration revealed in the nonselective boycotts like the 1963 New York school boycotts, the proposed stall-in planned to disrupt transportation on the opening day of the World's Fair, or the random violent protests of the 1964 summer urban ghetto riots. A letter in the Columbia University *Daily Spectator* (April 23, 1963) from a Negro undergraduate reveals the mood characteristic of many Negro youth, probably particularly of those destined by capacity and circumstances for leadership:

> The stall-in, the sit-ins, the school boycotts, the pickets, and all demonstrations of civil disobedience are only inevitable consequences of a long standing malfunction of our society. I sincerely wonder if those who came out so strongly against the stall-in have come out, are coming out, and will come out as strongly against poor public service in Harlem,

blatant police brutality in Negro areas, the inferior schools provided by the city for minority groups, discrimination in employment, and all forms of racial prejudice which prevent Negroes from their right to a first class citizenship.

The demonstrations by civil rights groups will become more indirect, more confused, more frustrating, and will alienate more "white liberals." They will continue until there is no longer any cause for them to continue. So I urge all interested parties to do more than verbalize their opposition to the effects; I urge them to direct themselves actively according to their capabilities to the cause of these effects. And until the cause is eliminated I will verbally and actively support irresponsible and responsible, indirect and direct, and overt and non-violent demonstrations which are aimed at the amelioration of our society. We have nothing to lose.

If demonstrations are often unwise and ineffective because they lead to retaliatory behavior without achieving specific goals, they must, nonetheless, be understood. This kind of fervent protest which defends both rational and irrational means to the desired end is a sign of the proud determination of many young Negroes to achieve their goals at whatever cost, and a sign of a loyal identification with the groups which shame had, in the past, prevented middle-class Negroes from sharing. It is a coalition against the observed "enemy" and, whatever its wisdom, must be heeded as evidence of the total intellectual and emotional commitment, the burning of the bridges characteristic of the impatient rising generation of Negro leadership.

Alternatives to Sound and Fury

If, however, disorganization and lack of discipline are permitted to develop into a primary weapon, the civil rights struggle will become a farce, unrelated to the resolution of basic and serious racial problems. Serious thought must be given to the problem of determining under what conditions certain techniques and demonstrations will be used. The argument that they will anger or alienate white friends is beside the point and unacceptable to thoughtful Negroes because white friends who refrain from anger at injustices but permit themselves to become angry at attempts to remedy these injustices are to a Negro irrelevant. Furthermore, such white friends and enemies are both more likely to be angered by methods that prove effective than by methods that prove inappropriate and ineffectual.

Student sitins, freedom rides, and bus boycotts were successful in the South, as noted earlier, because these methods dealt directly with desired objectives. They were clear and focused, and directly dramatized a specific injustice. The selective buying campaign in Philadelphia is an example of effective protest because Reverend Leon Sullivan and his associates organized it masterfully, pinpointed the targets, and were able to sustain and follow through on their demands as well as measure directly the degree of success. The NAACP campaign to bring pressure on industry has a similar strategy and may therefore be effective.

Some criteria for determining whether a boycott is an appropriate technique are if:

1. It is directed against a product rather than a service.
2. The economic damage or inconvenience is clearly to be borne by the proprietor rather than by the boycotters.
3. The goals and demands are clear and obtainable.
4. The action can be sustained until the demands are met.
5. There is minimum inconvenience to persons who are not responsible for the injustice.

Serious consideration should be given to the use of the boycott technique in dealing with the problems of education. There might be times when the boycott of schools is the most effective method of dramatizing and calling attention to long-standing educational deficiencies and ills, for example, in Boston, where as late as 1963, the school board insisted that there was no segregation and no "racial problem" in the schools; and in Cleveland, where the board sanctioned a policy of bringing Negro children to an allegedly integrated school but keeping them in separate classes. This kind of flagrant denial and degradation would seem to warrant the use of dramatic demonstrations where more reasonable methods failed.

But the objective can be attained most effectively if the boycott threat is not abused or used inappropriately. In New York City the school board had committed itself to desegregation, had reaffirmed the policy, and had embarked on at least a minimal desegregation policy. The problem here was to encourage the adoption and implementation of a more realistic, farsighted program. There was a question whether the boycott was an appropriate method to achieve this end. It may, indeed, have encouraged the use of similar methods on the part of the Parents and Taxpayers group and therefore the unification rather than the fragmentation of the opposition. The board now had to take into account a new, anti-civil-rights pressure group.

The possibility of eroding the moral strength and power of the civil rights movement is greatest if civil rights leaders permit themselves to be caught in the trap of rigidity and militancy for their own sake. Given the fact that the Negro in America does not have military, economic, and political power with which to wage his war for unqualified equality, he must rely upon a cold, calculating use of intellectual and moral power. He cannot permit himself to be shackled to gestures, slogans, and strategic clichés. He must be free to deal with the realities and he must be tough-minded as he seeks every advantage in a war of maneuver and propaganda. Irrationalities, emotionalism, and rigidity in the name of civil rights goals are no more acceptable than the irrationalities, emotionalism and rigidity of racism. The fight for racial justice is essentially the fight for the ascendancy of reason and humanity over ignorance and inhumanity.

Having said this, candor requires one to say also that it is ironic to observe that, more often than not, it is the more irrational and emotional appeals and demands which are responded to positively by those in control of political power. It raises a serious question about the value of a trained and disciplined mind when one is forced to observe that logical and reasoned arguments for social justice are so frequently ignored, while the threats of the demagogue are responded to.

Now that a "strong" civil rights bill has been passed, Negro organizations need to address themselves to the difficult task of planning and implementing a comprehensive and coordinated strategy.

This strategy requires effective machinery by which responsibility for decisions on specific objectives is delegated to appropriate groups and agencies; performance and effects of action are evaluated; and, if need be, some controls over inefficient, uneconomic, or ineffectual activities can be exercised.

Certainly a comprehensive plan and strategy must necessarily include decisions concerning the priorities and the energies to be expended and the methods to be used in eliminating racial discrimination and segregation in the key areas of education, employment, housing, voting and citizen rights and responsibilities, and public accommodations.

A general appraisal of the present level of civil rights activities suggests that it could be made even more effective through systematic programs for the gathering of information and intelligence, public education, and evaluation techniques and programs.

The case for planning is difficult to establish persuasively in a climate that demands immediate action and solutions. In the early stages of the Harlem Youth development project (Haryou), the most persistent criticism, from both responsible and sometimes irresponsible sources, was that there was no need for further study. These critics contended that planning and study are transparent dodges for the postponement of action and that those involved in the charade of research into the problems of disadvantaged youth were willing or inadvertent accessories to the perpetuation of the present injustices.

The most virulent statement of this position was made by an editor on the New York *Amsterdam News:*

. . . I'm fed up with social workers in Harlem because the average social worker in Harlem prostitutes the misery of the community and spends three quarters of his time trying to convert that misery into dollars and cents to put in his own pocket. . . .

So the folks downtown say in unison to the Harlem "expert":

"What can we do for these people to prevent this?"

This is what our expert has been waiting for. "I don't have all the answers, gentlemen," he says. "But I think I'm on the right track toward a solution to the problem. With about $250,000 I could pull together a research team of eminent social workers, psychologists, psychiatrists, anthropologists—the whole bit—and these men will come up with the answer for you in 18 months."

"In other words," say the City Fathers, "you need $250,000 to get started, is that right?"

And so the Harlem expert, whom you don't even know and who doesn't even know you, hops on the "A" train with a quarter of a million dollars of your money and mine to spend studying you.

The answer to these criticisms could not be made defensively or by claiming any magic inherent in a scientific approach to the solution of social problems. Attempts to interpret the planning stage as an inescapable antecedent, and an integral part of effective action were, at best, grudgingly accepted. This impatience with systematic planning must therefore be understood as an inevitable part of the high emotionality which permeates the racial crisis.

The *laissez faire* tradition so dominant in American history has had as one of its by-products a suspicion and aversion to systematic planning for human welfare and change. The implication is that desirable change will be achieved by natural, spontaneous development. Suspicion of planning, however related to a healthy concern for freedom, has its negative aspects. Intelligent planning, which rationally would seem obviously desirable, is rejected; for example, cities are allowed to grow at random without anyone effectively anticipating the problems of transportation, space, and esthetic needs. Planlessness is reinforced by apathy and by intellectual laziness. It has, furthermore, a potentially exploitative aspect. If one makes a virtue of not planning, then it is easier for individuals, under the guise of freedom, to use a situation for selfish ends. For example, if in building, one follows no rules or regulations as to safety, it can be interpreted as freedom for the builder but as denial of freedom to others. So, too, in the movement for social change in America's dark ghettos. A ghetto is not just a reflection of a struggle for power between those who wish to change and those who resist change, but a reflection also of primitive hostility to the creative use of human intelligence. Planning is not intrinsically a postponement of action, though it may be used as such. It is the rational approach to observed problems. It is a necessary prelude to effective action.

Ideology, Leadership, and Social Momentum

In reacting to the fervor of the present civil rights movement, it is easy to become preoccupied with the charismatic role of individuals and confuse this with the necessity for systematic strategy and planning for social change. It is sometimes forgotten that the historic Brown decision of the United States Supreme Court, which played a catalytic role in the present racial crisis, was the consequence of prolonged, nondramatic planning and of the activity of a highly trained legal staff in collaboration with social scientists and educators.

It is quite another matter to consider the strategy of deliberate compromise to be a sign of respectable evolutionary change. It may be the dilemma of the American Negro that he is torn between the reasonable and seductive appeals to be statesmanlike in his sense of timing and in his methods, and his deep and persistent awareness that past techniques of negotiations, discussions, and compromises are no longer consistent with contemporary realities. The successful movement of democracy in America and throughout the world has removed certain decisions from the Negro himself. Negro leaders can no longer control the pace of racial change in America. In fact they are no longer, if they ever were, literally *leaders*. Rather, they now seem to be mere interpreters or executives. This may be an important personal dilemma of those in a leadership role, but the imperatives of social momentum cannot be denied.

The basic structure, strength, and weaknesses of American society face increasing critical evaluation by a growing number of young Negro intellectuals. Probably James Baldwin, novelist and essayist, is the outstanding example and the most eloquent of these younger Negro social critics. In a bitter exclamation of futility and pessimism Baldwin quotes a prominent Negro, "I am not at all sure that I *want* to be integrated into a burning house." He quotes another as saying, "I might consider being integrated into something else, an American society more real and more honest—but *this?* No, thank you, man, who needs it?"

A further indication of the present mood of the younger Negro intellectual is the fact that he is directing his critical barbs not only at the inconsistencies and injustices inherent in American racism but is becoming increasingly critical—or more overt in his criticisms —of traditional Negro leaders and Negro organizations. While there have always been criticisms of these individuals and organizations from the more militant nationalistic groups of Negroes, it is significant in appraising the present mood of the Negro, particularly in the North, to note the relatively new fact that such criticisms, generally more reasoned and sober, are now coming from younger Negro intellectuals. It is another index of the complexity of the present level of strength and increasing morale of the Negro that it is possible to view these criticisms as evidence that the Negro in the North is now secure enough to assume the difficult role of self-critic and to demand that the Negro organizations become even more effective in obtaining complete equality in the shortest possible time. His anxieties lest these organizations and leaders show signs of fatigue or politically expedient compromise place him at polar opposites to those whites who tend to see organizations like the NAACP as extremist groups. The impatient younger Negro is more likely to see these organizations as more moderate and conservative than is consistent with his own sense of urgency. An additional dimension of this paradox is found in the fact that in spite of the sometimes hysterical criticisms of the NAACP by the more extreme nationalistic groups among Negroes, the more sober criticism from Negro intellectuals, and the strident, irrational criticisms and reprisals of white segregationists, the NAACP membership has risen at a faster pace among Negroes in the North than in the South during the past decade. It has also, like the National Urban League, which had further to go, increased its own pace and its sense of militancy in response to impatient pressure from younger Negroes.

As the lines of racial confrontation become more clearly drawn, some of the basic dilemmas of the Negro people take the form of apparent ideological differences and conflicts. The most obvious of these differences is found in an analysis of the relationship between the tactics and philosophy of Martin Luther King, on the one hand, and the Black Muslim movement, on the other. These two approaches appear to be dramatically and diametrically opposed. Martin Luther King preaches a doctrine of "love for the oppressor" at the same time that he offers an effective social action technique of nonviolent, assertive demand for civil rights. The Black Muslims preach a doctrine of black supremacy, hatred of whites, and total separation of Negroes from whites, who are characterized as "blue-eyed devils," morally defective and therefore incapable of offering the Negro justice and equality. In spite of these apparent differences, it would be a mistake to ignore the similarities in these two movements: Each reflects the Negro's basic impatience; each accepts, as a fact, the assumption that if the Negro is to attain his rights, he must do so primarily, if not exclusively, through his own efforts; each is an assertive reaction against the dawdling, tortuously slow pace of desegregation by the majority of whites who seem to Negroes to desire racial peace at any price; and each is in its own way militant and uncompromising.

For purposes of analysis, however, the most significant similarity between these two movements is the fact that they represent a basic dilemma and ambivalence within the Negro people as a whole. The Black Muslims reflect the reality of hatred and resentment which Negroes understandably feel. The Muslims are honest and defiant in their extreme expression of this genuine and understandably human reaction to injustice. The fact that they might be unrealistic, inconsistent, and irrational in the remedy which they suggest is not particularly relevant to the understanding of the psychological reality which they reflect.

Black nationalism, which has been accurately described as the contemporary descendent of the Garvey movement of the 1920s, is, like the Garvey movement, if not exclusively, a predominantly Northern urban social phenomenon. The national leadership and headquarters of the Black Muslims are located in Chicago. Their growing strength appears to be centered in Chicago, New York, Boston, Detroit, and Philadelphia. Recently there seems to be some evidence that the movement has gotten some foothold also in one Southern city, Atlanta. Their philosophy and that of other black nationalist groups is rather simple and direct. It is a philosophy rooted in hatred and despair and reflecting the American racist simplifications of the importance of skin color. The dramatic twist which these groups give to American racism is that they preach the supremacy of blacks and the inherent degradation of whites. This reversal is dramatic, disturbing, and terrifying to whites and to some middle- and upper-class Negroes as well.

The Black Muslims and most, if not all, of the other nationalistic groups appeal to the more marginal Negro. They recruit most successfully from the lower socio-economic and marginal classes. As C. Eric Lincoln has pointed out,* this group does a most effective job in rehabilitating its members. It is ironic that these essentially cultist groups are markedly more effective in raising the morale of their members, giving some purpose and meaning to their lives, than are the more acceptable social institutions and the traditional churches. The explanation for this irony may be found in the basic truth in the argument of the leaders of this group; namely, that our middle-class society, in inflicting or accepting the stigma and humiliation on the masses of black men, puts skin color above justice and humanity. These movements must be appraised as symptoms of the profound frustration, despair, and impatience found at all levels of Negro life in America and which have come to the surface within recent years. They cannot be dismissed as mere cults because the majority of Negroes have so far not joined them. The psychological complexities from which these cults draw their potential strength are shared by many Negroes of various social and economic groups. A Negro manicurist was quoted in a national magazine as saying, "You know those Muslims are telling the truth about white folks. I am not joining up, but I am not against them either." Lorraine Hansberry, the well-known Negro playwright and one of the more militant younger intellectuals, wrote, in a letter to the *New York Times Magazine*, ". . . I should not have hesitated to sit with, picket with, mourn with either Mustafa Bashire or Benjamin J. Davis or any other Negro who had the passion and understanding to be there [at

* C. Eric Lincoln, *The Black Muslims in America*, Boston, Beacon Press, 1961.

the UN demonstration of Negro nationalist groups over Lumumba's death]. The continuation of intrigues against African and American Negro freedom demands high and steadfast unity among Negroes."

Martin Luther King reflects another aspect of the general feelings of Negroes for whites. In preaching love he taps a part of the truth and, what is more, appears to have hit upon a highly effective strategy and weapon. In spite of pervasive problems of injustice, it is impossible for two peoples to have shared a common destiny for more than three hundred years without evolving bonds of identity and affection. The variations in skin color among American Negroes are all too striking and disturbing indications of the fact that the alleged hatred of the white man for the Negro was never complete and categorical. The Black Muslim's preachings of hatred of Negroes for whites, while a reflection of some aspect of the psychological reality, is also not complete. A major dilemma of the contemporary Negro, therefore, is to decide which aspect of his ambivalence should prevail; which is the more effective.

While Martin Luther King's initial impact among Negroes was indeed dramatic and national in scope, his personal leadership has been more effective in the South than in the North. The nonviolent, passive resistance, "love the oppressor" approach seems to have had some strategic effectiveness in the Southern Negro's struggle against those specific and flagrant types of segregation and discrimination found in the South, and to be consistent with the religious orientation of Southern Negroes to whom the Negro church has often been an ego shelter, a psychological refuge if not, heretofore, an instrument of social change. This philosophy and its related strategy and techniques do not seem to be particularly appropriate in dealing with the more subtle forms of segregation and discrimination of Northern communities. In general, patterns of discrimination in employment, political appointments, segregated housing, and *de facto* segregated education do not seem to be easily dramatized by boycotts, sitins, or the strategic philosophy of "love of the oppressor," in part because it is often custom and subterfuge rather than law that is the enemy. Under these conditions it is difficult to identify a specific oppressor even if one desired to "love" him into compliance with the requirements of justice.

There are more subtle problems involved in attempting to appraise the over-all struggle of the Negro in America. King's insistence that the Negro cannot afford to be corroded by hatred and must therefore discipline himself to love those who despise him is consistent with the Christian tradition and is the antithesis of the doctrine preached by the Black Nationalists. On the surface, King's philosophy appears to reflect health and stability, while the Black Nationalists betray pathology and instability. A deeper analysis, however, might reveal an unrealistic, if not pathological, basis in King's doctrine as well. It is questionable whether masses of an oppressed group can in fact "love" their oppressor. The natural reactions to injustice, oppression, and humiliation are bitterness and resentment. The form which such bitterness takes need not be overtly violent, but the corrosion of the human spirit which is involved seems inevitable. It would appear, then, that any demand that a victim love his oppressor—in contrast with a mere tactical application of nonviolent, dignified resistance as a moral rebuke with concomitant power to arouse the conscience and effectiveness of others—imposes an additional and probably intolerable psychological burden.

It has been argued that the proper interpretation of King's philosophy of love for the oppressor must take into account its Christian philosophical and strategic significance. This argument may be perfectly correct for a small minority of educated and philosophically sophisticated individuals. But it is unlikely that it can be accepted with full understanding by the majority of Negroes. Their very attempt to cope with this type of philosophical abstraction in the face of the concrete injustices which dominate their daily lives can only lead to deep and disturbing conflicts and guilt. The Gandhian method of passive resistance is perhaps less crippling than a Christian adaptation that calls for feelings of love as well.

It is more disturbing to reflect on the possibility that this aspect of Martin Luther King's philosophy has received such widespread and uncritical acceptance among moderate and liberal whites because it is less threatening and rejecting, making the guilt of whites easier to handle psychologically, and moreover not inconsistent with the stereotype of the Negro as a meek, long-suffering creature who prays for deliverance but who rarely acts decisively against injustices.

A Common Destiny

The issue of the rights of the American Negroes will probably not be resolved either by verbal or strategic preoccupation with love or with hatred. The issue may be more realistically resolved by less tenuous emotions, such as enlightened self-interest on the part of Negroes and whites, a shared destiny, and the imperatives of the contemporary threat to the national survival.

An inescapable reality is the fact that the American Negro is inextricably American. In spite of the psychological appeals of identification with Africa, and the temporary props to a sagging ego which can be found in occasional discussions and seminars about "our African heritage," the American Negro is no more African than he is Danish, or Irish, or Indian. He is American. His destiny is one with the destiny of America. His culture is the culture of Americans. His vices and virtues are the vices and virtues of Americans. His dilemmas are essentially the dilemmas of Americans. He cannot escape this stark fact, in spite of understandable attempts to evade the bitter reality that he has been treated, more often than not, as an alien in his own land. This bitterness has been compounded by the ridiculous, absurd fact that the darkest-skinned foreigner will be profusely apologized to if he is accidentally made a victim of American racism, that is, if he is mistaken for an American Negro and treated as such anywhere in America. The implication of these repeated "embarrassments" is that it is all right to treat a dark-skinned American as if he were subhuman, but it is embarrassing to the nation, and a reflection on our sense of decency and courtesy, to treat a dark-skinned African or Asian in a similar manner. This is pathetic and absurd. It defies even the pathological logic of racism. It also contributes to a major dilemma of the American Negro, the dilemma of identification with the rising status of his darker brothers throughout the world and his resentment of the preferential treatment which these individuals receive in his own land and which are denied to him. It is conceivable that some of this resentment might spill over from whites to Africans and Asians. It would be maudlin sentimentality to deny this possibility.

Various groups in Negro society have chosen, or moved unconsciously into, civil rights strategy positions which seem of sufficient consistency of character to justify an attempt to identify and classify them, with the usual injunction advisable in establishing all such categories; namely, that few individuals or groups fit precisely into *any.*

There is *the strategy of prayer,* applied for generations in the past, a strategy which relied on divine intervention. This strategy was doomed as a social instrument whatever it has meant in terms of individual solace because it was ineffective in producing direct evidence of social change. And solace itself may be inappropriate in the face of sustained injustice.

There is *the strategy of isolation* employed by the very few aristocratic or wealthy Negroes who choose to live apart from the aspirations and despair of middle- and lower-class Negroes, secure as possible behind their wall of privilege, electing conspicuous consumption instead of responsibility in an abdication of leadership.

There is *the strategy of accommodation,* practiced for generations by those in the Negro middle class whose aspirations could only be achieved by adaptation to white middle-class mores; the Puritan ethic of thrift, cleanliness, education, hard work, rigorously proper sexual mores. A sense of guilt about their own flight from the ghetto and their own personal success has now led many of these persons to a closer identification with the struggling Negro masses.

There is *the strategy of despair* of the Negro rural and urban masses. Despair does not seem properly identified as strategy and yet, in a real sense, it is; for to abandon hope—to withdraw—in the presence of oppression is to adjust to and accept the condition.

There is *the strategy of alienation* advocated by the Communists in the 1930s, who tried in vain to convince Negroes that a separate black republic was the answer to American racism. The Black Muslims and the Black Nationalists today follow the same strategy based on hatred of the enemy and pride in group identity. Like the Communists, the Muslims, too, advocate rigorous group discipline, ascetic self-control, unquestioning devotion to dogmatic ideology, defense of violence, and the unquestioned leadership of authority. This strategy of alienation is, in a sense, the most desperate of all, for those who follow it admit their total loss of confidence in the possibilities of democracy.

There is *the strategy of law and maneuver,* the technique of the NAACP and National Urban League who work within the existing systems of constitutional society and democratic capitalism, achieving significant gains by patient hard work, and by tough, relentless pressure on the groups that hold political and economic power, working with whites where practical. Such groups have often run the risk of being labeled "Uncle Tom" for proceeding at a pace too slow and complicated for the younger, militant civil rights leaders. They have, nevertheless, been effective, content with results even at the risk of poor public relations.

There is *the strategy of direct encounter,* the action patterns of the student sitins, the picket lines, and the boycotts, the strategy of CORE, SNCC. This strategy dramatizes flagrant injustices, involves individuals directly, and demands that individuals take sides. This strategy does not effect social change directly, but it impels the mobilization of social power to facilitate or to resist the desired change.

There is, finally, *the strategy of truth,* the method of the intellectual who has sought, through academic research, through drama, writing, and speaking to motivate others to achieve social change by the power of eloquent expressions, a fusion of reason and feeling. Theirs has been the belief that men's minds and hearts can be reached and that truth has the power to transform society. The strategy of truth is the most abstract and nebulous of all, and often seems the least effective; there is much evidence that truth fails when selfish power is threatened by it—or fails, as one must believe, in the short run. Nevertheless, the search for truth, while impotent without implementation in action, undergirds every other strategy in behalf of constructive social change. None could proceed toward democratic ends without it.

It is a temptation to try to select the particular strategy which will guarantee the solutions of the ghetto's multiple problems, but to succumb to this temptation inevitably drives one into some of the many fantasies or fanaticisms of the ghetto. Probably the ghetto's ills are not to be cured by any presently known single remedy. The more dramatic methods are likely to continue to punctuate the general apathy, alienation and despair of the ghetto. But the chances for any major transformation in the ghetto's predicament are slim until the anguish of the ghetto is in some way shared not only by its victims but by the committed empathy of those who now consider themselves privileged and immune to the ghetto's flagrant pathologies. If this social sickness is not fatal, then the combined energies and strategies of understanding and power in the society as a whole must be mobilized and given the force of sustained action to achieve actual changes in the ghetto so its people may have a realistic basis for a life of humanity and dignity. If racism has so corroded the American society that this is no longer possible, then no strategy or combination of strategies can transform the ghetto and save the society. In facing the future of the American ghetto, one cannot allow oneself the luxury either of hope or of despair.

9

BLACK AND WHITE:
THE GHETTO INSIDE

I remember coming home from school, you can guess how young I must have been, and my mother asked me if my teacher was colored or white, and I said she was a little bit colored and a little bit white. . . . And as a matter of fact I was right. That's part of the dilemma of being an American Negro; that one is a little bit colored and a little bit white, and not only in physical terms but in the head and in the heart, and there are days—this is one of them— when you wonder what your role is in this country and what your future is in it; how precisely you are going to reconcile it to your situation here and how you are going to communicate to the vast heedless, unthinking, cruel white majority, that you are here. And to be here means that you can't be anywhere else. I could, my own person, leave this country and go to Africa, I could go to China, I could go to Russia, I could go to Cuba, but I'm an American and that is a *fact*.

—James Baldwin, *The Negro Protest**

The great tragedy—but possibly the great salvation, too—of the Negro and white in America is that neither one can be free of the other. Each Negro is a little bit white, and every white is a little bit Negro, in the sense that neither is totally alien from the other. Both are caught in a common human predicament. Each needs the other, the white to be free of his guilt, the Negro to be free of his fear; guilt and fear are both self-destructive.

* Kenneth B. Clark (ed.), Boston, Beacon Press, 1963.

Yet the psychological distance, the hostility, the wariness, and the ignorance that keep the Negro and the white apart are over-whelming. As the civil rights movement gains in force and the two confront each other increasingly, they see that the courtesy they hid behind in the past was unreal. Beneath the façade lie deep feelings now being released in a torrent of words and responses. Though the expression of these feelings is proving painful to both Negro and white, there can be no healthy relationship between them without this present pain. The anger and bitterness of the Negro has opened many wounds, but his own wounds have been unhealed for what seems like forever. He now feels free—or rather, more free—to re-veal the extent of his hurt. The great tragedy will be if the white does not see or listen, with his heart as well as his mind.

A psychologist on the staff of the National Institute of Mental Health, himself white, wrote a revealing account of the Negro pro-test movement in which he commented on the new relationship be-tween Negroes and whites:

The awesome shame and guilt that might otherwise overwhelm millions of fair-minded and well-meaning whites in both North and South is held in check by ignorance of the shocking facts or assuaged by pernicious rationalizations. It is comforting, self-absolving, to believe that the Negro's innate shortcomings are responsible for his present condition, and hard to acknowledge that the circumstances we force him to live under may be the very cause of this condition.

Another fundamental that must be grasped is the magnitude of the present psychological gulf between whites and non-whites. The growing anger of the more vocal Negroes, fanned and fed by a growing im-patience, comes as a surprise to whites who live comfortably and peace-fully far removed from the major Negro centers. The Negro and *his* problems never impinge on their thinking, their world, their smooth running democracy. For them "sit-ins" and "stall-ins" and "freedom rides" are evidence of irresponsibility, of unreasonableness, of law-lessness, of radicalism that reinforce all the myths they have learned to believe. On the other hand, when such whites do come face to face with the Negro world they discover in themselves an entirely new response: fear. They sense the Negro's envy of the "privileged caste," they sense some of his bitterness. They see sometimes the flaring anger that injustice breeds. They realize for the first time how far most Negroes have been forced into a world apart, a world so unfamiliar to the average white that it could as well be in a foreign land. And in this alien world they discover a complement to the white man's rejection: the Negro's distrust. For the failure of the white man thus far to deal honestly and fairly with his non-white fellow citizens has bred a suspicion so deep that very few whites are ever trusted. And out of this recognition of distrust springs an unreasoned, and often unacknowledged fear.

The people who know this best of all perhaps are the young whites currently working in the Freedom Movement. Sometimes the ambivalence of their young Negro co-workers in the Mississippi COFO project last summer was hard to conceal ("If any heads get smashed down there this summer, I hope it'll be that blonde rich kid's, not mine"). At least in the beginning, some Negroes felt the whites had joined the dangerous venture "for kicks." The distrust is so pervasive that *Ebony* magazine recently reflected it in a feature article on the ten white men Negroes trust most. Not respect, not admire, but *trust*. The gulf that exists is wide and deep. Bridging it will not be easy.*

Although the plight of the Negro in the ghetto and the chance of his escape from his predicament depend on his own strength, they depend also upon the willingness of the white to accept that strength. Negroes alone cannot abolish the ghetto. It will never be ended as long as the white society believes that it needs it.

Fantasy Barrier

For generations Negroes and whites alike have been blinded by fantasies which have kept both races apart and added to frustration and impatience even as they seem to project their opposites. An important first step is to examine these fantasies as the false comfort and delusions they are.

The fantasy of *accommodation* or *acceptance,* which used to be the primary pretense of Negroes, still affects some, particularly certain successful Negroes who surround their lives with typical middle-class daydreams. Just as the white of threatened status may trace his lineage to the "Mayflower" and seek refuge in the Daughters or Sons of the American Revolution, so the Negro may boast that his family were freed Negroes earlier than others were, or that his parents

* William F. Soskin, "Riots, Ghettos and the 'Negro Revolt,'" Staff paper, Office of Planning, National Institute of Mental Health, 1964.

"had money." Or, as one successful Negro professional, who lives in a beautiful home, is wont to say: "All Negroes need to do is prepare themselves, save money, invest properly, buy decent homes, and then there would be no more prejudice." A common fantasy is to deny one's own identification with the racial dilemmas: "I have no racial problem; I get along with all whites." So, too, a single Negro or a few Negroes on a prestige campus or in a church or a profession may "fit in beautifully," indirectly reassuring the institution that it is satisfactorily color-blind. The truth is that every Negro has a racial problem, repressed or otherwise, and that no American social institution is truly color-blind—to be color-blind in a society where race is relevant is not to be free but insensitive. Negroes themselves may encourage this fantasy, responding to the safety of the oasis, not sure whether it is a mirage and generally careful not to challenge the dream for fear of waking. But as long as whites take special pride in having "a Negro friend" or boast of inviting Negroes to their parties, as long as it is considered daring and "liberal" on campuses to have an interracial affair, the dream is a dream.

The fantasy of *acceptance* is a form of another pretense, the fantasy of *denial*. The Negro or white may seek to repress painful racial problems or conflicts. The white may deny any knowledge that Negroes are excluded from renting or buying homes in certain neighborhoods or that Negroes are prohibited from registering and voting in parts of the South or that the absence of Negroes in certain executive and management jobs reflects anything other than natural selection of the "best" applicants. Some middle-class Negroes tend to share these pretenses with their "white friends," hoping to avoid conflict and discomfort. To believe that one is a living example of the proposition that there is no racial problem for the hard-working, successful, sophisticated person of either race does bring some measure of satisfaction. Yet, to the extent to which either the Negro or white believes this and behaves accordingly, the psychological distance between Negro and white is increased even if it may, on the surface, appear to be otherwise. No genuine friendship can be based on a lie, even a congenial lie.

Acceptance and accommodation are no longer the most prevalent fantasies among Negroes. Today it has become fashionable, instead, as the civil rights movement grows in fervor, to move from appeasement to a stance of defiance, a new fantasy of *militancy,* though many Negroes who are now in the forefront of militancy were among the most accommodating yesterday, little interested in the patient, determined progress of groups like the NAACP.

But random defiance, no more than meek accommodation, is based on the facts of life. The pretense of the Muslims who call for a separate black state, and of the extremists who threaten to close down the public schools if immediate and total integration is not forthcoming, have in common a failure to face the truth. It is clear—or ought to be—that American society would not sustain a separate black nation. It is clear—or ought to be—that immediate and total integration of the schools is not possible in cities with large and growing Negro populations. It is clear that white middle-class parents will not endure "reverse busing," the transporting of their children into the heart of the ghetto to schools that Negroes themselves have said for years are inferior. For Negroes to justify any such demands on the grounds alone of militancy is to attempt to deal with a disturbing reality by wishful fantasy. Yet it has become fashionable to demand and to expect the unreal, and the fact that a particular strategy does not make sense is considered irrelevant to its virtue. Those Negroes who oppose extreme militancy run the risk that their commitment to justice will be called into question, that they will be derided as "Uncle Toms" who do "the bidding of the white man." If they try to point out that it would be more useful to consider strategies that will divide rather than unite the opposition, they are suspected of irresolution in their devotion to civil rights. This automatic separation into sheep and goats by those who have arrogated to themselves the right of such judgment reduces the range of realism available to both. Fewer alternatives of action are judged acceptable; there is less flexibility to adapt strategy to changes in circumstances and to take advantage of openings; there is less personal grasp on reality itself. Anyone who raises questions threatens this fantasy of *militancy.* But if there are fewer questions, there will inevitably be fewer answers.

The basic delusion of the American white, on the other hand, is the fantasy of *aristocracy*. The basic myth of racism is that white skin color brings with it superiority—that the white is more intelligent, more virtuous, more sexually controlled by the mere fact of being white. In the integration of schools, the white child is believed, automatically, to be ahead of the Negro child in performance and in potential. The movement of Negroes into a white community is considered to be a prelude to poorly kept lawns, raucous parties, lowered property values. When a white thinks of himself in relation to the Negro, he need not appraise his own strengths and weaknesses, but enjoy membership in a homogeneous and superior white group in which ethnic and class differences are erased. It is no accident that the whites most ready to accept the assumption of social superiority are generally those of the lower middle class, who are struggling to improve their own economic and social status.

The delusion of the "white liberal" is superiority of another kind —not of origin, or of status, but of the spirit. He takes pride in the fact that he is free from prejudice. The fantasy of *tolerance,* which a decade ago was, for the liberal conscience, adequate support, has been superseded by the fantasy of *purity*. The crowning insult which anyone can pay to an intelligent Northern white is to suggest that he might be motivated to some action, decision, or plan by racial considerations. He responds somewhat as follows: "We do not keep racial records. We do not even know the color of Mary or Jim. He is just like one of us." Northerners find it more difficult or more painful than Southerners to face their prejudices. For the liberal it is a matter of self-respect to be considered free of bias. Yet when brought to the test by the stark and seemingly extreme demands of Negroes, this confidence often gives way to a resentment and anger at the Negro, an anger accompanied by guilt: "These Negroes, whose friends we are, are now going too far; they are breaking the bounds of our tolerance." The white liberal, who thought he considered Negroes as "we," may now address them as "you people." If he is sensitive, he may be shaken to discover in himself new feelings of alienation and even hostility.

One is forced to ask the further question, disconcerting to anyone who teaches or writes, whether fantasy also afflicts those Negroes and whites who believe it is possible for race to be transcended, those who consider that what they think is actually relevant to power, those who have confidence that rational communication between whites and Negroes in America can affect the real decisions of society. It is the wish but, more than that, the belief of those who teach and write that intelligent, rational planning can and will determine the direction of events. Yet it is surely possible that this direction will be charted rather in response to emotion than to rational strategy.

Confrontation of the Liberals

The Negro thrust out of the ghetto has imposed upon white public officials and liberal whites in the North a struggle which in many respects presents a more complex level of racial turbulence than the conflict between Negroes and obvious segregationists. This struggle, in the final analysis, may be even more pivotal to the direction and rate of the civil rights movement in America than the solution of the South's own problems. The key to meaningful resolution is in the hands of that large majority of whites who conceive of themselves as liberal, moderate, and decent human beings. It is a cold, hard fact that the many flagrant forms of racial injustice North and South could not exist without their acquiescence.

On issues of social justice other than race—on the rights of labor, on civil and political liberties—an initially small and committed minority of whites worked incessantly to win over the uncommitted majority. Their role in abolishing child labor at the turn of the century is an example of the social effectiveness of a small group working in concert with the uncommitted majority. The difference between these crusades and race is that in race one's own status needs are at stake. No significant minority of white liberals can work in a totally committed manner for racial justice for long without coming in conflict with conscious or unconscious anxieties.

White liberals believe that if the right to vote, the right to an education, the right to a job, the right to a decent home, the right to ordinary courtesies, the right to protection of government are denied to anyone; they are protected for no one. But many liberals stop short, disturbed and apologetic, when the principle is appealed to in behalf of sexual equality and intermarriage. Guilt, insecurity, and anxieties are easily associated with the problems of race. It is not accidental that sex is the most powerful argument for maintaining the *status quo,* when all others fail. Among the most powerfully stated and unstated rationales for the maintenance of segregated schools is the insistence that Negro children are sexually precocious and will contaminate the otherwise "normal" white children. The implication of this argument along with the academic retardation theory is that Negroes are academically retarded, and white children are sexually retarded, and that it would, therefore, be catastrophic to mix them in integrated schools. Without regard to the validity of such contentions, it remains an overriding fact that the demands for equality before the law and the insistence that rights not be qualified by race cannot be curtailed or postponed *because* of the fear of whites that if Negroes are granted these rights, whites may find them sexually attractive. The problem for the white liberal is to choose his own sexual partners; curtailment of this important personal freedom—as important to his own freedom as to a Negro's—cannot be determined by restrictions of the civil rights of Negroes.

The liberal position, when applied to race, has been, for a multiple of reasons, somewhat tainted. In those areas of life where liberals are powerful—labor unions, schools, and politics—one is forced to say that the plight of the Negroes is not significantly better than it is in areas where liberals are not dominant. Labor unions are not "better" than management. In fact, Wall Street and industrial leaders appear to be more realistic about race than are rank-and-file workers. During the most effective period of political liberalism in this century, the Roosevelt New Deal era, when the oppressed without regard to race gained some measure of economic security, Negroes had to threaten to embarrass the Administration by demonstrations and a march on Washington in order to achieve an executive Fair Employment Practices order. Perhaps it is impossible for any person, any organization, any political party, to be consistently and totally liberal.

Again, in the schools—on the primary, secondary, and collegiate level—where one finds strong declarations against prejudice, there is overwhelming evidence of a devastating form of oppression, perhaps second only in contemporary society to discrimination in housing. Colleges and universities, the citadels of American liberalism, are devoted to the freeing of the mind from narrow restrictions and from error; yet when one looks at the faculties of interracial colleges, one finds fewer than three hundred Negroes, and probably no more than two or three in the position of department chairman; there are no Negro deans and no Negro presidents. Recently these colleges have gone out of their way to recruit Negroes—another revelation of the fact that race is still a dominant aspect in all areas of American life. The continued existence of Negro colleges, with their predominantly Negro faculties and administration, reassures whites and Negroes that there is equal professional opportunity for Negroes. Negroes are ambivalent about Negro colleges; even at best, they are ashamed of them, for such colleges are an anachronism: that they need to exist to give Negro students an education can only emphasize the fact that integration has not come to American education at any level.

Negroes are dismayed to discover that even when liberals are in apparent control of an organization, not only do they not rally their groups for an effective role in the fight against racial discrimination; they even tolerate a measure of discrimination within their own jurisdictions. Loren Miller, a Los Angeles attorney and a vice president of the NAACP, points out that because the liberal's historic concern has been with individual rights, he sees progress in the admission of a few Negro children to a hitherto white school; while the Negro, who also wants individual rights, nevertheless regards the raising of status of the group "to which he has been consigned" as his own immediate problem and spurns the evidence of individual progress as mere tokenism.

The problem is multisided. The liberal often is less in control of the political or other institution than the Negro thinks he is. Doubtless because many organizations, churches, and political platforms have frequently taken the liberal stance, Negroes have been misled into believing that liberals set the standards for society as a whole. But often, power groups have allowed liberals to have the satisfaction of the words while they kept for themselves the satisfaction of the deeds. Liberalism, because of its close relationship to the world of the intellect and the world of language, often assumes that the word *is* the deed. Politicians and industrialists and business leaders know better. For liberalism to be really effective, and to regain the allegiance of the Negroes, which it has in some measure lost, it will need to move from the verbal level to the actual level of power.

The ambivalent role of white liberals must be understood also in terms of the power of their own conflicting loyalties—their desire to maintain the liberal democratic image of themselves and their desire to maintain their identity in their "in-group," their friends, their family, their social cliques, who do not necessarily share all of their own liberal attitudes. The conflict between the individual and the groups to which he belongs is transferred to the individual himself; his own conscience is in conflict with his timidities. In some this conflict is resolved by a self-protective rejection of the Negro as "too impatient" and by the conviction that the good of the total society requires a more measured, gradual approach.

One of the dangers in the present white liberal ambivalence toward the Negro is that it has caused many Negroes to reject the "liberal" label as a designation for themselves. For a number of Negroes "liberal" has come to mean "white." They, too, are ambivalent, for they do not wish to feel alien to the liberal tradition with which they associate the concept of justice. Yet the liberal has become a curious and troublesome adversary, often harder to deal with than the bigot who, at the least, states his position honestly in unmistakable terms. The bigot will react with contempt and hatred to Negro criticism, but the liberal looks hurt and expresses his continuing and forgiving friendship, thereby creating in his Negro counterpart a sense of frustrated rage and guilt that adds to the psychological burden already difficult to bear—a burden seemingly doubly unjust. When a Negro responds with anger to an act or attitude that seems to him discriminatory, he is often regarded as having violated the rules of conduct among gentlemen. He has not been amiable. He would seem, therefore, to have no way out. The choice is to alienate his friends or to suffer a sense of self-alienation.

In a round-table discussion on "Liberalism and the Negro," conducted by *Commentary* magazine and reported in its issue of March 1964, James Baldwin tried to explain to a group of distinguished, mostly white liberals why the term "liberal" had begun to pall. The liberal, he said, was an "affliction" to the Negro:

What I mean by a liberal is someone . . . whose real attitudes are revealed when the chips are down . . . someone who thinks you are bitter when you are vehement, who has a set of attitudes so deep that they're almost unconscious and which blind him to the fact that in talking to a black man, he is talking to another man like himself.

In a provocative article, "Farewell to the Liberals, A Negro View," in the *Nation,* October 20, 1962, Loren Miller said that the liberal could be defined as one who sees "both sides" of issues, one who is "impatient with 'extremists' on both sides."

The Negro is outraged at being an extremist. Since he takes the position that the Constitution confers complete equality on all citizens, he must rest his case on the proposition that there is only one side; his side, the constitutional side. Whoever opposes, or even doubts, that doctrine is cast in the role of a foe, whether he calls himself conservative or liberal. The middle ground on which the traditional liberal has taken his stand is being cut from beneath him.

Whites, as well as Negroes, are caught up in conflict and ambivalence about race. They have been required to learn the language and behavior of prejudice at the same time that they learned the words and ideals of democracy. One obvious way to cope with the contradiction between the ideal and the real is to deny the existence of the real. White officials, confronted by Negro demands in Northern urban areas, often say with bewilderment that there is no policy of exclusion of Negroes, that "some of our best friends, in fact, are Negro," or that no Negro has "ever applied for a job in our firm." Such beliefs ironically can create the very reality they assert. In professions where Negroes have felt unwelcome by whatever means— advertising in the "white" rather than the Negro press, relying on employment agencies in white neighborhoods, hiring by word of mouth from friend to friend—few, if any, Negroes *do* apply; and the failure to apply, in turn, convinces the employer that Negroes are unqualified for or uninterested in his business. Nor is an open-door policy in a church or club in itself generally sufficient to attract Negroes; in a society in which race is a dominant influence, those who have in the past been excluded assume they are "not wanted" until the evidence to refute this assumption is forced upon them.

So, too, many liberal whites believe that Negroes prefer to live together, that they are drawn to each other as the Chinese may be in Chinatown, because of a shared culture. No one will ever, in fact, know whether Negro culture *does* bind its members together until Negroes have the freedom others have to live anywhere. A conspiracy of white-controlled financial and real estate interests has effectively blocked any significant outward movement from the ghetto in spite of the fair-housing laws or other concessions to democratic ideology. Every Negro who seeks to move outside of an all-Negro community is required to fight and insist upon this right; for while the law protects his right, it does not allow him to take for granted in the first instance that he will be justly treated. The law asserts that the legitimate and verbal power of society is not on the side of exclusion. It does permit those willing to make the test to do so; and offers assurance that the law will not be used against them. In the South the law has been used as an instrument for the perpetuation of racial *status quo*. In the North, the law neutralizes exclusion; it does not, however, prevent it. The law sometimes penalizes injustice when injustice can be proved, but the burden of proof is on the Negro.

Some Pivotal Realities

In many all-white suburbs, human relations committees and fair housing committees have now been organized by liberals to break down the housing barriers. Such campaigns are a fascinating illustration of the fact that the Negro is forced to consider himself special—otherwise, why would campaigns be needed to permit him to exercise the rights which the law assures him?

White liberals have been having a frustrating time finding Negroes who will offer themselves as test cases. For one thing, it is not particularly comfortable to be a test case. For another, middle-class

Negroes who break out of the ghetto are often themselves convinced that they are already accepted by whites—to be a test case would be to allow race to become salient again in one's life, to bring the ghetto nightmare along when all one has sought is effective escape. When whites learn that hosts of Negroes are not poised and eager to take advantage of their new hospitality, when white human relations committees search in vain for a Negro (a search Negroes often regard with ironic humor) they tend to take this failure as evidence that Negroes really do want to live "with each other" after all. Furthermore, job discrimination has reduced the proportion of Negroes who can afford to pay the high rents or purchase price of good suburban housing. Generally Negroes are able only to move into those communities where whites themselves have minimum social and economic status; in those lower-income areas, economic and psychological status is already so tenuous that whites cannot allow their security to be jeopardized voluntarily. When Negroes move in, such whites feel they have sunk a bit themselves. They fight back in self-defense, in the phenomenon known as the "white backlash." As the civil rights pressure increases, the identification whites feel with their own group, through the "neighborhood" (previously downgraded in Northern cities, now suddenly rediscovered), through fraternities, churches, social clubs, is reinforced. The mobilization of the white community to protect itself through organizations like the Parents and Taxpayers groups in New York City must necessarily increase as the pressure to take sides increases. This stark confrontation, even when hostile and terrifying, has at least the important virtue of honesty.

It is easy to forget the rather obvious fact that whites are competitive and hostile among themselves, among and within the various ethnic groups which comprise the dominant "white" population. This quiet but pervasive intrawhite competitiveness is merely intensified and considered normal when Negroes insist upon sharing the rewards and status symbols. Whites then tend to close ranks in what seems to Negroes to be a solid wall of resistance to their demands. There is a temporary decrease in rivalry among whites and a joining of forces. The Parents and Taxpayers group included whites of varying political and religious views and ethnic origin; Jews and Gentiles; Catholics and Protestants; Italians, Irish, Polish, and others.

Whites who are reluctant to join this protective homogeny are subjected to social coercion, ridicule, and harassment, and in extreme cases, to the forms of violence, like bombings, ordinarily employed only against Negroes. The appearance of a formidable coalition of white resistance forces demands a compensatory defense alliance between middle-class and workingclass Negroes, ordinarily suspicious of each other—the middle-class Negro escaping reminders of the ghetto, the workingclass Negro apathetic and cynical about the motives of the middle class. For when a middle-class Negro's home in a white neighborhood is bombed, all Negroes are angry. When a workingclass Negro adolescent is shot by a white policeman, all Negroes are bitter, although only marginal Negroes might actually protest through rioting in the streets. Any homogeneous white resistance to Negroes tends to cause Negroes to close ranks.

When liberals say that the Negro is ungrateful and insensitive to the predicament of less secure lower-middle-class whites, who do have much to lose by integrated housing and schools, Negroes understand that they are to permit the rate of change in their status to be determined by the willingness of whites to accept them as human beings. This is the heart of racism: when one accepts race as a relevant criterion for decision about when, under what conditions, and how fast the lower-status race should be granted equality. Any Negro who agrees to accede to the majority's power to decide his rights for any reasons other than purely strategic has already been damaged psychologically in subtle, tragic ways.

The liberal has often felt righteous in his role as protector of the Negro. He talked of freedom and therefore successfully separated himself from involvement in the restrictions on freedom. He did not face his own role as accessory. He wrote serious articles on race in *Partisan Review, Commentary, New Leader,* and other magazines. He invited Negro intellectuals to discuss their common problems with him. He lived in accordance with the ritual of commitment and concern but ordinarily without the substance. Negro intellectuals have often played the game with the same *élan.* Some became pets of the whites. But if they took the game seriously, they were lost. Many were saved by protective cynicism; some, by the ability to exploit their position.

Negroes generally felt that white liberals did not understand, for if there had been a real relationship between them, they would have joined in an anguished outcry, beating their own heads against the walls of power in a demand for justice. Whenever a *New York Times* editorial questions the democracy of laws against discrimination in housing, whenever a *Partisan Review* writer takes moral relativism seriously, whenever a Norman Podhoretz explores his hostility toward Negroes in the pages of *Commentary,* a Negro may praise the honesty which permits such free expression but he must also question the serious concern for him.

Perhaps it has been more important psychologically than the white liberal knew for him to serve as surrogate and spokesman for the disadvantaged. The liberal's compassion and pity for the underdog, particularly the Negro, has led to a role of symbiosis and interdependence between the white liberal and the Negro. Perhaps it was inevitable that as the Negro came to reject the role of underdog and sought to be treated as peer, he would increase the psychological distance between himself and the white liberal, and stimulate in his earlier white benefactor both resentment and alienation, which, in turn, would cause the Negro to feel contempt for the white liberal.

Negroes are now insisting on being their own spokesmen; they are asking the whites to join them, either as equals or even in subordinate roles; but it is abnormal in our society for whites to be in a passive or subordinate or even equal role with Negroes, and extremely awkward for many of them to make the necessary psychological readjustment.

The present question is whether the relationship between the white liberal and the Negro, who have needed each other in the past, will survive the test of transformation of roles from the dependence of the advantaged and disadvantaged upon each other to a common commitment to mutually desired goals of justice and social good.

If the civil rights struggle is going to be successful, it will require white participation and commitment, even though a number of Ne-

groes believe the white is no longer relevant. The simple fact of
arithmetic decrees otherwise. Negroes are one-tenth of the American
population. Without white support and without the white power
structure the civil rights struggle is doomed to failure. As Gunnar
Myrdal, at the *Commentary* conference noted earlier, replied to
James Baldwin, who had spoken, "Nevertheless, Mr. Baldwin, you
will have to rely upon the liberals because, as somebody said before, it's not the conservatives who are going to fight for the bigger
reforms which must be made . . . you will have to rely on the
liberals—even if sometimes they are not too clear and too courageous,
and even if they sometimes need you to give them a push. I think
the most encouraging thing which has happened in America in recent
years is the rebellion of the Negro group, because that rebellion will
help the liberals to get into power and do the job that has to be
done."

The white liberal must be prepared, in this turbulent period of
transition, to accept the fact that even his closest Negro friends will
feel some hostility toward him. For if the white liberal can delude
himself into believing himself color-blind, the Negro of insight and
sensitivity cannot. To a Negro, every white person is, in a sense, a
symbol of his own oppression. Almost every Negro who has white
friends and associates suffers from feelings of ambivalence; every
relationship of respect and affection that seems to transcend the racial
and to be merely human causes the Negro to feel some sense of guilt
and betrayal just because it does bring an experience of liberation
from the bonds of inferior racial identification other Negroes have
not been able to achieve. Many Negroes are caught in a gnawing
sense of doubt, hostility, and guilt that interferes with any genuine
affirmative relationship with whites—and even with Negroes themselves. The Negro tends to justify his own anxieties and ambivalence
in self-protective ways, fearing to yield to the temptation to become
a "show friend," ascribing to the white an inability to be a friend
to a Negro. It would be too painful to realize that the guilt of unfulfilled friendship is in some measure his own. He may tell himself: I needn't feel guilty because my white friend is not really free
to be my friend.

Subtle tensions may result when whites themselves who harbor deep feelings of guilt about Negroes attempt prematurely and with exaggerated warmth to establish close relationships with them. This puts a strain on the Negro and makes it difficult for him to adjust normally. If the Negro rejects the overture as an invasion of his individuality, the whites, in turn, may be bewildered and hurt, and regress to a safe level of hostility and alienation. Few, if any, are capable of racelessness. But whites who try to be free must have the courage to accept the inevitable chaos and confusion of a changing society. There will be inevitable irrationalities in any move to a higher stage of rationality and justice. Above all, one must not retreat in the face of pain. Anyone who cringes, who retreats to the insidious conviction that things were more peaceful and, therefore, better when the Negro knew his place may find temporary security, but he has chosen the way of the past and instability.

The mistake is to seek for purity at all, and the white liberal no more than the Negro ought to expect of himself a superhuman response. Original innocence, if such a thing has meaning, can never be regained; in contemporary society, no one, Negro or white, can be totally without prejudice. No one should expect purity of himself or others. Any genuine relationship between Negro and white must face honestly all of the ambivalences both feel for each other. Each must identify with the other without sentiment. The white must resist the tendency to attribute all virtue to the underdog; he must respond insofar as he is able with a pure kind of empathy that is raceless, that accepts and understands the frailties and anxieties and weaknesses that all men share, the common predicament of mankind.

Any white who dares to be free of the myths of race faces awkwardness and risk and a need to defend himself, even ironically, against Negroes themselves. For many Negroes prefer, unconsciously or not, a continuation of the double standard; their preference sometimes wears the guise of an insistence on interpreting lack of prejudice as itself evidence of prejudice. Negroes are so accustomed to prejudice that many find it easier to deal with it than with a single standard of judgment for all men. It requires strength and courage for whites to persist in the face of such rejection. It is a temptation to retreat into sentimentality instead, and to be caught in the net of condescension, to say, "I would not want to hurt you because you are a Negro," and to suffocate the Negro with respect. Any white who refuses to be trapped into such an escape, and reaches the point of total liberation, will see and understand and act freely. He can never retreat, no matter what the threats, either to the sentimental lie or to the traditional racist lie; for the Negro is watching and waiting, despite his cynicism and his suspicion, with the beginning of trust.

Those whites who are really committed to civil rights can make it clear to society at large that a significant minority of Americans will no longer accept equivocation and procrastination. But it is far easier to deal with racial problems by writing letters to congressmen than to demonstrate one's own freedom. Every individual who rises above the constrictions of race is a demonstration that this is really possible. Every time a Negro sees a group of secretaries—white and Negro—chatting over lunch; or children—white and Negro—walking together to school, he feels that hope is possible. Every time his white friend shows he is not afraid to argue with him as with anyone else, he sees that freedom is possible, that there are some for whom race is irrelevant, who accept or reject a person not as a Negro or a white, but in terms of himself. Only so can the real confinements of the ghetto be broken. The Negro alone cannot win this fight that transcends the "civil rights struggle." White and Negro must fight together for the rights of human beings to make mistakes and to aspire to human goals. Negroes will not break out of the barriers of the ghetto unless whites transcend the barriers of their own minds, for the ghetto is to the Negro a reflection of the ghetto in which the white lives imprisoned. The poetic irony of American race relations is that the rejected Negro must somehow also find the strength to free the privileged white.

GENERAL INDEX

241

Labor unions:
AFL–CIO, 46
Brotherhood of Sleeping Car Porters, 43
building trades industry, 37
discriminatory practices, 38, 41–47, 205
ILGWU, 43–45
liberals in, 230
powerlessness of Negro worker, 43
status of Negroes in, 42–43
La Guardia, Fiorello, 118
Landers, Jacob, 115
Landlords, slum, 30
Langner, Thomas S., 83n
Law, strategy of, 221
Leadership:
in changes in ghetto, 213–219
Haryou Leadership Training Workshop, 53
psychological problems, 188
religious leaders and social action, 183–186
role in schools, 148–153
Lehman, Herbert H., 160, 187
Lewis, Hylan, xviii, xxvii–xxviii
Liberal party, 43
Liberals, 18, 20, 228–234
conflict between individual and groups to which he belongs, 232
definitions, 233
fears about intermarriage, 230
intrawhite competitiveness, 235–236
need for Negro unity with, 240
Lincoln, C. Eric, 216
Lindesmith, Alfred R., 92
Little League, 108
Lomax, Louis, 195
Louis, Joe, 197
Lumumba affair, 194, 217
Lutheran Church, 179

McCloskey, Mark A., xxviii
Magazines, power in the ghettos, 172–173
Malcolm X, 14, 169
Maneuver, strategy of, 221
Manhattan General Hospital, 94
March on Washington, 201–203
Marijuana, 89, 90
Marshall, Kenneth E., xxvii

Marshall, Thurgood, 157
Matriarchy, in Negro ghettos, 70–74
"Mayflower," 225
Meany, George, 46
Metcalf-Volker Act, 104
Methodist Church, 179–180, 181
Negro Central Jurisdiction, 180, 181
Metropolitan Achievement Reading Test, 120n
Metropolitan Life Insurance Co., 57
Michael, Stanley P., 83n
Middle-class residents of ghettos, 55–62
Militancy, fantasy of, 227
Miller, Herman P., 35
Miller, Loren, 233
Miller, S. M., 49n
Mobility, social, in the ghetto, 55–62
Mohammed, Elijah, 7
Monro, John U., xxviii, 148, 149
Montgomery bus boycott, 165, 183
Moon, Dixie, xxviii
Moore, Justin, 118n
Motivation, in the school, 132–133
Muslims. See Black Muslims
Myrdal, Gunnar, 41, 205, 238

NAACP. See National Association for the Advancement of Colored People
Narcotics addiction. See Drug addiction
Narcotics Committee, East Harlem Protestant Parish, Inc., 91
Nation magazine, 233
National Association for the Advancement of Colored People (NAACP), 8, 43, 118n, 157, 158, 165, 167, 185, 191–192, 209, 221, 227 231
Legal Defense and Educational Fund, 157, 192
National Association for Mental Health, 84
National Council of Churches of Christ in America, 201, 205
National Institute of Mental Health, 224
National Scholarship Service and Fund for Negro Students, 38
National Urban League, xxviii, 38, 167, 185, 214, 221

Wagner, Robert F., 118n, 160, 185, 187, 193
Walkley, Rosabelle Price, 31n, 32
Wall Street, 189, 230
Washington, March on, 201–203
Wealth, in the ghetto, 189–190
Weaver, Robert C., 157, 191
Welfare. *See* Public assistance
Wesleyan Methodist Church, 179
"White backlash," 16–18, 202, 235
White, Stanford, 85
Whitney, John, 153
"Wildcat" civil rights leaders, 207
Wilkins, Roy, 17, 185
Williams, Franklin H., 157
Wilner, Daniel M., 31n, 32
Witmer, Helen, 100
Woolworth's, 9, 164

World War I, 26
World War II, 100
World's Fair, stall-in, 207
Wright, Richard, 191, 195

X, Malcolm. *See* Malcolm X

Yale University, 149
Young, Whitney M., Jr., xxviii, 17, 167, 185, 191
Youth in the Ghetto: A Study of the Consequences of Powerlessness and a Blueprint for Change, xiii, xiv, 93, 120n, 121n, 125n, 133n
Youth Occupational Training and Employment programs, 105

INDEX OF CITIES

Atlanta, Ga., 22, 215
Baltimore, Md., 23, 24, 25, 144–145
Birmingham, Ala., 22, 29
Boston, Mass., 14, 24, 86, 215
Bronx, N.Y., 59; *see also* New York City, N.Y.
Brooklyn, N.Y., 25, 59, 115; *see also* New York City, N.Y.
Charleston, S.C., 22
Chicago, Ill., 13, 14, 23, 24, 25, 112, 215
Cleveland, O., 13, 23, 24, 25, 112; *see also* Hough area in General Index
Detroit, Mich., 13, 23, 24, 113, 215
Houston, Tex., 23, 24
Kansas City, Mo., 24
Little Rock, Ark., 22
Los Angeles, Calif., 13, 23, 24, 25
Manhattan, N.Y., 48n, 57, 89, 113, 115, 125, 159; *see also* New York City, N.Y.
Memphis, Tenn., 29
Minneapolis, Minn., 24, 86–87

Montgomery, Ala., 18, 165, 168
New Orleans, La., 22, 23, 24, 25
New York City, N.Y., 14, 23, 24, 25, 31, 35–36, 39, 42–43, 44, 45n, 47, 59, 81, 82–85, 87, 88, 90, 112, 115–116, 118–121, 137, 148; *see also* Bronx, Brooklyn, Harlem, *and* Queens in General Index
New York State, 37, 113, 118n
Philadelphia, Penn., 14, 23, 24, 113, 215
Pine Bluff, Ark., 22
Pittsburgh, Penn., 24
Puerto Rico, 88
Queens, N.Y., 25, 59; *see also* New York City, N.Y.
Rochester, N.Y., 14, 24
St. Louis, Mo., 23, 24, 25, 84n, 86, 148
San Francisco, Calif., 25
Virginia, 118n
Washington, D.C., 13, 23, 24, 25, 29, 113, 201–203

About the Authors

KENNETH B. CLARK began his education in the Harlem public schools and was later graduated from Howard University and received his Ph.D. from Columbia University. In 1962 he returned to Harlem as an "involved observer," serving as the chief consultant and chairman of the board of directors of the Harlem Youth Opportunities Unlimited project (Haryou), from which *Dark Ghetto* arose. But, according to Clark, *"Dark Ghetto* is a summation of my personal and lifelong experiences and observations as a prisoner within the ghetto long before I was aware that I was really a prisoner."

In 1938–41 Clark was a research associate with Ralph Bunche and Gunnar Myrdal on the noted Carnegie study that led to *An American Dilemma.* He was president of the American Psychological Association in 1970–71 and of the Society for Psychological Studies on Social Issues in 1959–60. He is now Distinguished Professor of Psychology Emeritus of the City University of New York. Clark is author of, among other books, *Prejudice and Your Child, Pathos of Power,* and *King, Malcolm, Baldwin.* He lives in Hastings-on-Hudson, New York.

WILLIAM JULIUS WILSON is the Lucy Flower Distinguished Service Professor of Sociology and Public Policy at the University of Chicago. He is a MacArthur Prize fellow, a fellow of the American Academy of Arts and Sciences, a fellow of the American Association for the Advancement of Science, and president of the American Sociological Associaton. He is the author of several books, including most recently, *The Truly Disadvantaged: The Inner City, The Underclass, and Public Policy.* His home is in Chicago, Illinois.